Martin Sixsmith was educated at Oxford, Harvard and the Sorbonne. From 1980 to 1997 he worked for the BBC as the Corporation's correspondent in Moscow, Washington, Brussels and Warsaw. From 1997 to 2002 he worked for the government as director of communications and press secretary. Martin is now a writer, presenter and journalist, living in London. He is the author of two novels, *Spin* and *I Heard Lenin Laugh*, and several works of non-fiction, including Philomena, first published in 2009 as *The Lost Child of Philomena Lee*.

Also by Martin Sixsmith

Ayesha's Gift

A daughter's search
for the truth
about her father

MARTIN SIXSMITH

**SIMON &
SCHUSTER**

London · New York · Sydney · Toronto · New Delhi

A CBS COMPANY

First published in Great Britain by Simon & Schuster UK Ltd, 2017
This paperback edition published by Simon & Schuster UK Ltd, 2018
A CBS COMPANY

The author
holder:
form

ght-

A CIP catalogue record for this book
is available from the British Library

Paperback ISBN: 978-1-4711-4977-1
eBook ISBN: 978-1-4711-4978-8

Typeset in the UK by M Rules
Printed and bound by CPI Group (UK) Ltd, Croydon, CR0 4YY

Sopra la lontananza del suo fratello dilettissimo [BWV 992]

AUTHOR'S NOTE

Like, I suspect, many white Britons, I took little interest in Pakistan. As a country it appeared distant, alien and dangerous. Pakistanis in Britain were peripheral to me – I exchanged greetings with my friendly newsagent, read about extremists plotting to impose sharia law, and walked through streets of Asian faces when my football team played at Bradford or Aston Villa. Two events made me think again. An appeal for help from a young British Pakistani woman, followed by a tragedy in my own life, drew me into the writing of this book and, with it, an understanding of the shared concerns and common humanity that unite us.

The book grew from these facts, but it is not a factual documentary. The character named Martin is not me, although I share many of his thoughts and sorrows. Ayesha is not Ayesha, because the real Ayesha insisted that her identity be protected. As you read the pages that follow you will understand why all the main characters have been changed, locations altered and events rewritten. The whole picture of corruption and violence, the organised crime and the anguish of those caught up in them are terribly real.

PROLOGUE

I met her on an evening of November streetlamps and my breath rising in Piccadilly where a shaven-headed cabbie in a bulging overcoat raised his fist to a cyclist in orange, 'What did you want me to do – fucking run you over?'

I got to the bar early and chose a table in an alcove to watch her as she entered. My friends say I'm a *Luftmensch*, drifting into other people's stories but shying away from involvement. Maybe I don't like to get drawn into other people's misery. I didn't want to get drawn into hers.

When she appeared I was startled. I'd pictured an afflicted Muslim in veils and tears, but Ayesha wore a pencil skirt and high heels and held a smartphone in her hand. She was prodding the screen but getting nowhere. She remonstrated with a waiter, exasperated by the lack of signal. She hadn't glanced around, hadn't looked for me. When she did, she had none of the first-encounter diffidence such occasions normally produce.

'You're Martin.'

'Yes, hello. You must be Ayesha.'

'I'll have a glass of red. Cabernet sauvignon. French.' The

words were directed towards a waiter. 'Mike says you're a writer. So what are you writing about?'

Her question struck me as an interrogation.

'Psychology. Psychiatry. I'm writing a history.'

'Really? Which bit are you writing about right now?'

It's not that I resent people prying; it was more her assumption that she had the right to quiz me.

'Theory of Mind.'

'What's that?'

'Attributing mental states to others.'

'Yeah? What does that mean?'

'Think about it. It's being able to see that other people might not share all the same beliefs and desires that we have ourselves.'

'No. You'll have to do better than that. You won't keep readers interested with stuff like that.'

I gave in.

'Okay. Some people can't understand the minds of others. Very young children or people with severe autism don't realise that someone else might think differently from them. There's an experiment where we show a child a pack of Smarties and ask him what he thinks is inside. The child says "Smarties", but when the psychologist opens the tube it's got pencils in it. The psychologist closes the tube and asks the boy what he thinks his friend Susie, who hasn't seen inside the tube, will think is in it. If the child replies "Smarties", we can say he possesses insight – he realises that Susie can have a false belief. But if he says "pencils", it means he doesn't yet understand how the mind works. Children have to be four or five before they acquire theory of mind. And some people never do . . .'

'So why's that such a big deal?'

'Because it underpins the concept of empathy, for one thing. It lets us put ourselves in someone else's shoes. And in evolution it was a spur to human development. Knowing that the man in the next cave might have purposes in mind that don't necessarily reflect our own helped expand our intelligence. It meant taking on board that mental states can differ from reality, and that people's behaviour can be predicted by their mental states. You needed to grow a bigger brain if you were going to keep track of all that.'

'But we can never know another person, can we? I mean, truly know them . . .'

'Aren't we getting a bit philosophical? I didn't realise you wanted to see me for a seminar.'

Ayesha looked blank. 'I want you to work for me. I need to know you'll write things the way I want them written. You need to convince me that you're the right person to do it.'

The conversation had become a job interview for a job I never wanted, the tragic victim a hardnosed negotiator.

'Look,' I said. 'I thought we were going to talk about your father and what happened to him. Mike told me you were devastated and you wanted my help. But I can't help you if won't talk to me properly. And I'm certainly not going to write anything to order.'

Ayesha finished her glass of wine and waved to the waiter to bring another.

'Then I suspect we're not going to get on. I've worked in the City for long enough to know the importance of getting things clear. This is something that matters to me and I want it done properly. I'll pay you a fee – you can't be earning much from writing about psychology, for God's sake – but I'll need a proper contract with proper guarantees that you won't write anything I don't approve.'

I don't know why I didn't just walk out. It wasn't the money. My interest was in Ayesha herself, in her story, and in why she wanted it to be told.

'The point is that I can't write something I don't understand. I don't know anything about Pakistan. I don't know you. And if you won't . . .'

'But you wrote that other book, didn't you? The one about the mother and her lost son, wasn't it?'

I couldn't fathom where her hostility was coming from.

'That was different. I felt a connection with it. I can hardly feel a connection with your story if you won't tell me about it.'

She got up. 'Look,' she said, 'I don't have the time for this. I'm not in the business of haggling. I'm making you an offer. You need to commit to this project or I'm leaving.'

Ayesha was already picking up her coat from the chair beside her. She'd got her arms into the sleeves when the heel on one of her shoes broke. She stumbled back down.

I saw the change in her face; she looked exhausted and defeated. She was sobbing, the pretence of detachment gone. The tears flowed and Ayesha told me her story.

PART ONE

CHAPTER I

The phone call that sliced through her life had come three months earlier. Ayesha Rahman was in her mid-thirties, chief executive of an IT consultancy that she'd founded with friends from university. She had grown Rahburn IT from nothing into one of London's most sought-after, beginning with loss-making contracts for local firms, building up a portfolio of retail chains, then making a timely switch to work for public institutions and central government.

Success had brought Ayesha a good income and a reputation as an operator. It had swept her from backstreet Burnley in Lancashire to sophisticated society in London at a pace that had at times left her bemused. But she had enough self-belief to take it in her stride; if she felt unsure about her entitlement to sit at the top table she didn't let it show. She knew how to read people, to pinpoint their weak spots; and she had the steadiness of nerve to exploit them with a smile on her face.

Rahburn's decision to focus on Whitehall had followed the government's calamitous attempts to computerise NHS medical records. Contracts to rectify past mistakes were suddenly being offered and the big consultancies wanted them. Ayesha had pitched to the Department of Health and became such a frequent visitor at its Whitehall headquarters that the security staff gave her her own pass. The brief was for new networks that would allow the NHS to go paperless within three years. The government was putting a billion pounds into a new technology fund and winning a slice of it would make or break Rahburn as a public sector player. By the beginning of August success had seemed assured. Rahburn, along with two longer-established consultancies, was on the shortlist for a contract worth forty million over five years. Ayesha had made a storming presentation to the DH's board and the Director of IT Services had responded to her mix of brash self-confidence and flattering deference. When she suggested they meet for a drink he was delighted.

I didn't doubt Ayesha when she described how the fellow had been eating out of her hand. She was a good-looking woman with fine features and an air of serenity that men found charming. Her hair was dark and sleek, her complexion flawless café au lait. She wore designer dresses and understated jewellery that said she didn't have to try too hard. Her manner was one of urbane entitlement, the City woman who accepted admiration as her due; speaking to her on the phone you'd more likely take her for a product of Cheltenham Ladies' College than of Kahin Nahi in Pakistan.

A week after her pitch to the DH board, the Whitehall grapevine was unanimous that Ayesha had got the contract.

But one of the rival consultancies heard of her tête-à-tête with the IT Director and lodged a complaint with the department's compliance officer. Ayesha had done nothing unethical, but the love-struck civil servant had sent her a slightly too personal email and someone had leaked it. The DH had searched its departmental soul, wrung its hands and called Ayesha. A jumpy official on the end of the phone informed her that the competition for the IT contract was being reviewed and might have to be rerun with a new shortlist. He didn't say that Rahburn would be excluded, but Ayesha got the message from the tone of his voice.

The human psyche is not good at calibrating the level of unhappiness in which it finds itself. We feel overwhelmed by one set of reverses, only for them to be superseded by others even more distressing. Then we yearn for the previous afflictions that once had seemed unbearable, thinking how happy we would be to have our old troubles back again. A day after Ayesha received the phone call from Whitehall she took another, this time from her mother.

'Isha? Isha, dearest, is that you?'

Ayesha knew from the tremor in Asma's voice that something had happened.

'Yes, Mama, it's me. What is it?'

'Ya Allah! Tragedy . . . Tragedy upon us . . .'

'Mama, you need to calm down. Tell me what's happened.'

Her mother couldn't calm down. She was crying, shouting into the phone that her life was over, that she didn't want to live any more. She couldn't bring herself to put it into words; she would begin a sentence then break into sobs.

Ayesha told her to put down the phone and make herself a cup of strong *doodhpatti* tea, boiled up together with the milk. 'It will calm you, Mama. Don't do anything foolish. Just sit in the parlour and I will ring Bilal so he can come and help you.'

Ayesha picked out her younger brother's number on her speed-dial. Bilal lived in Burnley, five miles from the family home. By right, Asma should have rung him first – Pakistani women know that men must be deferred to; their pride must not be slighted. But Bilal was gentle and ineffectual; Ayesha had strength and resourcefulness. The family had come to rely on her, girl or not.

Bilal picked up. She could hear from the noise of a car engine that he was working. 'Bilal, I think you need to go round to the house as quick as you can. Mama just rang and she's in a state . . .'

'I'm driving, Isha. Can't you hear? It's Saturday night. I've got fares booked for the next five hours. I can't just drop everything . . .'

'I'm not asking you, Bil, I'm telling you. Drop off the fare that you're driving now and go straight round to the house, okay?'

Bilal did what he was told. Sixty minutes later he rang her back from their parents' home.

'I'm at the house, Ish. I've seen her and she says it's Dad. She's had a phone call from Guddu in Kahin Nahi and he's told her that something has happened to Dad. But she's so upset I can't get the details.'

'What do you mean, something's happened to Dad? Where is he?'

'In Pakistan, of course. He went weeks ago. Didn't you know? You're away in London, Ish. You don't know what's going on any more . . .'

'Tell me again, Bil. Dad's in Pakistan. And what do you say has happened to him?'

'It's not me saying it. It's Mum. She says Guddu told her. I don't know what it's all about. But it's serious. And Mama's in meltdown.'

Ayesha told her brother to put their mother back on the phone. She was a little more coherent.

'Isha, dear. Terrible news. Guddu rang. He says Daddy has died in Kahin Nahi.'

CHAPTER 2

Ayesha spent the next hours on the phone. She called Guddu, the brother of her father's mother in Kahin Nahi outside Karachi and the only member of the family there with a telephone. The first dozen attempts didn't connect, then she got a recorded voice that she recognised as her great-uncle's. Her Urdu was good enough to understand that the voice was asking her to leave a message.

'Guddu, it's me, Ayesha.' She spoke as calmly as she could. 'I'm calling you from London. Asma says something has happened to Dad, but we can't work out what. I know it isn't easy for you to call, but please . . . please would you ring me as soon as you can?' She paused and swallowed. 'Oh Guddu, I'm so worried. I'm so, so worried . . .'

Ayesha put down the phone and sat for a moment. It was after midnight. Getting upset wouldn't help anyone. She rang the Foreign Office, made a note of the out-of-hours duty number and called it. A sleepy female voice answered. 'FCO out-of-hours. This number is for emergencies only.' It was the first time that word had been spoken. 'Yes,' Ayesha said. 'Yes, it is an emergency.'

She explained to the woman what little she knew. She was alone and scared; making contact with the Foreign Office felt reassuring. The British government had the authority that she lacked. Its machinery would whir into motion and take charge of things.

'I'm sorry, but you'll have to ring back in the morning, madam,' the woman was saying. 'There isn't anything that can be done at this time of night. Ring again on the main switchboard number tomorrow.'

Ayesha blinked. 'Time of night? But my father is in trouble. I need your assistance. It's urgent.'

'I'm sorry, madam, that's not something we can help you with. And I thought you said your father had died. If he's dead, then there isn't a hurry.'

Ayesha had been buoyed by adrenalin, but things were starting to hit her now. Yes, she thought, perhaps it really is true; perhaps Daddy really is dead. She calmed herself. Guddu hadn't rung back. Until she heard from him, there was little she could do.

She tried to make the time pass by trawling the Internet for information on flights to Karachi. She found an early morning departure, glanced at her watch and saw it was leaving in less than five hours. Without thinking she opened the drawer with her British and Pakistani passports. She picked up the green one and slipped it into her handbag.

Her patience ran out; she rang Guddu again. This time he answered. 'Kahin Nahi 261813. Hello.' Guddu sounded harassed. Ayesha found herself unexpectedly on the verge of tears. 'Guddu, it's Isha. Are you all right? What's happened to Daddy? We've been hearing all sorts of things. I left you a message . . .'

Guddu was old and his native language was Urdu. Ayesha listened as he did his best to explain, but she was catching one word in three. She stopped him repeatedly to ask for clarification; the story was getting more and more confused. She picked up the word 'suicide' and asked Guddu what he meant. He said something complicated in Urdu then something incomprehensible in English. The old man was flustered, his words tumbling out at such bewildering speed that Ayesha asked him to stop. 'Guddu,' she said slowly and clearly. 'I think I should come to Kahin Nahi. Then I can see things for myself.' Her great-uncle understood; the relief and gratitude in his reply were unmistakable.

Fifteen hours later Ayesha emerged from the customs hall of Karachi's Jinnah airport carrying the single bag she'd had time to pack and plunged into the swirling sea of handwritten signs, shouting people and sweltering afternoon heat. The plane had coddled her in its familiar air-conditioned envelope, but this was another world.

In the terminal building Ayesha waved away the men in sweat-stained shirts who jostled her with cries of 'Car for you! Car for you!' and walked outside. Trusting to the safety of uniforms she buttonholed a taxi wallah and asked him to find her a driver for a journey out of town. She was worried that the man would laugh at her Urdu, but he nodded and led her to the parking lot. 'This is Jasir,' the man said. 'Tell him where you wish to journey and he will take you there in the lap of modern safety and comfort.' For the first time in twenty-four hours, Ayesha allowed herself the shadow of a smile. She negotiated the price with the driver and told him she needed to be in Kahin Nahi before sunset. She had managed to explain to Guddu that they should postpone Ibrahim's funeral to the last permitted moment.

The hour's drive passed in a flurry of anxiety. She hadn't told anyone where she was going; she hadn't slept; she felt feverish. Guddu had said suicide, but why would her happy, gentle father kill himself? If Ibrahim had died of a heart attack or in an accident that would be something she could understand. But everything she was being told seemed confusing. She wanted the truth but dreaded finding it.

Arriving in Kahin Nahi Ayesha hardly recognised the place. She hadn't been there for over twenty years. The small village had become a sprawling town. New roads ran at unexpected angles and Ayesha struggled to direct the cab driver to her grandmother's house. They made false starts along dusty streets with rows of wooden houses, some of which looked familiar but never led where she expected them to. A woman sitting at the roadside shelling peas shook her head when they asked for directions. Ayesha told the driver to mention the Rahman house and the woman asked which Rahman they meant. Ayesha said, 'The widow of Hassan, son of Mohammed.' Finally the woman nodded.

Ten minutes later they pulled up at a two-storey house with distinctive iron railings along the front. The canopies of the jacaranda trees around the building had spread extravagantly since she was last here and a herd of goats had colonised what was once the garden. She paid the driver and walked up to the house, expecting to be met by her grandmother or by Guddu. But the door was answered by a man she didn't know, and his perfunctory *as salaam alaikum* sounded unwelcoming. For a moment she feared she might have got the wrong house. She asked him in hesitant Urdu who he was, but the man told her to wait and closed the door. Ayesha's stomach knotted. The taxi driver had gone; she was alone in a town she barely knew, grappling with a language she barely spoke, embroiled in a mystery she could barely comprehend.

The door opened and Ayesha was surprised to see her Uncle Ahmed. She hadn't seen Ahmed for years, not since he and her father had fallen out so angrily that years of silence had followed, more than two decades of smouldering resentment between the brothers and chilly estrangement between the two branches of the Rahman family. Like Ibrahim, Ahmed had lived in Burnley, but they barely acknowledged each other's existence. Ayesha and her brothers were told to look away if they encountered Ahmed's children in the street.

Ayesha stared at her uncle, trying to square his presence with the events of the past twenty-four hours.

'Uncle Ahmed?'

The swarthy man with a waxed moustache stepped forward from the shadow of the doorway. Ahmed was wearing a shalwar kameez, with a prayer cap on his head. Ayesha, who had only ever seen him in English shirt and trousers, found his appearance disconcerting. When he leaned towards her she caught the smell of curry on his breath.

'My child.' Ahmed ushered her into the house. 'Come and rest.' He clicked his fingers to a serving boy. 'Tea for the memsahib. Serve it in the public room. Bring the armchair.'

Ahmed fussed over his niece, full of condolences. His sympathy was unnerving. She asked where her grand-mother was and Ahmed spread his hands. 'My mother is old; this tragedy has upset her mind. I have sent her to the house of her brother, Guddu, so he can care for her until her son is buried.'

Ayesha strained to take in what her uncle was telling her. 'Where is my father, Uncle Ahmed?' she said. 'What happened to him? How did he die?'

Ahmed tilted his head to the side, concern on his face. 'Ibrahim has been washed and anointed as the Qur'an enjoins us. He has been wrapped in the funeral sheets and will be buried before the sun goes down. As for the nature of his demise, the police station commander has recorded the death as suicide. I was not in Kahin Nahi when my brother passed. I have no further information.'

Ayesha put her hands to her face, hunched in the arm-chair in the public room. 'Uncle Ahmed,' she said, 'this has been such a shock. I had no idea Daddy was unhappy. I never ever suspected he would think of killing himself. Why would he do such a thing?'

'I repeat: I was not here when Ibrahim died, so I have no insight into his state of mind. If I may say so, you also have been living away from him. You did not know Ibrahim was unhappy, but perhaps you did not keep in touch with him as you should have. If you had stayed close, perhaps you would have known what was troubling your father. Perhaps you could have helped him.'

Ahmed's words stung her. The thought that she had neglected her duty as a daughter had been in Ayesha's mind since she learned of her father's death. But it was hard to hear it from an uncle who had never been his brother's keeper, whose coldness might have contributed to Ibrahim's despair. Ayesha was about to say as much, but kept silent. It was a shared tragedy; recriminations would help no one.

'You are right,' she said. 'I didn't do as much for him as I should have done. I know he wanted to see me more and hear more about what I was doing. But I had my job in London; my life was in London – that's why I couldn't be there for him in Burnley. It's not an excuse. I should have been a better daughter and now it's too late . . .'

Ayesha burst into tears. Ahmed soothed her. 'Don't cry, my child. Things happen in this world. People despair of life and it is no one's fault. We must trust in Allah. Life must take its course . . .'

Ayesha composed herself. It felt uncomfortable to share her grief with a man she hardly knew and whom her father had taught her to avoid. It struck her as strange that her grandmother would not be present at her son's funeral; and she wanted to speak to Guddu, who seemed to know the most about her father's death. But when she asked Ahmed to take her to Guddu's house, he shook his head. 'You must excuse me, my child. I have arrangements to make for Ibrahim's burial. Sunset is not far off and there is still much work to do.'

When Ahmed left, Ayesha rang Guddu's number on her mobile. Fifteen minutes later he was beside her, his old man's eyes bleary with tears. His narrow, veined hands were shaking with sorrow. When he embraced her she felt the fragility of his emaciated body. As a girl in Pakistan and on her later childhood visits Ayesha had always loved Guddu and she sensed that he loved her. He had the same openness of character and emotional frankness as his sister, Ayesha's grandmother, and her younger son, Ayesha's father. Guddu motioned her into the garden. They walked through the long grass that scraped their legs, scattering the goats, seeking out the shade of the jacarandas.

Guddu was anxious to tell her something and it was easier to communicate now face to face. In a mixture of Urdu and English he consoled her, squeezed her hand, shared her grief. Then he spoke about the night her father died. Ibrahim had been in Kahin Nahi for several weeks, he said, staying at his mother's house 'while he was carrying out his business'. The house was large and rambling; Ibrahim slept in a ground floor bedroom that opened onto a terrace overlooking the garden.

'I cannot be certain,' Guddu said, 'but now that I ponder upon it I recall several days on which unknown persons came to my attention in the vicinity of my sister's home. I paid no heed. But last night I was sitting with my sister in the public room, Ibrahim had retired and I was about to leave for home. At that point it seems to me that I heard voices whispering in the garden and they were speaking not Urdu or Sindhi but Pathan. I say again that I may be mistaken, but with the benefit of hindsight it appears to me that I heard several bangs or blows emanating from the part of the house where Ibrahim was quartered.'

Guddu glanced at Ayesha, trying to gauge the impact his words were making.

'My sweet girl,' he said, 'I do not wish to nurture unfounded suspicions, but subsequent events have given me food for thought. My sister became aware of Ibrahim's fate when she went to his room with his late-night cocoa. Finding him on the floor, she despatched the serving boy to alert me. I telephoned to the police station and spoke to the Station In-Charge, Inspector Iqbal Hafiz. I was surprised to learn that the police already knew of Ibrahim's death. Iqbal told me not to concern myself, that this was a case of suicide and his men were on the scene. When I hurried to your grandmother's house I found men in uniform already there. I asked to see my nephew's body, but was told that the bedroom had been sealed and Ibrahim's remains taken to the morgue.'

'But Guddu,' Ayesha said, 'how could the police have known that Daddy was dead? You had only just rung them . . .'

Guddu frowned. 'That has puzzled me. And there are other things. The police showed uncharacteristic efficiency in compiling their First Investigation Report, to the extent that they had it ready when I arrived. As the closest literate relative, I was told to sign the FIR on behalf of the family, confirming that Ibrahim had committed suicide. They would not listen when I spoke of the Pathans whispering in the garden or the noise I heard coming from Ibrahim's bedroom. It felt as if the policemen had their story fixed.'

'But that can't be right. The police wouldn't lie. What reason would they have? If they say it was suicide, then surely it must be.'

'Perhaps I am mistaken; I dearly hope I am. But Pakistan is not England, my love. Not everything here is done the way it is over there.'

It was less than twenty-four hours since Ayesha had learned of her father's death. To hear now that he may have been murdered and the police were somehow covering it up added pain that felt too cruel to bear. Perhaps it would be best to ignore what Guddu was saying, to let events take their course? That would be the simplest way, the easiest for her . . . But the thought of her dead father and the ordeal of his final moments would not leave Ayesha. She had failed him in life, she told herself; she must not fail him in death. Letting matters drop, simply accepting whatever might have happened to him would be a betrayal. She was not going to do that.

'So how do we find the truth?'

'There is a way,' Guddu said. 'It will not be pleasant. But if the police are unwilling to help, we must do things for ourselves. We must see your father's body. When I went to the morgue they refused to let me in. But even they would not have the effrontery to deny a daughter the right to see her father.'

Ayesha looked doubtful, but Guddu insisted. 'It is our only chance. You must open up the winding sheet and discover what state your father's body is in. We must not let them get away with this – for Ibrahim's sake . . .'

At the entrance to the morgue Ayesha and Guddu found

a group of men with cigarettes in their mouths and guns in their hands. Ayesha recognised one of them as the man who had opened the door of her grandmother's house. When she asked Guddu who they were, he frowned. 'They are the ones who kept me away from Ibrahim's body. I don't know who they work for, but they are powerful men, more powerful than the police.'

The men demanded Guddu and Ayesha's identification documents. They tried to bar their path. But Guddu spoke to them with an air of authority. When he told them that Ayesha was Ibrahim's daughter come to see her father the men exchanged hurried whispers. One of them took out a mobile phone and began tapping in a number, but Guddu forced the issue. 'Have you people no shame? She must be allowed to see her father. The Prophet, peace be upon him, will curse those who turn away an orphan!'

The men moved aside to let Ayesha into the building, but when Guddu made to follow they pushed him away.

It was dark in the morgue, the only sliver of light from a ventilation grille in the external wall. Ayesha's eyes grew used to the gloom. A row of shrouded corpses made her gasp. She forced herself to step forward, examining the tags on the bodies until she found the one marked Ibrahim Rahman. Pity, revulsion and awe washed through her. This final meeting with the father she had adored, fought with and consoled could not have been more unsettling. She needed time to make peace with him, but there was none; she craved the dignity of a measured farewell, but events were rushing her on.

She felt the contours of her father's body beneath the

tightly wound shroud, placed her hands on his chest, his arms and shoulders. But she could not bring herself to unwrap the cloth; the whiteness of the funeral sheet was all that lay between her and the horror beneath. She was turning away when she heard Guddu's voice. In the silent morgue it startled her; she couldn't see where it came from until she spotted a shadow at the ventilation grille. 'Ayesha, you must hurry. The men are phoning their bosses. Have you unwrapped him?'

Ayesha shook herself. 'I'm trying, Guddu. But it's not easy. I don't know what I'll find . . .'

'I know, love; I know. But you must do it. Do it for his sake!'

She located the loose end of her father's winding sheet and tugged at it. The material began to unravel. She made out the top of Ibrahim's head with the little bald patch he had taken such care to disguise with his Brylcreem and comb-overs. The familiarity of it jolted her; the thought that she would never see him again, never tease him about his hair, his paunch, his self-mocking pretence at manly vanity.

She pulled again at the cloth. Ibrahim's face was visible now, his eyes closed, his features serene. But there was something odd about the side of his head. She pulled away more of the shroud and saw it was covered in blood. Ayesha wanted to scream, but Guddu was whispering through the grille, urging her to press on.

To release the next fold of cloth she had to lift her father's head. She slid her hand under his neck, but it sank into his flesh. The back of his head was missing. Ayesha vomited on the floor. She counted the gashes that could have been caused only by the most violent of blows; she noted the weal around her father's throat where a noose of wire had buried itself in his flesh.

Guddu's voice came again at the grille. 'Ayesha! Put back the shroud! They're coming. They will kill us if they know we've opened the body!'

The men were shouting to her. 'Come out, memsahib! The sun is setting. We have to complete the burial . . .'

'. . . or the old man won't get his seventy-two virgins!' shouted another, and there was a burst of laughter.

Ayesha heard the warnings. She didn't doubt their lives were in danger. But she couldn't bring herself to do it. The thought that wrapping her father back in his funeral sheet would be the last thing she would ever do for him was too much to bear. She stood helpless over the body.

'Closing time, ladies and gentlemen! Drink up; we're closing.'

The voice of the bar manager interrupted her story. Ayesha was in tears. She had spoken for nearly two hours and held herself together with dignity. But the memory of her father's injuries, his ligatured neck and battered skull, had finally been too much. I placed my hand on her arm and she forced herself to smile.

'You're upset,' I said. 'Let's stop, shall we?'

Ayesha shook her head. 'I want to tell you everything. I haven't spoken like this to anyone. I'd like another drink.'

I looked to the waiter, but he made a gesture to say the bar was closing. 'Let me try him,' Ayesha said. 'I think he's Pakistani. I can use my Urdu.'

'Actually,' I said, 'I'm pretty certain he's Spanish.' We both laughed.

I could have prolonged our conversation – we could have gone to another bar – but the truth is I was happy to suspend Ayesha's tale. I had begun the evening with no interest in her story, but something had stirred. The narrative seemed to be settling into the plucky-heroine genre, a battle against dark forces with an outcome either tragic or triumphant. But perhaps not . . . Turning points are tangled things and the knots can be tricky to unpick. I knelt to examine the broken heel of Ayesha's shoe and managed to push it back into place. I told her it should last until the taxi got her home.

CHAPTER 3

Ayesha had repelled me with her caustic manner then filled me with sympathy. I surprised myself by how completely I took her side. She had a fierceness about her; to the world she appeared tough and unfeeling, yet I felt that I understood her. The arrogance hid a wounded girl who needed help.

I was curious, too, about her father, the enigmatic Ibrahim who had gone from fond parent to torture victim in what appeared to be a sadistic murder. In life as in fiction, we are drawn into people's stories by the lure of outcomes.

Ayesha's flat was at the top of a Victorian mansion block overlooking the Regent's Canal. She answered the door in jeans and a T-shirt. She was working on a pitch to the troubled Tesco group, an IT system that would fix the catastrophic glitches in their accounts reporting, boost the group's slipping image and bolster Rahburn's reputation. Meeting her again after the emotional intensity of the previous week's evening in the bar was awkward. Ayesha was, if not cold, business-like. I hardly expected the same confessional ardour, but I was surprised how far she had retreated from self-revelation. She had opened up too much; now she was irked, embarrassed, distant.

I sat on her white sofa and drank her black Nespresso. She was wary about why I had come back and why I had changed my mind about wanting to write about her. I tried small talk but I couldn't get her talking. I asked her to resume her story; she responded reluctantly.

She had succeeded in rewrapping her father's body before the men came to carry him off. They seemed suspicious but didn't say anything; perhaps they feared they would be blamed for letting her into the morgue. When she had tried to follow them, they pushed her away; women were not welcome at an Islamic funeral. She went with Guddu to see her grandmother, but the old woman was too distracted by grief to speak to anyone. At the funeral feast, she found some of the men who had been guarding the morgue talking to her Uncle Ahmed. When Ayesha told him she didn't believe her father had committed suicide, he frowned and asked what evidence she had. Guddu had warned her not to tell anyone about their discoveries in the morgue, so she told Ahmed she simply could not accept that Ibrahim had killed himself.

Ahmed left her in the care of his surly friends and came back two hours later with the Police Station In-Charge. Inspector Iqbal seemed flustered. 'I have some news. We have determined that Mr Rahman did not commit suicide. We have determined that Mr Rahman was murdered by the administration of poison. We have two miscreants in custody who have confessed to the crime. I have now sealed this dossier.'

Her father's death had become a murder. But why were the police talking about poison? Ayesha had found head injuries and ligature marks. Without telling anyone, she scoured the Karachi phone book and hired a private detective. Masood Jilani was a long-serving former policeman and had come across such scenarios in the past. He said the poisoning story smacked of a charade mounted by a police department bribed to cover up a crime. The arrested 'miscreants' would be part of the plot, paid to plead guilty to poisoning in the knowledge that when the case came to trial, months or years later, the judge would be told there had been no poison in the dead man's body. The prisoners would be released and it would be too late for the authorities to start looking for the real culprits.

Ayesha had been in Pakistan for over a week and needed to fly back to England. There was an IT contract that needed to be wrapped up and she didn't trust her deputy to clinch it. She told her great-uncle Guddu she would return as soon as she could, but her work kept her tied up in London for the next three months. That was the reason she came to me. A mutual acquaintance, Mike, had told her I could help with her investigation and then write about it in a newspaper or a book. Now she seemed to have cooled on the idea.

'So there you are. I've told you everything. You're up to date. There's nothing more I can tell you.'

I had been in her apartment for barely half an hour and she was ready to be rid of me. If I left now I felt I would never see her again. I tried another approach.

'Why don't you tell me some more about your father,

Ayesha? I need to know about him if we're going to do something about it.'

It worked. Ayesha slipped off her shoes and leaned back on the couch. When she began talking again the warmth had returned.

Ibrahim Rahman was born in Kahin Nahi, then a rural community on the outskirts of Karachi, in 1953. The Rahmans were landowners and conscious of their status. They belonged to one of the higher castes, living off the revenues from their land, farming some of it themselves and leasing the rest to other families. Ibrahim's father, Hassan, had fought in the war, serving in an Indian regiment along-side British units in the Far East. He had returned to Kahin Nahi in 1945 and married a cousin. They had had three girls and, despairing of having a son, had adopted the orphaned son of a second cousin. Two years later, Ibrahim was born.

The years following the war had been difficult. As head of the family, Hassan had the responsibility of preserving the Rahman land in a period of turmoil. The 1947 partition of India triggered mass migrations as Muslims flocked to the newly created Pakistan and Hindus fled in the opposite direction. The new arrivals needed somewhere to live and Pakistan was riven by clashes over property ownership. Hassan fought for the family's territory, but it wasn't easy. Land rights had long been contentious in the subcontinent, with disputes kindling vendettas that flamed into violence and murder. The British had set up a land registry in the late nineteenth century, but corruption and inefficiency meant that it remained an approximate business. Local officials known as *patwaris* were put in charge of the written records. Personal greed, bribes and threats could persuade them to falsify ownership documents in favour of their friends or themselves.

Hassan had to be careful. He paid money and homage to the patwari, knew whom to flatter, whom to court and whom to cajole. He was a local man, adept at intrigue. By the time Ibrahim was born, the family's prospects seemed secure. Hassan ran the land and oversaw the farming, leaving his wife to manage affairs at the house.

Ibrahim's earliest memories were happy ones. From the moment he could walk he spent his days with his father, tramping the fields, inspecting the cattle. At harvest time, he and his cousins would meet to gather the crops in a round of festive activity that united the family. Ibrahim learned the ways of the Pakistani countryside, absorbed its sights and sounds and smells and saw the way its character changed with the seasons. He soaked up the heat of the summer and drank in the rains that slaked the land in spring. Autumn beguiled him with its imperceptible progression, turning the world from green to brown; the crisp winter nights sent him huddling under his eiderdown.

A joyful childhood left Ibrahim with a love of his native land. In later years with Ayesha on his knee he embellished its charms. She grew up with an image of her father as a latter-day Mowgli living wild in nature's realm, never knowing when he would encounter charging elephants or be forced to run in panic from man-eating tigers.

Ibrahim's tales of the adventures he shared with his father endeared him to her. She loved this man who seized her by the waist and threw her dizzyingly, thrillingly high. She screamed for mercy, but knew he would not let her down; she learned the feel of him, the contours of his shoulders that she clung to in exhilarated terror, the warmth of his chest as he hugged her to him. She imbibed the smells of his body, the acrid fragrance of his sweat, the sweetness of his aftershave, the half-life of the spices he'd consumed the night before, the shiny Brylcreem that he plastered on his hair.

When Ibrahim recounted his life, his daughter heard it change and expand from one telling to the next, full of colourful variations that she later recognised as the bountiful fantasies of a happy imagination. When, older, she realised that Daddy had never slain leopards or fought off bandits and dacoits, she loved him all the more for it. He had cherished her so much that his fondest wish was to impress her with his valour, to convince her that he was the greatest, loveliest daddy who had ever lived. For Ayesha, he was.

In some of his childhood tales, Ibrahim spoke of his sisters and brother. In Pakistan, he told her, a family would educate only one of its sons while the other children would remain at home to help with the family's business. Ahmed was the elder, so he got the education. Ibrahim had no problem with that; the sons would inherit equally, and he had no interest in going to school. He was happy to wave Ahmed off to the madrasa and stay behind with Hassan to roam the land. The girls got no schooling because they were girls so it would have been a waste. When Ayesha interrupted to protest, 'But Daddy, *I'm* a girl!' Ibrahim would laugh and say, 'Things are different now, Ish. You'll get whatever you want. You know Daddy can't refuse you anything . . .'

For the young Ibrahim, the Pakistan of his childhood was open spaces and nature's bounty. But the legacy of Britain's presence in the country remained strong. The Asian homeland and the British motherland were divided by geography, culture and religion; after 1947 statues of Queen Victoria were pulled down and smashed, some of them replaced by bronze replicas of the Qur'an. But when things were hard at home, when monsoon rains washed away the crop, when violence and dissension threatened the family or the nation, the people looked to Britain. Britain held their dreams and their ambitions. They learned about it in books and films, in school and in the flighty comedies that came through their radios and TVs. A world where naughty vicars chased scantily clad women, where men dressed up in frocks and everyone saluted a matriarch in a gold coach carried ineffable fascination. It was a place the young wanted to experience and the old dreamed of, a distant paradise where life's troubles would be soothed by contented prosperity. 'To London!' was their equivalent of the Jews' 'Next year in Jerusalem . . .' Even the fulminations of the baleful Enoch Powell, the man who had lived in and known the subcontinent but took delight in demonising its people, failed to dampen the enthusiasm for migration to the foggy nirvana.

In 1965 Ahmed went. He had done well at school and completed his studies. Hassan respected his adopted son; he took pride in his achievements, but he never had the same affection for him as he did for Ibrahim, his youngest child and dutiful companion in the rural life he loved. Seeing Ahmed off on the boat to Southampton was not such a wrench in Hassan's heart. He gave him his grandfather's amulet for guidance in the new world and whispered words of advice in his ear. He told him to work hard, keep out of trouble and write as often as he could. But he didn't shed a tear as the boat left the quay.

Ahmed's passage had taken some manoeuvring. Uncle Kabir, a relative by marriage to Hassan's cousin, was already living in Lancashire and had agreed to be Ahmed's sponsor. That satisfied England's demand for financial guarantees from its new residents. But the British consul in Karachi was a stickler, renowned for his obdurate questioning and citing of rules. So Hassan and his wife decided to play safe. When they filled in the forms they wrote that Ahmed was Kabir's son, automatically entitled to join his father in the UK. At the visa interview the consul looked suspicious. But records of births, marriages and deaths in Pakistan are flexible things that can be moulded to suit many purposes. Members of a family marry their first and second cousins with bewildering regularity and the system of given and family names is so unregulated that Pakistanis themselves barely understand it. A harassed, red-faced foreigner is very unlikely to get to the bottom of things, and the consul didn't. He huffed and puffed then applied his stamp to the triplicated forms that would send Ahmed on his way.

In the week before Ahmed was due to sail, he drew Ibrahim into an adventure much darker than any he'd had before. It started as a joke. The boys in the village knew Amir and they knew his boasting. They were teenagers and most of them rubbed along together. But Amir was always talking about how rich his family was, how they had a car while others had to travel on foot, how his father could spend more in a day than the other boys' parents did in a year. Ibrahim, who was young, would listen and smile. Ahmed, older, got angry.

Ibrahim smiled when Amir said he was going to see Nour. Nour was a girl with long plaits and a slightly scared manner. She was pretty; the boys admired her from afar. When Amir boasted that he would do more, Ibrahim didn't really understand. Ahmed listened to Amir's prattle and kept his counsel.

When Amir disappeared from the village and Nour disappeared shortly afterwards, Ahmed went to see the girl's father. He told him he had overheard the young lovers' conversations and knew their plans. Nour's father, humiliated by his daughter's betrayal, thanked Ahmed and asked him to come with him; he wanted the young man's help to locate the lovers' refuge. Ahmed agreed and told Ibrahim to jump into the four-wheel drive with him. Was he looking for safety in numbers? Did he want a twelve-year-old to witness the wages of dishonour? Or did Ahmed know that what was about to happen would shock and scar his brother for ever? However much he thought about it in the years that followed, Ibrahim could not find the answer.

Both boys saw what happens to a daughter who betrays her family's honour. Ahmed and Ibrahim saw Amir being hanged. And they saw Nour buried alive. They saw her trying to clamber out of the pit, catching their eye in a desperate, imploring panic that Ibrahim never forgot. Angered by her struggling, Nour's father smacked her head with the spade he had used to dig her grave and she fell back in. The men took it in turns to shovel the earth onto her quivering body.

When Ahmed sailed for England, Ibrahim was left with the memory of Nour's last moments. It kept him awake then soured his dreams when he slept. Ahmed had shrugged and mocked him. 'These things happen. It's the will of Allah. Get used to it.'

Ibrahim tried to harden his soul, tried to tell himself he must accept the absence of kindness and mercy in the world. But it wasn't easy. He wondered what he would do if ever he were to have a daughter who betrayed him in the way that Nour had done. Would he too enforce the just retribution that the code of honour demands?

With Ahmed gone, Ibrahim blossomed. He was his own man now. He went into the world, met new people and learned from them. He was no longer the simple country boy at home only in the fields. He frequented the town, learned the ways of commerce and saw what sort of thing makes money and what is merely a waste of time. Unlike Ahmed, Ibrahim was sociable and open. He had a frankness about him that endeared him to people. He could talk to anyone, from a chai wallah to a professor.

Ibrahim's ambitions grew with his confidence. The life of a backwater like Kahin Nahi was no longer enough. He asked his father if he too could make the trip to England, but Hassan was reluctant. Ibrahim was his favourite, destined to take over the stewardship of the family's lands as the baton passed between generations. Ibrahim persisted. Hassan tried to be firm, but he loved his son and wanted him to be happy. Soon after his sixteenth birthday, Ibrahim followed in his brother's footsteps.

Ahmed had been working in England for four years and had saved enough to buy his brother an air ticket from Karachi to London. To satisfy the British authorities he acted as Ibrahim's sponsor and financial guarantor, and on an October morning in 1969 the two were reunited in the terminal of Gatwick airport. Ahmed had borrowed a car from a Pakistani friend who ran a cab firm in Burnley and driven down before dawn. As they headed north the brothers drank tea from Ahmed's Thermos flask and ate cold samosas out of a Tupperware box. Ibrahim marvelled at the roads, the cars, the houses and the newness of everything. Ahmed, sophisticated cosmopolitan, mocked his bumpkin brother and boasted of the life he had been living in Albion's bright delights.

When Ahmed said they were approaching Burnley, Ibrahim's stomach tightened. This was home now. He felt the thrill of anticipation, the dread of the unknown. As they drove by the terraced houses he pictured the lives of those who resided behind the lace curtains and pot plants. His heart filled with hope. Britain was the land of opportunity.

Kabir's house looked like all the others. The paint was peeling and the windows were dirty, but when they dragged Ibrahim's suitcases into the hallway the smell of curry that leached from the carpets, the ceilings and the bright patterned wallpaper was comfortingly familiar. Two Pakistani men ran down the stairs and out of the front door with a cheery *as salaam alaikum* in the characteristic burr of Kahin Nahi.

Ahmed saw Ibrahim's look of surprise. 'It's not just you and me who live with Uncle Kabir, 'Brahim. There's a dozen of us. Don't worry – we're all from Kahin Nahi. There are no outsiders.'

'But Ahmed,' Ibrahim said, wide-eyed. 'How can everyone fit in? Where does everyone sleep?'

'All in good time, brother,' Ahmed said. 'You'll get used to things. It's different from at home, but we manage.'

Ahmed told Ibrahim to put his bags in the back bedroom. There were two rooms upstairs and each had four beds. All but two of them were occupied by sleeping men huddled under blankets.

'We sleep in relays,' Ahmed said. 'It's not a problem, because we all work at the mill and we all do different shifts. Different shifts at work . . . different shifts in bed! Come on, I'll show you the kitchen.'

In a room downstairs an iron pot was bubbling on the stove. 'We keep the curry cooking round the clock,' Ahmed said. 'There's always someone who needs a meal, so we just add more ingredients as the day goes on. On Sunday afternoons everyone sits around the pot and we eat and smoke and talk, just like at home. Abdul's in charge of the cooking; he makes the curry and the chapattis and we all chip in to the cost. Life is sweet, little brother.'

On Monday morning, Ahmed took him to the mill. It was bigger than anything Ibrahim had seen, a looming hulk of blackened brick towering over the terraced streets, shading out the light. Inside, the noise engulfed him; the air shuddered with the *moto perpetuo* of machinery, cogwheels spinning, shuttles flying in the complex cross rhythms of the industrial dance. Men hurried back and forth with hammers and oil and bobbins, midgets beside the dark machines. Wisps of cotton hung in the air like clouds of icing sugar dusting the rumbling lathes.

The foreman weighed Ibrahim up. The man was a north Punjabi and Ibrahim struggled with his accent. In his eagerness to please he heard himself gabbling obsequiously in reply to the fellow's questions. 'Where are you from? Are you legal over here? What experience do you have? How will you show your gratitude if I take you on?' Ahmed had told Ibrahim what to expect. He would receive no pay for the first month and the foreman would take a cut of his wages for the next six. After that the arrangement would be reviewed, with the level of future contributions dependent on Ibrahim's work rate and on his participation in the complex scams that the foreman outlined to him.

The mills were owned by white bosses, but the workforce was almost exclusively Pakistani and Pakistani work practices had taken root. The foreman and the shift masters demanded a sliding scale of bribes in return for getting or keeping a job, for promotions and for the right to take holidays. The workers got their pay in cash every two weeks and there was no point in complaining if some of it was missing. Phantom employees were put on the payroll, clocked on, clocked off and paid at the going rate with their wages shared among those in charge according to the level of respect their position commanded. The bookkeepers were Pakistani, too, so the bosses never learned of the money that percolated out of their accounts.

Pakistani communities in Britain bring with them the

customs of their homeland, and Pakistan does not work in the same way that Europe does. Formal law, formal justice and formal policing are not the order of the day; society runs along other lines, with patronage, respect and honour taking the place of codified rules. Law is clan-based, family and tribal, administered by powerful men whose rulings are imposed by force. And when Pakistani tribes settle in Britain, they settle together. The population of east Bradford hails from one region of Pakistan, that of north Rochdale from another. Clan structures, practices and accents are all preserved.

The area of Burnley where Uncle Kabir had settled was a mini Kahin Nahi. The men who passed through his house, staying for a week, a month or a year as they strove to establish themselves in Britain, were from the same suburb of western Karachi. They shared a common background and common tales of life back home. In the evenings they returned from the mill, ate their curry and chapattis, smoked their cigarettes and reminisced about the past. When things were going well they would talk about their women, their ambitions and their plans for the future. Then it was time to wake the others who were on night shift and take their place in bed.

The camaraderie, the shared memories and the familiar codes of conduct made it easy for Ibrahim to settle. He was a young man and the future was his. England delighted and surprised him. Shortly after his arrival he came out from his shift in the factory to find the world magically transformed. The grimy buildings and litter-strewn streets had vanished and in their place a pristine veil of white had made the universe anew. Ibrahim marvelled at the miracle, ran to tell his housemates and slid headlong on the icy pavement.

There were things that were less easy to accommodate. In his first months in Britain he found the country's easy-going ways and lax morality disconcerting. After Pakistan's fierce insistence on the dictates of honour and religious observance, the Britishers' addiction to drink, their love of gambling and their displays of sexual depravity shocked him. But Ibrahim acclimatised. He was a nice-looking boy, tall and gangly with a shock of thick black hair and a winning smile. The 1970s were dawning and he looked good in flared jeans and denim waistcoats; he grew a moustache that gave him the air of a young Omar Sharif. Pakistani boys were still not that common in Lancashire and Ibrahim discovered that he held a fascination for English girls who didn't mind cocking a snook at their fuddy-duddy parents. For three liberating years, he went out, forced himself to drink shandy and improved his English with the help of crackly LPs by David Bowie and Herman's Hermits.

For all his accreted Britishness, Ibrahim's heart remained Pakistani. Unlike some of his friends he didn't pine for the old country, but he kept in touch with his family, writing letters that took a fortnight to arrive and eagerly awaiting replies that took even longer. He attended the mosque on Fridays and tried to pray five times a day, *Salat al-fajr* at dawn, *Salat al-zuhr* at midday, *Salat al-'asr* in the afternoon, *Salat al-maghrib* at sunset and *Salat al-'isha* at midnight. When he forgot, he reasoned that he was young and Allah would probably understand.

The Pakistani code of social precedence had followed its sons to their new home and few questioned its demands. Social rank derived from age, wealth, influence and the position a man occupied in a family. The system of castes and clans seemed mysterious to outsiders, but those who belonged to it understood every nuance. Families were assigned their place on the scale according to the history they brought with them, the land they owned or the connections they had with the dynasties of Pakistani politics. Kabir was venerated as the patriarch who had brought the Kahin Nahi boys to Britain and the father who replaced their fathers. He demanded and received money and deference; even when he was wrong he was right. They may have resented having to pay homage, having to assuage Kabir's vanity and rapaciousness, but they did it because that was how things worked.

The same relationship of entitlement and debt ran right down the social ladder. Each man knew to whom he owed respect and from whom he could command it. Even those at the bottom, the poor, the progeny of insignificant families and despised castes, accepted their fate as the immovable equation of life. It had been thus since time began, and there was little chance of it changing.

But for all its feudal stability, the system imposed demands. For individuals and families to preserve their place in the pecking order they had to be constantly on guard to defend it. Maintaining respect and protecting honour were paramount requirements; losing face, allowing oneself to be disrespected was fatal. If a family let an insult go it could be shamed and ridiculed, its authority gone.

The result was that insults, real or imagined, were answered with shattering force. Implacable violence was the response to loss of face; those who didn't avenge a slur were weaklings and cowards. And slurs were everywhere, from disparaging remarks to insufficient toadying, the failure to pay bribes, the refusal of a wedding proposal or a marriage that went wrong. A girl could dishonour her father by declining an arranged marriage or falling for the wrong boy. A boy could dishonour his parents-in-law by abandoning or divorcing their daughter. All these offences demanded immediate, manifest retribution.

Young Ibrahim did not question the ways of his homeland. He was obligated to his older brother because Ahmed had brought him to England, acted as his sponsor and taught him the customs of English life. Ahmed was owed respect and Ibrahim gave it.

Ibrahim's footloose years came to an end in 1974. He was twenty-one and it was time to marry. From Kahin Nahi Hassan wrote to say that the family had found him a bride; Asma was seventeen and Ibrahim's first cousin. They had met as children when they helped to harvest the crops on the Rahman estate, but they hadn't seen each other for years. Hassan enclosed a photograph so Ibrahim could picture his future partner. As both families had agreed on the match, Ibrahim knew there was no point arguing; he wrote to say he would be pleased to marry Asma.

In the early summer he flew to Karachi and took the bus down rutted roads to Kahin Nahi. He was back for the first time in five years and the place struck him as primitive. The countryside he had loved when he walked out as a child with Hassan seemed arid now, the animals malnourished, the villages impoverished.

But Ibrahim found Asma a willing and grateful bride; she was pretty and personable and her family had provided a generous dowry. For them, Ibrahim was a catch. Marrying 'an Englishman' was a sign of status. It meant their daughter could bank on an invitation to join her husband in Britain; there were bureaucratic hurdles to leap, but their grand-children would be British.

The wedding was low-key. Ibrahim had told his foreman that he was getting married, but a week off work was the best he could negotiate. When he returned to Burnley he was joshed by his housemates. They quizzed him on his wedding night performance and asked if the beautiful Asma had appreciated his virility. Ibrahim smiled and took it in good spirits. When the letter came three months later tell-ing him that Asma was pregnant, he showed it to his friends and they slapped him on the back.

Ibrahim was growing up. A married man had respon-sibilities and he lived up to them. Every month he sent a portion of his salary by Western Union transfer to Asma's father in Kahin Nahi. Every month Asma's father wrote to thank him and to explain why Ibrahim would need to increase the amount of money he was sending. Urgent repairs were needed to the family home, an unex-pected tax bill had come in, a member of the extended family had had another baby. The flow of money from Pakistani men in the new world to families in the old was a fact of life. Some of Ibrahim's mates grumbled about the feckless folk back home and their insatiable demands for cash. But Ibrahim shrugged and sent them what they asked for.

Ibrahim worked hard because he owed it to his future family and because he was a young man who liked to please. When the foreman offered him overtime he did it; when they told him to sign a dodgy worksheet he signed it. Ibrahim liked Burnley life and Burnley liked him. His old girlfriends stayed friends; some would have liked to stay more, but Ibrahim thought of Asma back in Kahin Nahi and told them he was spoken for. On his birthday they helped his Pakistani housemates stage a party, first at Uncle Kabir's and then at the pub on the corner. Several of the English girls were married or going steady and they brought their partners. Young working-class white men, they were suspicious of the Pakistani boys but drink and jollity helped bridge the divide.

The following weekend some of them invited Ibrahim and Ahmed to Turf Moor. Burnley had just been promoted from the second division of the Football League and were storming up the table in the top flight. Their opponents were West Ham United, the stadium was packed and the fiesta was on. No one noticed two non-white faces among the 18,216 who passed through the turnstiles; Ibrahim and Ahmed were part of the crowd and part of the fun. When the white boys chanted 'Up the Clarets!' and 'Super Dobbo!' they did the same. They barely understood the rules of the game, but it was exhilarating to sing and shout, to share in something that Englishmen felt passionately about. When Geoff Nulty put Burnley ahead with a rasping volley into the top of the net, their white friends included them in the communal embraces. They bought them pork pies at half-time and didn't notice when the brothers slipped them uneaten into their pockets. In the second half West Ham's Graham Paddon equalised with a scuffed shot that crept over the line to silence the home fans. Ibrahim sensed the change that swept over the terraces and motioned Ahmed to stop shouting. The rest of the game was played in a mood of frustration; there was discontented muttering as the crowd streamed out of the ground. Ibrahim and Ahmed said goodbye to their friends and set off down Brunshaw Road to walk home. At the corner of Irene Street a gang of youths set on them, attacking them with bottles and sticks, kicking them as they lay on the ground, shouting, 'Kill the Pakis! Up with Enoch! Send the bastards home!'

The doctor in A&E told Ahmed that he had two broken ribs and Ibrahim that he was lucky not to lose his sight. Some of the boys at Uncle Kabir's nodded sagely in an 'I told you so' way. Abdul the chapatti maker produced a leaflet he'd found lying on the ground in the Open Market and everyone gathered round the curry pot while the English speakers translated it out loud. It was from an organisation called the National Front and it carried extracts from a speech by an MP called Enoch Powell:

In fifteen or twenty years there will be in this country three and a half million Commonwealth immigrants and their descendants. Whole areas and towns across England will be occupied by sections of the immigrant population. We must be mad, literally mad, to permit the annual inflow of some 50,000 immigrant dependants. It is like watching a nation heaping up its own funeral pyre. So insane are we that we actually permit unmarried persons to immigrate for the purpose of founding a family with spouses and fiancés whom they have never seen – and I am making no allowance at all for fraudulent entry.

The reference to fraudulent entry provoked a little nervous laughter. Most of those present had bent the rules in one way or another, and all of them had fiancées in Pakistan waiting to become part of Powell's statistics. The MP went on:

The native English population find themselves made strangers in their own country. They find their homes and neighbourhoods changed beyond recognition, their plans and prospects for the future defeated; at work they find that employers hesitate to apply to the immigrant worker the standards of discipline and integrity required of the native-born worker; they begin to hear more and more voices telling them that they are now the unwanted.

There was some tittering at the mention of corrupt work standards, but the mood was edgy.

The idea that immigrants can be integrated into our population is a dangerous delusion [the leaflet concluded]. We are seeing the growth of vested interests in sharpening

racial and religious differences, with a view to the exercise
of domination over the native population. As I look ahead,
I am filled with foreboding; like the ancient Roman, I see
the River Tiber foaming with blood.

At the end of the reading there was silence. One of the
younger boys asked if this meant 'the English are going
to send us all back home'. But Uncle Kabir, who had sat
immobile throughout, stood up slowly then loudly and
deliberately farted. As the room collapsed into laughter, he
folded the leaflet three times and lit it on the gas jet under
the curry pot before dropping the burning ashes into the
bin.

Ahmed and Ibrahim's injuries were slow to heal, but they
couldn't afford to miss work. When they turned up at the
mill their fellow workers averted their eyes, thinking how
easily they could have suffered the same fate. Racism was
rising as the British economy slumped.

Ahmed and Ibrahim didn't speak about the attack or
the effect it had had on them, but Ibrahim sensed that his
brother blamed him. Ahmed made disapproving references
to Ibrahim's 'so-called white friends' who had taken them
to the football game then left them to fend for themselves.
Ibrahim tried to explain. 'I think those miscreants must
have been West Hammers people,' he said. 'Because
Burnley people love us.' Ahmed snorted and walked away.

At the next kitchen gathering, Ahmed spoke about the
danger Pakistani people faced in Britain and how they
must band together to protect themselves. Several of the
men agreed; the only way to be safe was to build strong

communities and keep the whites out. Ibrahim spoke, too, but with an apologetic smile. 'The whites aren't all racists,' he said. 'The people I know are ordinary folk like us. We don't want to cut ourselves off from everyone, do we?' The reaction from the rest of the room took him aback. A welter of voices damned the English and warned about the dangers of trusting any of them. Ibrahim tried to object, but Ahmed waved him to be quiet. 'Brother,' he said, 'I am your senior. You owe me respect and I order you to stop seeing your whites. They have brought shame upon us and pain. I will not permit you to expose us to such hostility.'

Ibrahim bowed his head and sat down. Ahmed was his older brother; to argue with him in public would be an affront to his dignity that neither of them would be able to live with. But the following day on the way to the mill, Ibrahim reopened the discussion. 'I'm not arguing with you, Ahmed. Of course you're right about the racists. But the way to deal with them isn't to retreat into ourselves. We'll end up living in ghettoes. Why don't you try and learn English, brother? You'll get on much better in this country. You could be a part of things.'

Ahmed laughed. 'You saw what the National Front wrote, didn't you? They don't want integration – they say it will never work. So why should we even try? They don't want us, 'Brahim, so why should we want them? This is our country too, you know. We need to get whatever we can out of it.'

A month later a letter came from Kahin Nahi informing Ibrahim that he was a father. Asma had gone into labour unexpectedly. She had endured the ride along bumpy roads to the hospital. She hadn't complained about the heat and the flies, the primitive maternity unit and the lack of hygiene during the birth. But she cried when the doctor told her it was a girl. By the time the letter arrived in Burnley, Ibrahim's daughter was already three weeks old.

'And that baby was me.' Ayesha sat up on the couch and looked in my direction. 'Apparently my dad read the letter out to his mates and said something like, "I'd rather have had a boy, but never mind." I think he was just playing it cool, though, because that night he went out to the pub and bought drinks for the whole bar. He was only twenty-two, so at that age you don't want to be too sentimental, do you?'

'I suppose not,' I said. 'But can I ask you something? You said this all happened in 1975, right? So doesn't that make you nearly forty? I thought you told me you were thirty-four . . .'

Ayesha grinned. She had a luminous smile that I hadn't noticed when I first met her; she could probably convince people she was whatever age she told them she was. 'In my business, you need to be young and bright. Let's say thirty-four is my professional age. How old are you?'

'Almost old enough to be your father . . .' I stopped myself. 'I'm sorry. That's not a very sensitive thing to say under the circumstances.'

'Don't worry,' Ayesha said. 'I don't find it offensive. There's something I quite like about it . . . Can I ask *you* something? Why are you here? Is this just an opportunity for a book for you?'

'It's partly that.'

'And what's the other part?'

'I suppose I'm interested in you.'

'As a person? Or as a character?'

We laughed.

'Both . . . I'm interested in you and in writing your story. I don't want you to pay me a fee, though.'

'Yes, you said that. Why not?'

'Because if you're paying me, you'd think you had the right to tell me what to write. It's to do with integrity and telling the truth.'

'Really? So you'd be telling the truth, would you? You wouldn't be changing and embellishing things to make the drama better? Are you sure about that? And how could I be sure you wouldn't write something I don't like?'

'You'd have to trust me. Not everything can be guaranteed by money, Ayesha. Sometimes you have to put your faith in someone.'

CHAPTER 4

I woke to the phone ringing. The clock said 5.30am.

'Martin, are you awake?'

I recognised her voice.

'It's 5.30, Ayesha. What's the matter?'

'My detective in Pakistan says he's got news. I want you to hear it.'

'You want me to hear . . .? You mean we are going to write this? I thought you . . .'

'Of course we're going to write it! Can you be here by seven? I've set up a call.'

An hour or so later the door to Ayesha's flat was open so I walked in. She was haranguing a telephone operator somewhere in Pakistan and gestured for me to fetch coffee from the kitchen. When I came back she had Masood Jilani on the speakerphone.

'Listen, Masood,' she was saying, 'I've got someone with me whose Urdu is even worse than mine – he doesn't have any. You're going to have to speak English. And this line is terrible, so you'll need to speak very clearly, okay?'

'Wilco, Miss Rahman. All understood.' Masood Jilani's voice carried the 4,000 miles from Karachi with military precision. He hadn't spent twenty years in the Pakistani police for nothing. 'Report in hand. Awaiting your go-ahead.'

Ayesha glanced at me with a mixture of amusement and pride. It hadn't been easy finding the best private detective in Kahin Nahi, but by luck or judgment she'd got him.

'Thank you, Masood. Please go ahead.'

In English garnished by archaisms that persist in the subcontinent decades after being ditched in the motherland, Masood Jilani outlined the results of his investigations in the weeks since Ayesha had left Pakistan.

'Miss Rahman, I beg leave to report. Despite negative machinations from the competent authorities, I have complied with your instructions and secured an independent autopsy on the subject Ibrahim Rahman. Hold-ups were encountered because the police opposed exhumation then refused to make available testing facilities. But my colleague Nazir, working in the coroner's department, ensured the post mortem was carried out to the highest standards. The results confirm beyond doubting that your father was murdered in most brutal fashion, viz. blows to the head with blunt instrument at a time when the victim was bound hand and foot and a ligature noose pulled around his neck. Cause of death was either asphyxiation from said ligature or catastrophic trauma from repeated blows. The forensic technician who attended the autopsy says he has rarely seen such damage to a human cranium. In his opinion it was caused by sledgehammer blows wielded onto the rear of skull while the victim was being pinned down on a concrete floor. In light of ligature marks on wrists and ankles, it is unlikely that Mr Rahman would have been able to defend himself.'

I saw Ayesha's face fall and her lip tremble. She struggled with the horror but refused to surrender to it.

'Thank you,' she said. 'That confirms what I have believed to be the case since I saw my father's body. I have not been imagining things. And now we have a clear picture of what we are dealing with. But, Masood, can you tell me who could have done this? Who could have murdered my father in such a brutal way?'

Masood Jilani was reluctant to speculate. 'I am not in a position to answer this question at the moment. My inquiries are at an early stage. But I must inform you that such crimes are not uncommon in Pakistan. There are dangerous men here who control many things and do not fear retribution for their actions. Organised criminals traffic in alcohol, in land, in drugs, in people and they do not care whom they murder to protect these interests. It could have been any of these, any one of them who had a score to settle with your father.'

Ayesha shook her head. 'I don't think that's possible. My father was just an ordinary man. He had no connection with that sort of thing. He was a taxi driver, Masood, not a Mafioso.'

'I understand, Miss Rahman. But it is my job to ask questions. As one of your great European detectives said, "I suspect everyone and I suspect no one." I would be indebted to you for whatever information you can furnish about Mr

Ibrahim's business activities. In my experience, this is an area which often provides fertile soil.'

'Business activities? He didn't have any,' Ayesha said. 'He was in Pakistan to look after his mother. She's in her eighties and very frail. He was a good man doing a good deed . . . and now he's been murdered . . .'

On the other end of the phone line, Masood Jilani did not sense the emotion that had gripped Ayesha. 'Be that as it may. But I need to know everything about your father or we will simply remain in darkness. I must know about his financial affairs, business associates, land, property. Did he have enemies? Were there feuds? And I need to know about his personal life, his emotional involvements. I cannot tell you how many times I have encountered men who have a second family hidden away, with a wife and children in Britain and another family in their home village. I cannot exclude such a scenario in your father's case. And that can be a powerful motive for murder.'

'That's completely impossible. I don't believe any of that can be true about my dad. He was so gentle and open, and so *transparent* – he had no secrets from anyone.'

Masood Jilani coughed. 'But that, I'm afraid, is the nature of secrets; they are things that no one knows about or even suspects. If they did, then they would not be secrets . . .'

'No, Masood. Not in this case. Everyone loved my father. He had no enemies.'

Ayesha spoke with complete conviction, with total faith in the man who had cared for her and protected her all her life. She was insistent on Ibrahim the innocent victim and I wanted her to be right. Her claim that her father had no business interests in Pakistan left me uneasy – I remembered that Guddu had spoken of Ibrahim 'carrying out his business' while staying at his mother's house – but I said nothing. Ayesha felt vindicated by Masood's discoveries; she had been right not to accept that her father's death was a suicide, and now she wanted retribution.

'Why don't you go and confront the police, Masood? We know for a fact that my father was murdered, and they are doing nothing about it. Why don't you talk to Inspector Iqbal?'

Masood counselled caution. 'The police are powerful, sometimes treacherous. Your great-uncle Guddu was right when he told you not to reveal to them what you discovered about the body in the morgue. I know how the police work and they can be as dangerous as the criminals. We need to stalk this tiger.'

'Well, the key thing is to find the killers,' Ayesha said, 'and to make them pay for what they did to my dad. I'll take your advice. Get on with your investigation and tell me what you find. Then we'll decide what we do about the police. The person I have with me here is an investigative journalist. Martin's going to help us with our search, and the book he's going to write will expose the things that go on in Pakistan. You should copy him in on everything you send to me.'

When Ayesha put down the phone, I thanked her for including me in the correspondence with Masood; it felt like a sign of trust. She nodded. 'You see why I want you to write about this. I want you to know exactly what went on, so you can shame those who did it.'

The sun rose in the bay window overlooking the canal. Things seemed to have eased between us, the memory of my last, frosty visit to her apartment apparently forgotten. But other tensions remained. Ayesha wanted me expose the men who had killed her father, and that raised the prospect of personal danger for me as well as her. And we differed over who would have control over the book, who would lead and who would follow.

I got up to leave, but Ayesha offered to show me her flat. On a bookshelf there were photos of a young man in chinos and a blue shirt. I asked who it was.

'That's Peter. We're pretty much engaged.'

'Pretty much? What does that mean?'

'It means I'm not sure. What about you? You're married?'

'Yes. Twenty years.'

'I see. A good experience?'

'Are you asking my advice?'

'Maybe.'

'How long have you and Peter been together?'

'Nearly six years, but we've had to keep it secret. Peter's white; my family wouldn't have approved.'

'Okay. But you haven't married Peter in all that time, so what makes you think you'll do it now?'

Ayesha frowned. 'I don't know if I will . . . Perhaps . . . My father would have been heartbroken if I'd married Peter; that's partly why I didn't. But he's gone now and somehow I feel free. It's terrible to think that I'm free because my daddy's dead. He left me bereaved and liberated; a punishment and a gift all at the same time . . . I can't get my head around it.'

'I don't think you have to, Ayesha. You don't need to feel bad. You loved your father; and you love Peter, don't you?'

'Maybe. When marriage was impossible, I never had to ask myself if I loved him enough to marry him . . .'

The conversation had taken an awkward turn. I was opening the door to leave when Ayesha threw her arms round me. 'Thank you so much,' she said. 'I'm so glad I came to you.'

CHAPTER 5

Embarking on a new book offers the fascination of a beginning with many endings. But for a book that springs from real events the devil, perversely, is in the uncertainty. Might those involved back out with the thing half-written? Might they disagree over how the story should be told? For the author it is an unsecured emotional investment in a venture that can founder on many rocks. The tone would be a challenge. Ayesha's story was full of drama; the book would have to tread a path between underselling and overplaying it. And the form was a dilemma. Would it be a factual documentary? A dramatised version with imagined scenes and dialogue? Or should the whole thing be fictionalised? Would 'Martin' appear as a character, and if so would it be me or a fictitious avatar? Names, places and some events would in any case have to be changed to shield those at risk. The story revolved around a murder, the perpetrators of which were still at liberty. Naming them would expose the victim's family – and potentially the writer – to reprisals.

Christmas came. On Boxing Day I found an email from Masood Jilani, addressed to Ayesha and copied to me as she had instructed:

Dear Miss Rahman

I beg to report that I have been following leads as per your commission and I fear I have discovered something unsavoury. Were you aware that your father has been a regular visitor to Pakistan for the past eleven years? May I inquire if you were aware of the purpose of these visits?

Yours respectfully,

Senior Inspector (retired) Masood Jilani.

The tone of the message was ominous. I emailed Ayesha. She did not reply directly, but copied me on her response to Masood:

Dear Masood,

No, my father did not tell me about his visits to Pakistan. I have been living away from the family home during the period you refer to. I believed he was visiting Pakistan to care for his mother, my grandmother. If you have any indication to the contrary, please let me know.

Masood's reply came almost at once:

Dear Miss Rahman,

I do not wish to leap to conclusions. But I have discovered that your uncle Ahmed has also been coming here – regularly, like your father. I have investigated the identity of the fellows you encountered in Mr Ahmed's company and I regret to inform you that these men are gangsters. Furthermore I have discovered that your late father was engaged in substantial business activities in Kahin Nahi, viz: he was buying up land, many acres of it, and building a mansion on it. I am reliably informed that the bathrooms of this mansion have golden taps. Do you by any chance know where Mr Ibrahim was getting the money from?

A week went by and no further messages arrived in my inbox. Ayesha had stopped copying me on her correspondence with Masood. I emailed her, but she didn't reply. Had Masood uncovered 'something unsavoury' about her father that she didn't want me to know about?

My fears of Ayesha pulling away seemed to be coming true. But at the same time the suggestion that Ibrahim might have been less than an innocent victim piqued my imagination. Ayesha herself was becoming darker and more complex.

In mid-January she rang to suggest we meet for a drink. She had been thinking about things and wanted 'to discuss our relationship going forward'. Rather than invite me to her flat, she suggested the bar on Piccadilly where we had first spoken. The conversation began awkwardly.

'Look,' she said, 'I know you're not stupid. I should never have asked Masood to copy his emails to you, but it's too late to undo that now. You're wondering what Masood has come up with. Okay, I'll tell you. You'd probably find out anyway if you wanted to. He thinks my dad got caught up

in some crooked business in Pakistan and that's the reason
he got murdered. Masood says he's got solid information. I
don't believe it. So that's where we're up to.'

She seemed to be closing down the conversation, but I
felt she wanted to talk. I asked if there was anything she
would like to share with me. She sat for a moment.

'Okay. Masood rang me. He's very polite and very . . .
Pakistani, if you know what I mean. He dresses everything
up in circumlocutions, but basically he's traced one of the
men I saw talking to Ahmed at my father's funeral. The
guy's name is Javed Shafik and it turns out he's a big shot in
Pakistani organised crime. Masood says he's a drug-dealer,
a kidnapper, a blackmailer, a people-trafficker – you name
it. But the police can't touch him because he's got protection from the local politicians, or even national politicians
for all I know. Masood says that's the way things are done
over there: the mafia guys do the political parties' dirty
work – beating up the opposition, bumping them off – and
the politicians give them big hand-outs from state funds.
Masood says there's a scam that's going on in Kahin Nahi
involving extortion rackets and kidnappings. He doesn't
know much more, but he's going to keep digging.'

'That sounds dramatic.' My thoughts were with Ayesha,
but I probably had half an eye on the book. 'So does Masood
think your dad was killed by these crooks?'

'No, that's just it. Masood thinks my dad and Ahmed
were involved in the scam . . . that they were crooks
themselves.'

CHAPTER 6

A week went by with no word from Ayesha. I rang and emailed but she didn't respond. I took the tube to Maida Vale and knocked on her door. She seemed unsurprised to see me.

'I was wondering how long it would be before you came to doorstep me. Once a journalist . . . So what do you want?'

I asked if she had heard any more from Masood Jilani and she said she hadn't. But she had been thinking about what he'd told her.

'Look, Martin, I'm as keen as you are to find out the truth, only for different reasons. I need to understand what my father was doing in Pakistan – it turns out he's been going there for ten years or more. Masood's got it in his head that Dad and Ahmed were part of some international criminal ring, but the whole thing seems ridiculous to me. I'm going to talk to my mother and see what she knows about Dad's trips. I'll go up to Burnley next week. You can come with me if you want. You know so much about the story, you may as well find out the rest.'

Ayesha had a sports car and she enjoyed using it. I had barely slid into the passenger seat before she put her foot down. The length of the Kilburn Road we sat in silence. Approaching the North Circular she clicked the CD player; it was the Lamento from Bach's B-flat capriccio. I recognised the pianist as Leon Fleisher and Ayesha smiled. 'So you like proper music then? That's nice. Peter's a Ska fan.'

Long drives in a small car are an imposed intimacy. The car was fast but the journey was slow, the M1 nose to tail with traffic.

'I bet the motorways weren't like this when Ahmed drove my dad up from Gatwick in 1969,' Ayesha said. It felt like a cue. I asked her if she would tell me the rest of her father's story; last time, she had stopped at her own birth in 1975.

'Yes, right; that's when I came on the scene. Dad was over here but Asma hadn't got her visa yet. She and I had four years in Pakistan together. It's astonishing how much I can remember about it. Everything was so different; I think it must have burned itself into my brain. I can remember the sunshine, the heat, the smells of the cooking as if it's happening now, not thirty years ago . . .'

'. . . or nearly forty years ago . . .'

'Okay, there's no need for that,' Ayesha said, smiling. 'It seems Dad came over to see us from time to time; he must have come at least once, because my mother Asma got pregnant with Bilal. He was born in Kahin Nahi like me. I can't remember much about that. What I do remember is my grandfather, Hassan, and how strict he was. I was terrified of him; the least little thing and he'd be yelling at Mum and me. It must have been all those years he spent in the military. My great-uncle Guddu was the one who looked after me. He was so lovely, just like his sister, Hassan's wife. I remember he used to take me outside and let me play in the dirt with the worms and insects. I think the bugs must have been much bigger in Pakistan and much more colourful; I can see them crawling up and down the stalks of grass in our garden. Guddu used to sit smoking his cigarettes and reading *Dawn*, the Pakistani newspaper, and he just left me to it. I always felt safe, because I knew he was looking after me.'

'It sounds idyllic. What was it like when you realised you were leaving to go to England?'

'It was a shock. The flight from Karachi to Heathrow was very early in the morning and everyone was in tears. Guddu was beside himself; he thought he would never see us again. I think I must have slept on the flight, because the next thing I remember is being at Heathrow and Dad and Ahmed were there to meet us. I had hardly seen Dad before then, and apparently I didn't want him to pick me up or kiss me.'

'And what were your first impressions of Burnley?'

'The cold! And the gloominess of everything. That's what I remember. I'd been used to sunshine and wide open spaces. So coming to Burnley you were suddenly in this dark place with brick buildings everywhere and rain and fog the whole time, or at least that's what it felt like. I got used to Ibrahim being my dad, though. I think he felt a bit guilty that he'd left us on our own over there, so he made a big effort to be nice to us. And despite what he told his mates about wanting a son, it was me who was his favourite. He was always buying me things – Barbie dolls and a plastic kitchen range to play on, with plastic knives and forks and pans and everything. He must have loved me because he spent a fortune!'

'Was he still living with Ahmed and the others at Uncle Kabir's house?'

'No, he'd moved. He'd got a little semi in quite a nice neighbourhood. He was still working at the mill, so he must have done lots of overtime and saved everything he could. The thing about Ibrahim is that he always aspired to be English. He wanted an English way of life, for him and for us. And he wanted us to be middle class.'

'He wanted you to be English?'

'Yes. So, for instance, Ahmed and the other men who'd been living at Uncle Kabir's all went on to buy houses in Pakistani neighbourhoods. They wanted to stick together. But Dad didn't. He was adamant that we were going to live in a white neighbourhood where there were no immigrants. And the people there liked him. He spoke the funniest English you've ever heard. Everyone was "chuck" and "luv" and so on, but with the strongest Pakistani accent. Mum's English is even worse. They were both insistent that we children should learn English properly, so we wouldn't have an accent.'

'Well, I'd say it worked. You sound like you went to the poshest of public schools.'

'I didn't, though! We went to the local state school then the comprehensive. But we had home tutors, including one who came to give us elocution lessons. Ibrahim was obsessed with us speaking well. He said it was the only way to get on.'

'What about religion? Did you have Muslim schooling as well?'

'Every night. We'd have a quick snack when we got home from school, then we'd go to the mosque for an hour of Islamic teaching. I say Dad wanted us to be British, but there was a sort of duality about it. We'd have an English tutor on Saturday then an Urdu tutor on Sunday. Mum and Dad spoke Sindhi at home, but they also made us learn Urdu, because it was all about moving up and getting on. Urdu is the official language of Pakistan, so if you speak it people can tell you are educated. Dad was an intelligent man, but he wasn't educated. He always used to say that if he'd had an education he would have made something of his life.'

'What do you mean about duality? Between being British and being Pakistani?'

'Yes. Mum and Dad wanted us to be British but they also considered themselves and us to be Pakistani. Very much so. And there seemed to be no sense of any conflict about it. Perhaps they were naïve, but they thought they could have both – being British with all that implies in terms of opportunity and better standards of living, but retaining their Pakistani identity. Back then when I was growing up, it seemed possible. I'd say that was the happiest time of our lives in England.'

'It sounds happy. But those were the years of Enoch Powell and the National Front, weren't they? Did that sort of thing never affect you?'

'It did, but not for a while. At first everything was fine. Asma loved the life here, and she loved Ibrahim for giving it to her. Neither of them seemed to understand that there would be challenges – like racial prejudice and their kids struggling to fit in. That would all come later.'

'When did Ibrahim stop working at the mill and start his own business?'

'In the 1980s. He saved up to buy his first cab and get a taxi licence from the council. Then he bought an office; it was an old terraced house in central Burnley. And we began to move up in the world. The minicab business expanded so much that he had to start employing other drivers.'

'An immigrant success story?'

'I suppose so. Dad's ambition was always to own property. When he'd earned enough he bought what he called a "dream home" in the suburbs, away from the town centre. I think he bought it for my mum, really. It was an Edwardian detached with high ceilings and big rooms and lawns for us children to play on.'

'So is that where your mum, Asma, still lives? Is that where we're going to see her now?'

'Yes. I just need to mention something before we get there. A few years after we moved in, the house next door turned into a squat. That really upset Mum and Dad. They had got on well with all the neighbours, they loved the street and they'd been very happy there. But when the squatters arrived there was a constant stream of racial abuse. They would climb over the fence making noise in the night, kicking over our milk bottles, trying to scare us. I remember Mum ringing me in tears and saying they'd been in the garden urinating on her vegetable patch. She said she'd have to dig everything up and start all over again; but she never grew anything after that. They had to keep all the curtains drawn. As soon as they opened them, next door would start pulling faces or exposing themselves and shouting. Mum and Dad complained, but the council did nothing. I was away in London by then and Dad tried to protect me by not telling me the extent of it. If he'd told me I could have done something. Then one summer they threw stones at Dad as he was cutting the grass and they hit him. He was so shocked. It soured everything for him.'

'It must have been terrible.'

'It was really depressing. I think it changed my dad. He felt that everything he'd achieved was being destroyed. He said he hated the house now; he could never be happy or at peace again. He stopped being the easy-going dad we'd known. He started having long silences when he wouldn't communicate. And his temper got bad; he'd get angry over silly little things.'

'I can understand that. And you've got two brothers, right?'

'There's me, then Bilal, then Tariq. Tariq was born after Asma came to England.'

'And you were saying earlier that it's the boys who get the privileges – help with education and things.'

'Well, that's the Pakistani way, the Muslim way. But my dad treated us equally, unlike most Muslim men. I've seen how badly some of them treat women, including their wives and daughters. Ibrahim was never like that. He always encouraged me to get an education. I won't say he boasted about me when I got into Cambridge, but he was proud of me. Uncle Ahmed didn't like it. He told Dad, "She'll get too big for her boots," and when Dad laughed at him, Ahmed said, "You, too, Ibrahim; you're getting too big for your boots." But Dad didn't care. The whole point of coming to England was to make the most of every opportunity.'

'Your uncle Ahmed seems to crop up a lot.'

'It's always been a bit of a mystery to me that they fell out, because when they were children in Pakistan Dad and Ahmed were close. They were the boys in the family and Granddad was proud of them. As you know, Ibrahim was his favourite – he was the youngest and he stayed at home with Hassan. Ahmed was adopted, but they treated him like their own. He was bright and did well at school. Dad had a lot of respect for him. Ahmed was his big brother, he was Dad's senior; and Dad was very governed by respect for family and giving people their due. It was partly the Pakistani system of rank and social standing, but I think he was genuinely keen to see the best in folk. Dad liked people and he wanted them to like him. I never heard him criticise anyone unfairly or have a go at them behind their back.'

'Yet you said Ibrahim and Ahmed fell out. What was that about?'

'I think it was complicated. When I was a girl, Dad used to tell me about his childhood and how proud he was of coming over to England as a teenager in 1969, all on his own. But then he'd say, "Well, your uncle Ahmed was here of course," and there was a sort of frown in his voice. When you're little you can sense these things. If I asked him about it he'd say that Ahmed had been his sponsor and showed him how things are done in England and found him work. But he said that put him in Ahmed's debt. If I asked him to explain, he just shook his head.'

Ayesha had turned off the motorway and was navigating her way through Burnley town centre. I wanted to hear more about the brothers' quarrel; she said she would talk further on the return journey. The conversation in the car had been our friendliest and it felt as if the mistrust between us was diminishing. In a pleasant suburb on the far side of town we pulled up at Ibrahim and Asma's dream house.

CHAPTER 7

Ayesha had warned me that her mother had been depressed since Ibrahim's death. She had been up to see her a couple of times but the weight of Asma's grief had left her unable or unwilling to talk. We found her sitting alone, a tiny, diminished presence in the high-ceilinged front room. The curtains were closed, most of the furniture appeared to have been removed and what remained was pushed against the wall. The floorboards were bare; our voices echoed in the unheated space.

Asma roused herself to greet us then brought plates of rice and meat from the kitchen that she laid out on folding tables. The act of serving food heartened her; a brief smile crossed her face and I glimpsed some of her daughter's radiance in her eyes. She had Ayesha's delicate features and glossy black hair, but her face was lined with care. Asma seemed wary of my presence and I wondered if Ayesha had properly explained who I was. I remembered what she had said about having to keep her relationship with Peter a secret. When I told Asma that I was a writer she nodded, but I wasn't sure she had understood. She began to speak in Urdu, but Ayesha interrupted. 'That's not polite, Mum. Martin only speaks English.' Asma nodded again and was silent.

Ayesha spoke about her work, about life in London, about her old schoolfriends from Burnley. When she asked about Bilal and Tariq, Asma said, 'Your brothers are well.' The conversation seemed awkward. It was unclear if Ayesha had told her mother what she had discovered in Pakistan. I wondered how Ayesha would broach the subject they were both avoiding.

'Mama,' she said finally, 'I've been worried about you. You don't talk to me properly when I ring you. You don't tell me what's been going on. You don't seem yourself . . . Are you sure you're all right?' Asma smiled but her eyes were heavy with sorrow. 'Yes,' she said. 'Please do not worry about me. I have a lady from the council who is coming to see me. And I am watching *Strictly Dancing* on the television.' Ayesha glanced at me, amused, embarrassed, worried. She tried again. 'No, I mean how are you feeling? How are you coping? It won't help just pretending that nothing has happened.'

Asma thought for a moment; then she spoke reluctantly. 'I am . . . sad, Isha. Life without 'Brahim is hard. He was important in all our lives. How can we be happy without him?'

Ayesha took her hand. 'Yes, Mama. I know. It's the same for me. And for Bilal and Tariq. We loved him. We always will. But Dad isn't coming back, Mum. He just isn't. We have to get on with life . . .'

Asma nodded. 'Of course. That is right. I am getting on. Getting on with life.'

Ayesha was staring at the floorboards, her voice little more than a whisper. 'I love you, Mama . . . And I loved Dad. He was always good to me. I miss him . . . so much. I know what it must be like for you . . .'

Asma gave a sob and hugged her daughter. The two women were caught up in the intensity of their grief, oblivious to my presence.

'Where are you, 'Brahim! Where are you, my husband!' Asma's wail rose from deep within her. 'Why have you abandoned me? Why have you gone from me, my love?' The warmth of their embrace was a fleeting shield against life's horror, but Ayesha pulled away.

'Mum . . .' She paused, as if weighing up what she had to say. 'Mama . . . I need to ask you something. Why did you not tell me when Dad went on all those trips to Pakistan? And did you know why he was going there? It's important . . .'

Asma wiped her eyes. 'I didn't tell you, Isha, because Daddy told me not to. He didn't want to worry you. Granny was ill in Pakistan. He was going there to look after her . . .'

Her mother's explanation was the one she wanted to believe, but Ayesha wasn't sure she could do. 'Mum,' she said, 'is that really why he went there so often? People are saying there was a different reason . . . That he was involved in some sort of land deal and building a mansion with golden taps . . .'

Asma shook her head. 'Oh, Isha, don't ask me this.

Daddy never told me . . . He never told me about these things . . .'

'But you suspected something? You knew it wasn't just for Granny that he was going there?'

'No. I don't know anything. It isn't my business. We can't bring Daddy back . . .'

'But don't you want to know what happened? Don't you want to clear Daddy's name? Isn't there anything – anything at all – you can remember that might explain why people are saying such bad things about him?'

'All I know about is that girl who died. Is that what . . .?'

Ayesha cut her off in Urdu. She glanced in my direction and saw that I had heard.

'I meant business activities, Mum. Don't worry. I can ask Bilal and Tariq . . .'

Ayesha stood up; I was wondering if she was signalling that the conversation was over when a key turned in the front door. There was a voice from the hall and Ayesha's brother Tariq walked in, shouting into a mobile phone. Ayesha tensed; Asma leapt to her feet, but Tariq made a point of ignoring them, anger in his face. He finished his call and addressed the two women in Urdu. His questions were an interrogation; the subject was unmistakably me.

'So what are you here for?' Tariq turned to me, hostility in his voice.

'I'm here because Ayesha invited me. I'm a writer. I'm hoping to write about what happened to your father.'

'Oh, you are, are you? And why would you want to do that? My sister's idea, is it?'

Ayesha intervened. 'Tariq, don't jump to conclusions.

Martin's going to help us find out what happened to Dad. He's an investigative journalist; he's done this sort of thing before.'

'We don't need his help. What's the point? He can't do anything that we can't do for ourselves.'

'No, Tariq. We're not getting anywhere with the Pakistani justice system. Martin's going to write a book. He's going to tell people how corrupt the whole thing is and how murderers can . . .'

'Shut up, Ish! Listen to me. That country is third world. You can write what the hell you want about them and it won't make a bit of difference. You're not going to shame them into telling the truth just because some stupid English journalist writes a book about them!'

Tariq was fierce; like an Asian Heathcliff blown in from the Lancashire moors, his eyes filled with rage. The women seemed in awe of this angry, wayward child; Ayesha told me later that she and Bilal barely spoke to him and his visits home were rare. He had come now to confront the intruder who was inserting himself into the family's story.

'You can't help us.' Tariq placed himself menacingly in front of me. 'You don't understand how things work in Pakistan – it's no use relying on the police or the courts or appealing to what's right and what's wrong. The only thing that works over there is violence. The only way to sort this out is for me to go and slit those guys' throats, the guys who did it to Dad. That's what I'm planning to do. So stick that in your book!'

I said that on balance I didn't think he should go slitting any throats just yet; that it would spoil the whole storyline.

Tariq didn't laugh, not the glimmer of a smile. Ayesha hastened me out to the car.

The drive back to London was subdued. I asked if Tariq was serious about his plans for revenge but Ayesha didn't reply.

'I was telling you about Ibrahim and Ahmed,' she said. 'You wanted to know why they quarrelled.'

I nodded. She was evidently more comfortable talking about some things than about others.

'Okay. Well, the first thing I can remember is when we were children. Ahmed had a boy and a girl and we played with them sometimes. But Ahmed's wife, Sania, was a horror. She was always telling us off. One day she came round and started ranting at Mum. She was angry because she said Tariq had been rude to her daughter. Asma just laughed, but Sania started lecturing her and telling her she needed to teach her children manners. It was trivial, but it brought a lot of things to the surface. I think Ahmed and Sania were jealous of us. Everything we did, they had to copy. If we got a new car or had our garden done, they did the same. Sania would tell people all sorts of lies about us, and within the Pakistani community gossip is really powerful. We were very English in that sense, because we weren't prepared for it; we were shocked by her behaviour and it caused huge problems.'

'What about Ibrahim? How did he deal with it?'

'He found it hard. There was one occasion when Ahmed attacked my father, I mean physically attacked him. Sania had said something to Tariq and me and we had answered her back. Ahmed came over and things deteriorated. That was the beginning of the end. Ibrahim believed in honour and family respect, but this was too much.'

'So what did Ibrahim do?'

'He should have challenged Ahmed; that's what the Pakistani honour code demands. You mustn't allow anyone to disrespect you. But it all happened when Dad was really depressed by the abuse he was getting from the squatters next door. He was getting abuse from the white racists and now abuse from Pakistani bigots in his own family. I think Dad felt nobody wanted him, that he didn't belong anywhere. He withdrew into himself and did nothing. He was in a bad way.'

I had been listening to Ayesha's account, waiting for a chance to mention something else.

'Ayesha, can I just ask you about something Asma said? She mentioned a dead girl. What did she mean by that?'

Ayesha's knuckles whitened on the steering wheel.

'No, she didn't,' she said. 'You must have misheard.'

CHAPTER 8

I didn't see Ayesha for over a week after our trip to Burnley. There had been too many instances of her concealing or trying to conceal potentially important information. I understood her desire for her father to be innocent and for any book to portray him in a positive light, but working relationships like these have to be based on trust.

I asked Ayesha for a meeting and she agreed we should have one. I suggested a time but she said she was busy; I suggested another but she wasn't sure she could make it. I asked her to pick a date and she did so, but texted at the last minute to say she was tied up. The same thing happened again. Ayesha's excuses became less and less credible.

I told her she would have to make her mind up: if she wanted to be part of the book I was planning, she would have to commit herself. Otherwise I could either drop the whole thing or write a fictionalised version of the story without her input. She rang to invite me to her apartment.

On the way to Maida Vale I resolved that I would not leave without clearing the air, without getting to the bottom of all the hints and half-revelations. Ayesha said she had arranged another conference call with Masood Jilani, the private detective in Kahin Nahi. She hoped I would take my invitation to be present as an indication of her good faith. She apologised for her silence, said she had been feeling particularly sad and thanked me for my patience.

Masood Jilani rang punctually. He had news of the police investigation into Ibrahim's murder and the news wasn't good. Inspector Iqbal, the Kahin Nahi Station In-Charge, had released the two miscreants he had been holding on suspicion of poisoning Ayesha's father.

'It was a charade from the very start,' Masood said. 'Just as I told you, the police were arresting these fellows only for fobbing us off. And look, they succeeded. You have gone to England, Inspector Iqbal has got you off his shoulders and now he can collect more bribes from whomever is paying the cover-up. We are back at number one square.'

I spoke first. 'Masood, I'm sorry, that sounds ridiculous. If everyone knows the police are on the take and that they're arresting people and releasing them on a whim – or on payment – why don't the authorities stop it? Surely the Pakistani government wouldn't tolerate such blatant corruption . . .'

Masood found my ignorance exasperating. 'It is very simple, Martin sahib. In rural areas the police have to be self-financing. They don't get money from the government, or at least not enough to operate on. In the old days they were entitled to food and support from the community; local farmers had to bring them milk and bread. But that has gone. So now they have to find ways to supplement their inadequate salaries. In big cities police skim off the profits from illegal operations like gambling and prostitution. But there is less of that in the countryside, so they need other revenues. And chiefly that means raking in money from crime perpetrators and crime victims. They take bribes from both sides; from criminals wanting to avoid prosecution and victims wanting the criminals prosecuted. The outcome of a case depends very often on who pays biggest bribe.'

I tried to interrupt, but Masood was in full flow.

'One very common trick of rural police is that they prepare two First Investigation Reports, each implicating different people. So they can tap both sets of suspects for money to get one FIR acted on and other one thrown out. Also they insert as many names as possible in FIR to increase number of people who will pay to get their name taken out. And since actual criminals are usually wealthiest of all, they pay biggest bribes and get excluded from the investigation.'

'But what about my father, Masood?' Ayesha asked. 'What have you discovered about him?'

'Well, this is what I am trying to tell you, Miss Rahman; but Martin sahib deflected me with somewhat irrelevant questioning. I beg leave to report I have discovered more about those mafia types I was mentioning before, especially about Javed Shafik and those extortion scams I was referring you to. Javed Shafik is kingpin in Kahin Nahi and it appears he is threatening farmers and small landowners until they sell him their land for only just a song, then he makes big profits by selling it onwards. He also has close acquaintanceship with political classes, and in this latest instance I am hearing he got a bogus contract from the government ministry to build some hydro dam freshwater supply scheme near to Kahin Nahi. He would get a very large payment, but the contract and construction are all fictional; payment is just a reward for Javed Shafik's boys bumping off politicians' opponents or other such deeds. Well and good. But the problem for Javed is he has to make some steps to actually building this damn dam. At very least he needs to acquire that land on which he has told the political wallahs he would build it. And actually this looks bad for us. Because I have suspicions that your uncle Ahmed was involved in Shafik's scam dealings and now I fear your father was also. Why? Because that land I mentioned Ibrahim was buying up is slap bang in middle of the territory where this dam is supposed to be built!'

Ayesha's face fell. 'So you think my father was in cahoots with Shafik . . . with the land mafia?'

'At the moment, memsahib, I do not have all the facts; but there is one way of finding out. You remember that tiger I was previously stalking? The Kahin Nahi Police know more about this caboodle than they have been divulging. So I have served notice on our friend Inspector Iqbal. I recently paid a visit to police headquarters and asked them some very relevant questions. The police boys I spoke to were excessively friendly; and that usually means they have something to hide. When they realised I suspected their game, they offered me money. I told them to keep their bribes. They are covering up for someone, memsahib, but

Masood Jilani is no shrinking violet. I shall force whoever is behind this to come crawling out of the woodwork!'

When Ayesha put the phone down she looked so distressed that I abandoned my intention to confront her. Three days later she rang to say she needed to see me urgently. She'd had a telegram from Kahin Nahi. Masood Jilani had been shot. He was in hospital with a bullet in his spine.

CHAPTER 9

Ayesha had asked if she could come to my house. I thought it strange, but felt I could hardly refuse. I offered her coffee. She was trembling.

'The hospital says Masood's in a critical condition, Martin. He could die. And if he doesn't he'll probably be paralysed for life. All because he was trying to help me. God knows who shot him, but it has to be because he was asking questions . . .'

'Ayesha,' I said. 'This isn't your fault. Masood's a professional; he was doing it because that's his job. He was a cop for long enough to know the risks. So don't blame yourself.'

'Yes, I know. But don't you see what this means? Whoever shot Masood wasn't just warning him, they were warning us. These people are so deeply implicated in whatever's been going on that they don't care who they murder. They've killed my dad and they tried to kill Masood. If we carry on they'll kill us, too!'

Masood's shooting changed things. A one-off murder had escalated into something much more sinister. But I was reluctant to give up. When I was a reporter working in war zones, my cameraman used to say that incoming bullets seen through the camera lens appear as safe as watching them on television; the viewfinder distances you into detachment. And writing a book had the same effect. Processing life into words on the page, real people into characters inured me to danger; the threats, violence and tragedy were part of a plot I felt I could control.

'Look, Ayesha, I don't think we should give up just yet. You and I both want to know what happened to your father. We owe him that, don't you think? You said you felt guilty about letting him down; I'm worried it will haunt you for the rest of your life if you don't do the right thing now.'

I heard the mendacity in my words, but continued.

'You need to do this for yourself and for your mother as much as for him. And don't worry; I'll be with you. We're in this together. The book is just incidental . . .'

Ayesha's face was a mask.

'But what we do need is trust between us. Whenever I was in danger as a journalist I knew I could trust the people I was working with – my producer, my cameraman – and that's what kept us alive. So I want you to be open with me. I know there are things you've been hiding. From now on will you tell me everything?'

Ayesha nodded. 'Yes,' she said. 'It isn't easy. I'll try.'

I leaned forward and took her hand. 'Thank you. I promise you won't regret it. What happened to Masood is dreadful. But if we don't want the same thing to happen to us, we need to be absolutely clear what's going on here. You need to tell me: were these people gangsters that your dad fell foul of . . . or were they crooks he'd been working with?'

Ayesha hesitated. She wanted her father to be innocent, but the question of the land and the extravagant house in Kahin Nahi preyed on her mind. What had Ibrahim been involved in? Where had he got the money from? He had been a loving father, but had his disillusionment with England and his desperation to help his family drawn him into crime? Everything in Pakistan seemed to revolve around bribery, corruption and lies; maybe it was the nature of Pakistani society that had changed him.

'We all have different people within us,' she said. 'Perhaps I never really knew him at all.'

'Perhaps none of us ever understands our parents. But I don't want us to have secrets from each other, Ayesha.' It felt like the right moment to press her. 'Why don't you tell me about the dead girl your mother mentioned when we were in Burnley?'

'Yes. I may as well . . . You'd probably be able to find out by going back through the newspaper reports . . .'

She seemed uncertain; I squeezed her hand and she didn't withdraw it.

'You remember I told you about the terraced house my dad bought to use as an office for his taxi business? Well, something happened there; something that got Dad into a lot of trouble. It was before I moved away to go to university. I can remember him coming home late one night in a terrible panic . . .'

Ayesha stopped. I feared she was thinking better of it, but she resumed.

'I heard him whispering to Asma in their bedroom, then he was up and down the stairs all night. The next day he didn't go into work. He spent the morning on the phone ringing people; he spoke quietly so I couldn't hear what he was saying . . . Then the police came . . . There were six of them and they had a warrant to search the house. They pulled the place apart, emptied drawers and shelves, turned over mattresses, ripped up carpets. It was horrible. They kept Dad under guard in the spare room while they were going through his things. Then they took him away without telling us what was going on. Mum and I were in a terrible state . . .'

Ayesha swallowed hard.

'It seemed a girl – a white girl, a teenager – had been found dead in the back yard of Dad's office building . . . Her name was Kelly Stafford and she was sixteen. It seemed like she'd fallen from the top floor of the house. No one knew why she was there or what had happened, but the police decided that Dad must somehow have been involved. They weren't saying how the girl had died, if she had fallen accidentally or what, but the local newspapers got hold of the story and suddenly there were headlines all over the place about "Burnley teen murder" and "Who killed Kelly?" and so on. It was a nightmare.'

Ayesha's story shocked me, but I didn't want to deter her from telling the rest of it.

'Okay. So was Ibrahim involved? You said he came home in a panic . . .'

'He was in a panic because one of his drivers who'd been at the office had seen the girl's body lying in the yard. I don't think Dad was anywhere near the place. This driver had rung Dad to tell him about it. Dad had no idea who she was or why she was there. And the guy was ringing him, asking him what to do. So of course he was in a panic. None of them knew what to do. They're all Pakistanis, all taxi drivers; of course they're going to be petrified about what happens when the body gets found. They'd be the chief suspects. Pakistanis are always to blame for everything. So yes, of course they should have reported the body straight away; but you can understand what they were going through.'

'I suppose so. But what had actually happened? Was there foul play involved?'

'What happened was a nightmare. It turned into four years of harassment and persecution. The police really had it in for my dad. It turned out that the girl, Kelly, had absconded from a council care home in Manchester. No one knew how she'd got to Burnley. The forensic investigation concluded that she'd fallen from the fire escape at the back of the house . . .'

'Okay, so perhaps she could have been trying to break in . . . Could she have been climbing the fire escape and fallen off?'

'Yes, of course she could. And that's what I think happened. That's what any reasonable person would think, right? But the police went after Dad and after the drivers who were working for him. Because they were Pakistanis. They kept coming round to the house with more and more warrants. They seized Dad's bank books and the accounts for his business. He had no idea what they were after. It was like they suspected him of being a criminal master-mind; they treated us all like criminals or drug dealers or something . . .'

'And was Ibrahim being held in custody all this time?'

'No, they didn't have anything on him, so they had to let him out. But they set some ridiculous level of bail and he really struggled to find the money.'

'But if there was bail it means he was being charged with something, doesn't it? If they were just releasing him, they wouldn't be asking for bail?'

'Yes . . . No . . . It was complicated. Actually it was really to do with the other guy, the driver who'd rung Dad in the first place. The first thing the police did was to search Dad's offices, where the girl had fallen from. And in the top-floor bedroom they found some blankets and some half-eaten food and things. So the police were making out that she'd been living there and that she'd fallen, or thrown herself or been pushed out of the window. Well, Dad knew nothing about any of that. The house was on four storeys – it was an old Victorian place – and he only ever used the bottom two floors. Upstairs it was just like some storerooms for junk; he never went up there. But the drivers did. They used to use part of the top floor as a smoking den when they were on their break or waiting for a fare. And the driver who phoned Dad right at the beginning to say he'd found the body was a strange fellow; I never liked him. So if there was some foul play I think he might have been mixed up in it. I'm pretty sure the phone calls Dad was making that morning after he came home in such a panic were to this driver, trying to find out what had really happened . . .'

'But why didn't Ibrahim report all this to the police straightaway? Didn't he realise that waiting and doing nothing would throw suspicion on him?'

'Look, I told you already. He was in a panic. Pakistani people hate to get involved with the police – they're the white man's police; they aren't on our side. And I don't think Dad really knew what the driver fellow had been getting up to. At one stage the guy seemed to admit that he'd known the girl, Kelly; that she'd been his girlfriend or something and that maybe she had been living in that top-floor bedroom without Dad knowing about it. Then the guy changed his story and said she must have broken into the house and been squatting there. So Dad was confused. If she had been living in his house, or – even worse – if she'd been there because of one of his drivers, he just thought it's all going to land on his plate and he's going to take the rap for it . . .'

'So what were they charging him with, if they were demanding bail from him?'

'Failing to report a death. And they were saying to him that if it turns out not to be an accident then he'll be charged with perverting the course of justice. So Dad's petrified. He's very suspicious about the driver who discovered the body. He's thinking he should tell the police about his suspicions, but he's worried about the consequences. So Dad ended up having to maintain his story that the girl must have broken into the office and hidden there without anyone knowing. But the police didn't believe it. They kept hauling him in for questioning and they obviously leaked it to the press, because Dad's face was in all the papers.

His face, not any of the drivers who worked for him. We couldn't understand why my father was being so demonised and the other guy was never mentioned . . .'

'So do you think there really was foul play, even if your dad wasn't involved in it?'

'I don't know. I can't believe my dad could have done anything like what they were accusing him of. The whole time he was being interrogated and pilloried in the press, he stuck consistently to his version of things – that he didn't know the girl, didn't know she was living in the house, if indeed she had been, and they couldn't prove anything other than that. In the end he was convicted of not reporting a death. There was no murder charge for anyone. But the police wanted someone to be punished so Dad got a really harsh sentence. He got three hundred hours of community service. He ended up sitting at home, depressed and not knowing what to do with himself. He felt it was so unfair; that British society had treated him really badly . . .'

'So he didn't feel British any more? He'd become an outsider again?'

'He felt his reputation and his standing in the community had been completely destroyed. He'd got caught up in something terrible and he'd been unfairly treated. I've got massive regrets that I didn't do more to help him during that awful period. That really haunts me . . . And the worst thing was that Ahmed revelled in Dad's humiliation. He didn't come to his aid or defend him as a brother should do. When it was all in the papers and people were talking about it, Ahmed went round saying, "Oh yes, Ibrahim could well have done it . . ."'

CHAPTER 10

It seemed clear what we should do and where we should go – Pakistan. But when I put it to Ayesha she wasn't sure. Her recent experiences in that country had scared her. Her temerity in confronting the thugs at the morgue, her willingness to examine her father's body now seemed foolhardy in the extreme. She regretted having employed Masood Jilani, both because of what had happened to him and because it had tipped off dangerous people that she was pursuing them. When we met to discuss how to proceed, she had printed out the official travel advice from the British Foreign Office and insisted on reading it to me:

'"There is a high threat from kidnap, terrorism and violence throughout Pakistan. The Foreign and Commonwealth Office advise against all or all but essential travel to different parts of the country. There is a particular threat of kidnapping against Western nationals. British nationals of Pakistani origin have been targeted by criminals as they are often perceived as being wealthier than locals. Criminal violence is common, including armed carjacking, robbery and murder. It is difficult to predict the safety of daily activity—"'

I tried to interrupt.

'No. Listen . . .' Ayesha said. '"The number of kidnappings for ransom of Westerners has increased. British nationals of Pakistani origin are at particular risk. British and other kidnap victims have faced extended periods of detention. While some were ultimately released, others have been killed. The long-standing policy of the British government is not to make substantive concessions to hostage takers . . ."'

'Okay, I get it,' I said. 'When – if – we go to Pakistan we should be careful. I'm not arguing with that . . .'

'*If* we go. But don't you see the other point I'm trying to make? Why does the Foreign Office make such a big thing out of "British nationals of Pakistani origin"? It's because they are prime targets for kidnapping and violence. And don't you think my father might have been one of them? A kidnap-gone-wrong would explain lots of things, like the men Guddu says were spying on Dad when he was at my grandmother's house; the fact that his wrists and ankles were bound . . . Maybe they were trying to take him away, but he resisted and they beat him so badly that they ended up killing him . . .'

'Yes, it's possible. Of course it is. So long as we don't have any confirmed leads, all explanations are possible. I see there's a long section in the Foreign Office guidance about the threat from terrorist and extremist religious groups targeting foreigners, so I suppose it's even possible Ibrahim was killed by them . . .'

'You're not taking me seriously, Martin. Terrorists blow people up; they blow up buildings and hijack airplanes. And anyway, Dad was a Muslim. We can rule out terrorists. But I'm right about kidnapping, aren't I? Dad could just have been in the wrong place at the wrong time. What do you think?'

'I think it's a possibility. And, to be honest, I think you are keen on that explanation because you want your father to be innocent. You want him to be a victim of chance, of fate, of misfortune. You want it because that's easier for you to cope with, easier than thinking he might have been a criminal, mixed up in some crooked business, and that he died because of his own . . .' I stopped. 'I'm sorry. I didn't mean that how it sounded. I know you're having a hard time. And I know you loved your father. But all I'm saying is that we have to be realistic; we can't let sentiment cloud our judgment . . .'

Ayesha had clasped her face in her hands and was rocking back and forth, racked by sobs. If I had thought that I'd learned to understand this complex, contradictory woman, here was proof that I hadn't. The emotional strain building within her had been so intense that it took only the slightest brush on a fragile nerve to provoke her collapse.

'Ayesha . . . I'm so sorry. That was stupid of me. Of course we must work on the assumption that Ibrahim was innocent. And of course I'm not going to force you to return to Pakistan. There's lots we can do without going there . . . What about the Foreign Office, for a start? Your dad was British, wasn't he?'

'Yes. He had a British passport . . .'

'Then we must get the Foreign Office onto this,' I said. 'It's their job to look after Brits abroad . . .'

Ayesha shook her head. 'He had dual nationality – British and Pakistani. When I tried the Foreign Office they said that makes a difference . . .'

'Nonsense! If Ibrahim was British, he was British. And the government needs to recognise it . . .'

Ayesha was rummaging through the printouts she had brought with her.

'I don't think it's that simple, Martin. When I asked the Foreign Office for help they were polite, but they quoted their rules and regulations about how much, or how little, they could help. Here, look – it's in the FCO guidance: "If you or your father were born in Pakistan, you might be considered a Pakistani national by the local authorities even if you don't hold a Pakistani passport, and the British government may be prevented from providing the full range of consular assistance . . ." That's the problem with Dad: he had both nationalities, so the Foreign Office doesn't want to know.'

'Then we need to pay them a visit.'

'Yes, I suppose . . .' Ayesha wiped her eyes. 'The FCO fobbed me off, but you're a journalist; perhaps they'll be worried what you might write about them . . .'

She had regained her composure.

'So . . . how about a deal?' she said. 'If you get us a meeting with a minister at the Foreign Office, then I'll consider coming to Pakistan with you . . .'

CHAPTER 11

I wrote to the Foreign Office. But first I wrote to the professor who had supervised my studies as a postgraduate psychology student ten years earlier. I told her I was worried about a friend and she asked when we met if I was sure this friend wasn't actually me. I smiled and said it wasn't; we sat down to talk.

Denise was in her sixties, an expansive, noisy Jewish woman who combined her academic career with work as a counsellor-therapist. She overflowed with natural empathy and emotional acuity; her kind eyes and ample bosom had comforted many sufferers of distress. I told her what I knew about Ayesha's experience as the daughter of a murdered father, how she had repressed her grief and anger, and how fragile her equilibrium now seemed. Denise said post-traumatic stress disorder affects the majority of those who lose a close relative in violent circumstances, and Ayesha was almost certainly suffering from it.

'Bewilderment, shock and grief are all deepened when there's no clear explanation of why a person has died. And trauma deliberately inflicted by other humans is the hardest to come to terms with, much harder than deaths in natural disasters. An unsolved murder allows the imagination to conjure up endlessly disturbing thoughts.'

'Most of the time she seems so normal and so in control,' I said. 'Almost too in control, if you know what I mean; as if she's calculating everything like a business deal. Then at other times she completely disintegrates.'

'Classic PTSD. The stronger the person, the harder they fall. The first proper case studies were soldiers in the First World War. These were brave men, so they held themselves together during the day but at night they were overwhelmed by nightmares and panic. The doctor who treated them, a fellow called W. H. Rivers, said the brave person's shame about acknowledging his own fear sets up a vicious circle that makes everything worse.'

'You mean the Freudian repression thing? Denying there's a problem?'

'Yes. Not talking about things; not finding any answers. The mind of your friend must be weighed down with all sorts of painful questions – who did this? Why did they harm my father? What was my father doing and thinking when he was killed? How much did he suffer? And was there anything I could have done to prevent it? When those questions remain unresolved, the mind works itself into a hyper-aroused state; it is constantly agitated, tortured by unknowing. Sufferers can't sleep, can't find rest. Eventually they can't hold it together and you get the sort of dramatic collapses you described your friend as having.'

'And do we know why the impact of deliberate killing is harder to process than that of other violent deaths? I mean if Ibrahim had died in a train crash, for instance . . .'

'Well, there's been research on it. I can give you the references if you want. I think it's to do with interpreting the intentions behind the death. A train crash isn't the result of a single person's ill will, but murder is. Deliberate killing is seen as an attack on our human integrity, which causes anger and a loss of trust in other people. Mistrusting others can verge on paranoia – it's very damaging for mental health . . .'

'Well, I wouldn't say Ayesha was paranoid, but she certainly has trust issues – not least with me.'

'I think you need to show understanding, Martin. When there's no logical explanation for a dreadful event like a murder it makes life seem terrible and meaningless. I'd say your friend is looking for meaning. If you could establish that her father was murdered by terrorists, for example, she could perhaps create a narrative that lends validation to his death – she could see her father as an involuntary participant in the struggle for freedom and democratic values, or something similar . . .'

I laughed. 'Oddly, we discussed exactly that scenario and Ayesha ridiculed me for saying the murder could have been terrorist-related. She's probably right. I wouldn't want to rule it out, though. Is there anything practical I can do to help her in the here and now?'

'There are always things we can do to help. For instance, experience with mass disasters suggests that taking relatives to the scene can be therapeutic. There's a Norwegian researcher who studied the effect of the Anders Breivik massacre in 2011. When he compared the mental health of family members who went to the site of their relative's death and those who didn't, he found less PTSD in those who went than in those who stayed at home. Why? He says it's to do with getting an understanding of what happened at the moment of death, with feeling physically close to the departed person and with being able to say goodbye. It isn't easy to visit the place where your loved one died in such a terrible way, so overcoming your resistance and fear is validating in itself. It feels as if you are doing something for the dead person, a kind of symbolic ritual that can help cleanse you of feelings of guilt.'

'Do you think I should tell her that the way to end the horror is to go back again and confront it?'

'Perhaps. Forcing yourself to do something unpleasant can be beneficial if it's handled properly. And just doing *something* is usually better than giving in to hopelessness or sinking into apathy. The best thing would be to solve the crime, of course . . .'

'Ha! I'm working on it!'

'. . . or in the absence of solving it, perhaps just writing about it will help. The book you're planning could be quite validating if your friend thinks you are telling her story in the right way. It could bring a measure of comfort, a sense of compensating for the pain or putting it in perspective. But you do need to tell it in the right way. Relatives are sensitive about how their loved ones are remembered because they are the ones who knew them, not you as a writer.'

I rang Ayesha to tell her about my conversation with Denise, but she didn't want to listen. There was an edge in her voice. When I asked if something had happened she said, 'Yes. I'm marrying Peter.' She sensed my hesitation. 'You're surprised? You don't think that's a good idea?'

'Ayesha, I don't know Peter . . . I'm not sure I know you. If that's what you want, then of course it's a good idea. Many congratulations.'

'You don't sound very convinced. If my dad were here, I don't think he'd be saying congratulations. He'd be trying to dissuade me . . .'

'Well, I'm not your dad. Getting married is a big decision, but it's *your* decision. You and Peter have to make it. No one else can do it for you.'

'Well, precisely! Because no one else cares about me. There's no one looking out for me; no one I can trust. I thought I could trust my dad and he's dead; I thought I could trust Masood Jilani and he's let me down; I thought I could trust you . . .'

CHAPTER 12

Women think that pouring one's heart out over lunch is a single-gender sport. But it isn't. Men approach self-revelation cautiously: first the football, then the job, the finances, the children, relationships, physical then mental health. A trusted confidant is a safety valve and mine was my brother. When I told Tom that my life was beset by unpredictable women, he grunted understanding. For the next hour he and I were two Henry Higginses lamenting la différence. I said Ayesha was becoming volatile and I was getting jumpy. If she pulled out of the book at the last minute, I could see months of effort going down the drain. We finished our lunch on the unsatisfactory understanding that I had little choice; I would have to cross my fingers and press on.

The following day I had a reply from the Foreign Office to say my request for a meeting had been noted. There was no confirmation that the request would be granted, but it gave me a pretext for ringing Ayesha. She greeted me with joy in her voice.

'Martin! The very person I was hoping to hear from! . . . Fantastic that you've got the FCO to acknowledge our existence. Thank you so much. I've been assembling the correspondence I had with them after my dad died – before I got involved with you – and I think we should go through it together. It's such a beautiful day. Why don't you come over for a coffee?'

I hid my surprise. I didn't point out that our last exchange had ended with her accusing me of being uncaring and untrustworthy. When I arrived she gave me a hug.

'So lovely to see you, Martin. I think we're going to get somewhere now. So, thank you for all your help. Here are the letters . . .'

I tried to ask about Peter and wedding plans, but Ayesha was laying out documents on the coffee table, accompanied by a running commentary.

'I told you how the Foreign Office gave me the brush-off when I rang them the day Dad was killed? That really annoyed me. The woman on the emergency helpline was completely useless. I didn't go back to them until after I'd been to Pakistan, so that must have been late August or early September. Here's the first letter I got my lawyer to send them . . .'

'You mean you've had lawyers liaising with the FCO? Ayesha, why didn't you tell me?'

'It doesn't matter. I'm telling you now. So here's my lawyer's first letter.'

Ayesha passed me a copy. It was from a firm of Manchester solicitors who had addressed their query, some-what hopefully, to 'The Foreign Secretary, The Foreign and Commonwealth Office, London'. The letter set out the facts of Ibrahim's murder and requested the British government's assistance in bringing his killers to justice. The Rahman family, it said, had reason to believe that the Pakistani police investigation of the crime was beset by ineptitude and possibly corruption. So would the Foreign Secretary please use his best efforts and those of the British High Commission in Islamabad to ensure that justice was done?

From the reply, dated two weeks later, it was clear that this was not the first such case the FCO had had to deal with. It was from Farooq Khan, desk officer with responsibility for consular matters within Pakistan, and began by expressing sympathy for the family's loss. The rest of the two-page document was an exercise in wriggling.

I appreciate your client's concerns about the investigation of her father's death and her desire to bring the perpetrators to justice. Unfortunately the Foreign Office is not permitted to involve itself in police investigations in foreign countries. We are also limited in the assistance we can provide to dual nationals in the country of their other citizenship. The British High Commission in Pakistan has been in contact with the Karachi police authorities, but any investigation remains a matter for them and we cannot oblige them to release any information. We recommend that your client engage a Pakistani lawyer, who will be able to address her concerns about the conduct of the police in that country.

I understand that your client is worried about her personal safety if she were to travel to Pakistan, but the

*FCO is unable to provide protection to British nationals
overseas. We can provide a list of private security
companies. We can also provide a list of international
funeral directors if your client wishes to repatriate her
father's body to the UK.*

*I wish to assure you that we have done everything within
our power to assist in this tragic case, and we are satisfied
that we have provided the appropriate consular assistance.
My colleagues in Karachi will continue to monitor
developments.*

Yours faithfully,

Farooq Khan, Desk Officer, Pakistan.

'A complete cop-out!' Ayesha said. 'They don't give a
damn. I wonder how they'd be acting if it was a white
Englishman who'd been murdered. They'd be pulling out
all the stops; the story would be on the news bulletins;
there'd be questions in parliament. My dad they think they
can sweep under the carpet and no one will care. Well, I
care! And I'm not going to let them get away with it. I got
my lawyer to write them a stinker of a letter.'

She gave me a copy to read.

Dear Farooq Khan,

*Our client engaged a local solicitor in Pakistan
immediately following her father's death. The solicitor
has advised her that there is no possibility of a fair and
objective police investigation without the payment of
bribes. The Rahman family does not have the means to
pay the amounts necessary and the solicitor is unwilling*

to challenge the police as he fears for his own safety. This is understandable given the shooting of a local private detective.

Our client is doing all she can to get justice for her father, but she lives in the UK, has limited financial means and is scared to travel to Pakistan. She desperately needs practical assistance from the FCO. Why, for instance, is the FCO not liaising with the Home Office and the Metropolitan and Lancashire police forces? Why is the FCO not supporting our client's demands for a new investigation? Could you at the very least ascertain if the authorities have accepted the results of the autopsy our client arranged to be carried out on the exhumed body of her father? In sum, we hope for a more constructive response from you.

Yours faithfully . . .

'How did they respond to that?'

'You can judge for yourself. Here's their reply.'

The authorities in Pakistan have confirmed the exhumation of Mr Rahman's body and they acknowledge the results of the autopsy that Ms Rahman arranged to be undertaken. My colleagues in Karachi have contacted the police authorities and they have informed us that an investigation is in progress. As such, the FCO cannot make any further representations on your client's behalf. We advise your client to pursue any allegations of failings by the Pakistani authorities through the proper legal channels. The Pakistani courts are empowered to impose sanctions on police and other authorities. As you will appreciate,

the FCO cannot insist upon the Pakistani authorities
conducting their investigation in a particular way.
  Yours faithfully,
  Farooq Khan.

'A fat lot of use that is,' Ayesha said. 'Okay, they've spoken to the police, but those are the very guys Masood Jilani said were being paid to cover up for the murderers. They're hardly going to throw their hands in the air and tell the truth just because the British High Commission asks politely how things are going. There needs to be real pressure on them. That's the only way we'll ever get anywhere.'

'I suspect you're right. And I'd say the only way we're going to get the FCO to apply that pressure is by a bit of arm-twisting. We need to get this meeting fixed so we can talk to the minister instead of just writing to low-level officials . . .'

'I'm not being negative, Martin, but I think even you might struggle to get a minister. I've spoken to other British Pakistani families in our position and they've had to wait months or years for a meeting with anyone. But when that white girl, Lucie Blackman, was murdered in Tokyo the government invited her parents to meet the Foreign Secretary within a week. It's depressing, but I think there are different values for white Britons than for us.'

That evening I was thinking about Ayesha and Peter, her future husband, wondering how he felt about the travails of the family he was marrying into. Peter was white, a Londoner, and evidently struggling to understand his fiancée. Ayesha had told me that Peter couldn't fathom the guilt she felt about her father's death or her sense of regret that she had somehow let him down by neglecting the Pakistani side of her heritage. He told her she was being unfair on herself. He was comforting, but she didn't want comfort; she was angry and disconsolate by turns.

Ayesha's sudden determination to marry Peter puzzled me. I wondered if her desperate situation and the loneliness and vulnerability she was feeling were pushing her into a step she had previously resisted.

The phone rang. My brother's voice sounded distant, muffled. He wanted to pick up the conversation we had had over lunch. He wanted to tell me something, but he wasn't making much sense. I suspected he was drunk. 'I can't hear you, Tom,' I said. 'Can you speak up? What are you saying about Tara?'

'I'm saying she wants to kick me out . . .'

We think our troubles are unbearable, then others come along that make us nostalgic for the old ones we once thought so hard to endure . . .

PART TWO

CHAPTER 13

My schedule was busy, Tom lived 180 miles away and it was a trek to get there. I should have gone to see him, but I crossed my fingers and hoped he would be okay. He and Tara had been married for twenty years; they had two children, a nice house and a dog. I told myself they would argue, reconcile and get on with things. But the thought that I was letting my brother down nagged at me.

There was better news from the Foreign Office. They were prepared to meet Ayesha and me. No minister was available, but the department would be represented by senior officials. Could we come to a meeting in three weeks' time?

Ayesha compiled a list of questions and objectives for the meeting, ranging from broad strategy – how to pressure the Pakistanis into re-opening the murder investigation and how to ensure it was done honestly this time, to fine detail – what had happened to the clothes Ibrahim was wearing and to the ropes that were used to bind him; had these been sent for DNA analysis and if not, why not?

She told me we must press the FCO on the department's policy regarding dual nationals; she felt they had been using Ibrahim's status as an excuse for not helping his family, and that much of the reluctance was due to a shadowy racism that allowed government officials to differentiate between white and non-white British subjects.

We turned up at the appointed time and were ushered into a conference room in an FCO annexe. A smart young Asian man rose to greet us.

'Hello. Farooq Khan. I'm the desk officer you've been corresponding with . . . And with me here' – he turned to a middle-aged woman in a starched blouse and sensible shoes – 'is Marjory Thompson, Head of Country Casework for India and Pakistan, my boss. Also, Superintendent Jerry Whitehead from the Metropolitan Police's International Unit has joined us to answer any questions that fall in his remit.'

Farooq Khan began to express his condolences about the 'tragic events' that had brought us together, but Ayesha cut him short.

'I'm going to start by showing you a photograph of my father,' she said. 'Because I want you to know that we are talking about a real person. Ibrahim Rahman was my dad, a loving husband and father. He isn't a statistic that you can file away in your archives. The investigation of my dad's murder has been a farce. The Pakistani police made two arrests that were based on false confessions. The exhumation and the independent autopsy that I insisted on proved these men were not the culprits. They were arrested because the murderers had bribed the police to arrest them, while the real criminals were allowed to go free. Now, despite all the noise and all the promises, there is simply no investigation going on. Things have ground to a halt. The police have pocketed their pay-off, the murderers are carrying on with their criminal activities and no one is doing anything about it.'

'Well, hang on a minute—' Farooq Khan interjected, but Ayesha overrode him.

'Turning to our experience with the FCO: for months we were fobbed off with endless discussions about citizenship and whether my father was a mono or a dual national. This is not acceptable. While that was going on, the crucial time to ensure a proper investigation was being wasted.

'Then the FCO told us that HMG does not send representations about individual cases to foreign governments, but the fact is that they do. I can cite specific instances of this happening. I have written six times to the UK High Commissioner in Islamabad and have received not a single reply. This is unacceptable.

'I want you to tell me why the FCO has constantly given us reasons why it *cannot* help us, instead of looking for ways in which it *can* help us. Why has the FCO defined my father's status as a dual national, when he'd lived in Britain for over forty years? And why are you so reluctant to assist us when we are a British family residing in the UK?'

Farooq Khan opened his mouth to answer, but his boss motioned him to silence.

'I am sorry, Miss Rahman. If you have been given the impression that we treat dual nationals differently from mono nationals, that is a misunderstanding . . .'

'But in Farooq Khan's letters to me he says explicitly that the FCO cannot offer us assistance because my father was a dual national.'

Marjory Thompson gave Farooq Khan a glance.

'That is incorrect. The FCO provides exactly the same level of assistance for dual nationals.'

'Okay. Thank you,' Ayesha said. 'So I would like us *all* to note that this will not be a problem from now on. But the fact remains that the Pakistani authorities have not carried out any proper investigation, and they will not do so unless you take some positive steps to force them into it.'

Farooq Khan cut in.

'But there is an investigation underway. The FCO has asked the Pakistani authorities for updates on the investigation, as it does with all cases. They have promised to provide updates, but you have to be aware that their way of doing things is very different from what might be done in the UK. We represent HMG in Pakistan and we must respect the local ways of doing things. We cannot interfere in local cases . . .'

'I'm afraid that is nonsense,' Ayesha said. 'The FCO has intervened directly in numerous similar cases – all of them, I have to say, involving victims who were white. In the case of my father, you have done virtually nothing; and when you have done something you have consistently failed to keep me informed of what is going on.'

'The problem is that we don't have the right to ask them for information about the investigation . . .'

'The problem is that there *is* no investigation!'

'Yes, there is! The Pakistani authorities are telling us that there is an investigation . . .'

'That is simply wrong. They might say there is, but it isn't true. Can you tell me what they are doing?'

'It isn't for us to do that. You should get your lawyer to ask them for an update on the investigation.'

'The police are doing *nothing*! There has been no analysis of the results of the second forensic investigation . . .'

'It isn't our role to force the pace of the investigation. We cannot—'

'Force the pace! The second forensic examination was done months ago!'

Jerry Whitehead, the representative from the Met Police's International Unit, looked uncomfortable. He was in his fifties, almost certainly serving out his time before drawing his pension, but he appeared to be taking Ayesha's predicament seriously.

'So it's been months since you had your father exhumed and there's been no progress since then?'

Ayesha nodded.

'Exactly,' she said. 'I know that could never happen in the UK, but things are very different over there. And what I am concerned about is that the more time goes by, the less useful any forensic evidence will become. Not to mention the increased likelihood that they will lose key items, like my father's clothes, which already seem to have been mislaid.'

Marjory Thompson tried to calm things.

'The problem is that this is all happening on sovereign Pakistani territory. The authorities say there is an investigation going on and that means we can't intervene. If you are unhappy, the best way is for you to take it to the court.'

'We've already done that. But you know as well as I do that there is such a backlog – hundreds of cases – and the delays are terrible. You can never get a judge to hear an application without bribing him. And in our case it's already too late, because the murderers have paid such massive bribes that we simply can't match them. I am telling you that the only way to get justice for my father is for the FCO to start making robust diplomatic representation to the Pakistani authorities.'

Marjory Thompson shrugged. 'Well, I'm afraid we are not going to do that, because the Pakistani authorities say there is an investigation that is going on . . .'

Farooq Khan seized his moment; his boss's reprimand had caused him to lose face in front of Ayesha, a Muslim woman, and he didn't like it.

'Yes. That is absolutely correct. What we don't want to do – and what we must not do – is to upset any diplomatic ties with Pakistan. That is our paramount consideration . . .'

'Really?' Ayesha shot back. 'That's what you consider paramount? More important than bringing murderers to justice? More important than my father? More important than a human life?'

'We are confident our colleagues are dealing with this case in the best possible way . . .'

'You are confident? Well, *I* am not confident. The Pakistanis only do anything when there is real pressure on them to do it. We *need* pressure to be brought to bear . . .'

'That's just not the way we operate. Pakistan tells us there is a case going on and we can't go pestering them for details of the case . . . We are not representing you in Pakistan; only your lawyer can do that. We can only give you assistance within the remit of our consular powers . . .'

'But there has been no progress. All I am asking is for you to give us robust assistance to help get something done . . .'

'I'm afraid there is no point in us promising you robust assistance – we cannot do this,' Farooq Khan said. 'Our colleagues in Pakistan say the Pakistani authorities are getting annoyed about all the inquiries they are receiving from us. If we consider that this matter is in danger of upsetting diplomatic ties with Pakistan, we may have to cease our assistance to you. We cannot jeopardise our ties with Pakistan. Our colleagues in the High Commission tell us—'

I raised my hand.

'Excuse me, but can we just be clear? Are you saying the inquiries about this case are annoying the Pakistani author-ities and that the FCO might have to stop being involved in the case because of this?'

Marjory Thompson caught the whiff of bad PR.

'No, that is not correct. I'm sorry, what Farooq says is wrong . . .'

'Oh no, it isn't!' Farooq Khan was loath to let another woman disrespect him, even if it was his boss. 'I have been the desk officer on this case and the Pakistanis are saying we are approaching them too frequently and it is causing problems . . .'

Marjory Thompson stood up; Farooq Khan fell silent.

'The FCO will continue with its assistance,' she said with an air of finality. 'We will continue to do what we can. I think this meeting is coming to a close. If you have no further questions, I think we should finish . . . Now if we can talk off the record, I am of course very sympathetic to what you have been going through . . .'

It had been nearly a month since I had had lunch with Tom; nearly a month since my brother phoned me in a state of evident distress. I had emailed him and got no reply; it was weighing on me that I hadn't made any further efforts to check he was okay. I rang his home number and Tara replied. I asked how Tom was doing and she said, 'Fine.'

CHAPTER 14

Ayesha was tough and determined. She had risen to the top of London's IT industry where women, especially Asian women, have to be ruthless to succeed. And now she was driven by a passion that stemmed from love for her father, regret for his passing and, perhaps, a tacit sense of guilt that she had not done more to save him. She was exorcising her pain through the search to discover who had murdered Ibrahim and why. Her passion and anger had sliced through the bland assurances of the Foreign Office officials, but when we met again a week later, Ayesha was full of regret that she hadn't insisted on concrete undertakings from them.

'I'm kicking myself, Martin. We had them on the ropes and we didn't pin them down. It's my fault – I should have got specific promises from them, but I let them get away with a few expressions of goodwill. I don't know how it happened – it's not like me to be so unfocused.'

'They were always going to resist getting into specifics,' I said. 'Maybe they genuinely are limited in what help they can give us. In any event, I'd say the best thing we can do now is to help ourselves. We need to do what I suggested earlier and go to Pakistan, don't we?'

Ayesha was silent. For all her bravery she was reluctant to return to Kahin Nahi. When I asked if she was afraid she nodded vaguely.

'Ayesha,' I said, 'we had a deal. You promised that if I got us a meeting with the Foreign Office, you would come with me to Pakistan . . .'

'I didn't say that; I said if you got us a meeting with a *minister* at the Foreign Office. I think we need another meeting and this time we really do need to see the minister. Will you help me?'

There was little point arguing. I wasn't sure how I would persuade the Foreign Office to serve up a minister, but Ayesha was determined to exhaust every possible option before considering a trip to Pakistan. My own contacts in Whitehall were long gone and I no longer had the clout of working for a national news organisation, so I cast around for advice, beginning with my former BBC colleague Aled Parry-Jones. Aled was a big, practical Welshman who had spent several years as the Corporation's Islamabad correspondent.

'Bloody Foreign Office!' he said when I told him how Ayesha had been treated. 'Always trying to shuffle off responsibility. Give me a few days. They owe me a favour after the episode in Balochistan. I'll see if Alistair Smart will talk to you. He's the minister responsible for south Asia and he's not a complete idiot; he may be some help. How's the book coming on?'

'Slowly. And I'm writing it in real time, so I've got no idea where the plot's leading – if Ibrahim really is the hero Ayesha wants him to be, or some despicable crook. And because Ayesha keeps blowing hot and cold about cooperating with me, I'm worried I'm going to end up with half a book and no way to find out how the story ends!'

Aled laughed. 'Ha! The miseries of being a writer! Just wait until you have real problems to deal with! You'll have enough of that when you get to Pakistan.'

'What do you think of the story?' I asked. 'Does it interest you?'

'Yes, but I've spent years out there. I have to say, the dynamic between British Pakistanis and Pakistanis in Pakistan is pretty fraught. There are all sorts of jealousies and resentments between them. I've come across quite a few murders like yours, usually connected with land disputes or family feuds. There was one I was thinking of writing about myself. But it turned out to be such a nest of vipers that I dropped the idea.'

'I was drawn to Ayesha's story precisely because of its drama and the emotions it has stirred up,' I said. 'There's something elemental about the passion and pride, the anger and hatred that exists in Pakistani culture. We've lost that in the West; it's as if our society has been mollycoddled and gone soft. In Pakistan there's still that untamed fierceness that you associate with legends of heroes and villains from ancient times. And then I find Ayesha herself fascinating; as a person, I mean. She's suffered so much and she's been so brave. But there's a lot I don't understand about the Pakistani mentality, or at least about Ayesha's. At times she seems completely opaque; she wants to solve her dad's murder but she's scared of discovering what's behind it. She's constantly trying to make me write the story the way she wants it written, as though she's worried that something terrible is going to emerge.'

'Okay. Look,' Aled scratched his chin. 'I wasn't going to mention this, but it strikes me there's a pretty big elephant in the room. You said Ibrahim was a taxi driver when he was suspected of involvement in that girl's death, right? So think about it. Who were the guys behind the scandals in Rochdale and Rotherham and Oxford? It was Pakistani men abusing white girls. And who were the people organising it all? In nearly every case it was Pakistani taxi drivers. They're the ones who were running the gangs, ferrying the kids back and forth, collecting the bookings and the money. You should read the cuttings. I'm not saying Ibrahim was one of them, but it's worth looking at. I wonder if that's what Ayesha's worried she'll discover . . .'

I got home late, with a notebook full of questions and a headache. There was so little firm ground, so many certainties that had crumbled at the first challenge, so much that seemed alien and incomprehensible.

Clicking on the Internet I entered the search terms, 'Child abuse; taxi drivers; Pakistani'. The screen filled with lurid newspaper headlines and stories of crimes carried out in cities across the country.

Police say vulnerable girls across Rochdale and Heywood were subjected to grooming by a network of men, mostly taxi drivers. Nine men of Pakistani heritage were jailed for crimes including rape, trafficking and child sex abuse . . .

The report concluded that approximately 1,400 children were sexually exploited in Rotherham between 1997 and 2013 . . .

Girls as young as 12 or 13 were being trafficked around the north-west of England. Men who worked in the take-away trade or as taxi drivers – professions that gave them unsupervised access to young teenagers – were grooming girls by offering them gifts, getting them hooked on drugs or alcohol, then forcing them to have sex. Victims were driven between Rochdale, Oldham, Bradford and elsewhere to have sex with men . . .

The facts were shocking, and the attitude of the rapists towards the girls sickening:

All the girls were white, all the accused were Asian Muslim men, and they displayed a searing contempt for their victims. 'You white people train them in sex and drinking,' one of the accused told the jury, 'so when they come to us they are fully trained.'

Girl E had only just turned 13 when Sajid picked her up in his taxi and plied her with vodka before raping her. She later said Sajid and his co-defendants 'treat white girls as easy meat'. Another victim said: 'Pakistani men pass you round like a ball, they're all in a massive circle and put a white girl in the middle.'

Two themes recurred throughout the reports – that the crimes were largely organised by taxi drivers; and that many of the girls were vulnerable children from care homes:

> The gang's victims were typically in care or on 'at risk' registers, their isolation from their families having turned them to drink, drugs or both.
>
> Men from other cities would visit for £100-a-time 'sex by appointment' set up by the Oxford gang, who would also transport their underage sex slaves by taxi to London and Bournemouth to be abused.

My email pinged. It was a message from Tom with the subject heading 'Highly Confidential PLEASE'.

Hiya Martin,

Are you in London? We have had plenty of drama up here. I have just started taking drugs. No, sorry, start again . . . I haven't taken any illegal substances for decades, but my GP has put me on Prozac. I have taken two a day as prescribed and am totally unable to spell! I got lost last night (don't let Tara know that I am telling you this bit, please). We were walking the dog in Thornberry Park, having taken my first Prozac tablet, and I thought Tara was following me but she wasn't. It took me and the dog four hours to walk home. In the meantime, Tara had called the police thinking that I had killed myself. Apparently there were four police cars and a helicopter looking for me. After walking all the way through Crofton,

Walton and down the dual carriageway, which is a very fast road without pavements, I realised I had no house keys. I thought I would find Tara at home, but instead I found a police car with a searchlight looking for me. This is what I put on Facebook . . .

'I have just had a meeting with an interesting member of the constabulary. We had to sit in his police car for half an hour and he passed the time by showing me pictures on his iPhone of handbags, quilts and dresses that he makes in his spare time on his sewing machine. Perhaps the oddest thing is that he showed me a picture of himself wearing his latest creation. Life couldn't possibly get any stranger, could it? He waited with me until someone came to take care of me, and as he left he said, "I haven't enjoyed any of my police work as much as I've enjoyed talking to you tonight." Potential boyfriend then?'

Love, Tom x.

I found Tom's message worrying. He reported the episode with his usual humour, but he didn't want me to talk to his wife about it. I replied immediately.

Wow! That's a dramatic series of events! Will you tell me more when I see you the week after next? The main thing is that you are ok. I think the Prozac is a good idea if you are feeling bad. I am guessing that getting lost was a side effect of a medicine you aren't used to yet. I particularly liked your story of the policeman and look forward to hearing more about him. But I really don't think you should take him on as a boyfriend . . .

See you soon. Lots of love.

PS I will of course keep all this confidential xx.

Tom wrote back:

Yes, it was the Prozac. But don't you think it should be prescribed only with some kind of tranquiliser? I have looked it up on the Internet, as has my fantastically loyal, beautiful and absolutely wonderful wife. 99% of people using it for the first time say that their depression deepens for the first one to two weeks of use. There are reports of people who previously had ideas of self-harm or suicide becoming violent towards other people in the first few days of taking it. One man stabbed his wife to death and then killed himself. I have told Tara to keep all knives locked up for a while! Joking of course – I absolutely love her to death (. . . sorry!) x.

CHAPTER 15

Aled kept his promise. The Foreign Office wrote to say that Ayesha and I would be welcome to come and meet Alistair Smart, the minister with responsibility for India and Pakistan. The meeting would be off the record and there could be no promise of special treatment, but the government was anxious to demonstrate its commitment to protecting the interests of all British citizens in all parts of the globe.

Walking into Whitehall, where I had worked as a senior civil servant for five years after I left the BBC, brought back memories. I recalled the horror that would grip civil servants when ministers were forced to engage with members of the public, especially those with complaints. Their driving imperative was usually to minimise the fuss without making concessions; to manage the minister's fears of negative publicity and restrain the politician's impulse to offer promises that would be awkward to keep.

We were escorted down the FCO's marble corridors

by a secretary who brought us to Farooq Khan's office. He greeted us politely but distantly. We were taken into a wood-panelled room where Farooq's boss, Marjory Thompson, was leaning over the shoulder of a balding, chubby man at a mahogany desk. The two of them were leafing through a file of papers, but rose to greet us.

'Ah, Ms Rahman, I presume,' the man said, proffering then withdrawing a hand as he remembered that Muslim women are not permitted handshakes. 'And you are Martin – I recognise you from the television. Well, you are both very welcome. Please take a seat; we have sandwiches here and Farooq will take your orders for tea or coffee.'

Farooq scowled.

'As you know, Ms Rahman, I am the minister who keeps an eye on your part of the world . . . I mean, on the part of the world where your father so tragically lost his life. I recognise of course that you and your family are good Lancastrians – Burnley, if I remember correctly. Anyway, I believe Marjory has cleared up the misunderstanding about the dual nationality thing. I am most keen that we at the FCO take good care of all our UK citizens, Lancashire or Yorkshire – I'm from Yorkshire myself, but don't let's allow that to come between us!'

Ayesha looked at me and raised an eyebrow.

'Now, what I would like to do today – and thank you for coming here to see me, by the way – what I would like to do is to put your minds at rest. I have spoken to my colleagues in the British High Commission in Islamabad and they have assured me that everything possible – I stress, everything possible – is being done to bring those responsible for Mr

Rahman's . . .' he glanced at his notes, '. . . for Ibrahim's death to justice. No stone left unturned, as they say . . .'

'I'm sorry, minister,' Ayesha was struggling to sound polite. 'I fear you haven't been given the latest information. The investigation by the Pakistani authorities into my father's murder has ended. They are no longer pursuing the case. There is no activity whatsoever. And despite all our requests, the British High Commission has failed completely to demand an explanation. I am at my wits' end. I have come here because I regard you as the only person with the ability to help me and my family. And I am sure that Martin, who is planning to write about this, would say the same thing. Martin's book already has plenty of villains; what he needs now is a hero!'

Ayesha's speech took me by surprise and, judging by the look on Alistair Smart's face, him too.

'Well now, Ms Rahman, that is very kind of you . . . Very, er, kind. And of course I would wish to play a positive role in this matter; a very positive role. I must say that actually there is a presumption against HMG getting involved in proceedings in foreign countries. And there are limits to what we can do. On the other hand, I have had five or six conversations about deaths in Pakistan in the last year . . .'

Marjory Thompson sensed the danger of ill-considered concessions.

'Ms Rahman, we have had this discussion many times. You claim there is no investigation, but the Pakistani authorities are telling us that there is one. You can see our difficulty . . .'

Ayesha's eyes remained fixed on the minister; the civil servant was a distraction.

'Minister, I beg you to believe me when I say that we know there is no investigation. I have personally discovered that the perpetrators have successfully applied to the High Court in Pakistan to block the opening of any reinvestigation. Effectively that has put an end to things. Now we can see how powerful these people are, both in terms of their political contacts and the money they have access to, neither of which we have.'

Ayesha had not mentioned anything to me about a High Court application. When I glanced across at her, I had the impression that she winked. But Alistair Smart was taking her claim seriously.

'Well now, I'm not sure that I know what to make of that. I must say I find it hard to believe that the High Court of any country would take a bribe from murder suspects. Don't you agree, Farooq?' The minister, playing for time, had turned to the most junior person in the room. 'You are Pakistani. Is it credible in your experience that the highest echelons of your country's judiciary would be amenable to such a thing?'

'Minister, forgive me,' Farooq Khan said. 'I am hardly Pakistani. I am British. And my family came from Bangladesh, not Pakistan. But if you ask me about Pakistan, I would say anything is possible in a society as corrupt as that.'

Marjory Thompson appealed for calm.

'Farooq, please! I think that is quite enough. Minister, I wonder if I might have a word?'

She spoke into the minister's ear in a conspiratorial whisper, waited until he nodded and then addressed the room.

'Ms Rahman, I am pleased we were able to have this meeting. I think we have clarified several important issues. The minister has kindly agreed that, exceptionally in your case, the Foreign Office will approach the Pakistani High Commission here in London to inquire about the progress of the police investigation into your father's death. We will find out how much more we can get from the Pakistani authorities. We will speak to the High Commissioner and ask him to ask the Pakistani police—'

Ayesha rolled her eyes. 'It's no good just asking for a general update—'

'We can make it clear that HMG is concerned. We can ask for more detailed information, which your lawyer in Pakistan can then follow up. I should say that families often feel there is no proper investigation being carried out. In many cases, the killers are local and the family has suspicions that they are being unfairly protected. I will also ask for the question of your unanswered letters and emails to be looked into.'

The meeting was over. The minister and the senior civil servants picked up their papers and rose from their seats. Ayesha tried to prolong the conversation, but Marjory Thompson cut her short.

'Farooq will show you out. Thank you for coming. And please be assured that we are doing everything possible to resolve this issue.'

At the exit Farooq Khan could contain himself no longer.

'You know something?' he said, turning to Ayesha. 'You

Pakistanis take up more of our time than any other nationality, and you're never grateful! I've been in all the meetings about your case; your endless letters and complaints are driving us round the bend. Marjory says Pakistanis are always murdering each other over honour feuds and land disputes and family quarrels. She says there's just no way the Foreign Office can spare the time and resources to get involved. So my advice to you is to get out of here and go and ask your Pakistani friends to sort things out for you!'

Ayesha tensed; she looked ready to punch the man. I hurried her out into the street, and as I did so my mobile phone buzzed. It was a text from my sister-in-law. 'Martin, please ring when you can. I need to talk to you about Tom.'

I hesitated. Tara's text sounded urgent; but Ayesha was furious, pulling at my sleeve until I followed her into the Red Lion pub across the road.

'Get me a red wine, will you? We need to decide what we're going to do about the fiasco we've just been subjected to. I can't believe they treat people like that and think they can get away with it! Get the drinks, will you . . .'

When I returned from the bar, Ayesha gave vent to her anger.

'It's my father's death that's made me face up to this, Martin, made me think about who I am. I used to think I was British and I used to think I was Pakistani too; but now I know I'm neither. What I discovered in Pakistan, all that cruelty and dishonesty and corruption, has made me realise I'm not Pakistani; my DNA is different from all that. But since I've been dealing with the British establishment, it's made me realise I'm not British either. With the Foreign

Office, it's like they theoretically recognise me as British, but the way they treat me it's clear they don't. I'm sure Farooq was telling the truth when he said they regard us with contempt. It feels like utter rejection. And at the same time, I'm having to reject my Pakistani side. As a family we're in no-man's-land. We don't want to be Pakistani because we're treated so badly over there: it's all about money and there's no sympathy or value for human life. And then there's this rejection from the British authorities. I feel in a complete muddle. Who are we as a family when our father struggled so hard for us to be British, and we feel British and we feel our loyalties are to Britain? Then at the same time we're told we're not Pakistanis, because people in Pakistan say, "Well, if you were really Pakistani you'd know how to deal with this: you'd know that you have to pay bribes and kowtow to these people and so on", but that's not in our DNA. Nobody is willing to accept us. So I've decided I have to take responsibility. It's my responsibility to stick up for my father and take this case forward. I know the risks that involves, but I have to do it because nobody else will: the Pakistani authorities say, "You're a British kid; why don't you ask your British government to help you?" And the British say, "You're Pakistani, so sort it out with your people over there." Before this whole thing happened, my line at dinner parties was, "I'm so lucky because I have the gift of two cultures", but the gift's gone. I thought I had two worlds, two identities at my fingertips, but now I have none . . .'

Ayesha's outpouring of alienation was upsetting. I sympa-thised with her predicament. But I couldn't help thinking that perhaps the FCO had a point – the honour feuds and the murders carried out for reasons that in the West would seem ridiculous did make it difficult for the Foreign Office to intervene.

It was late and I was tired. I put Ayesha into a taxi and agreed we would meet again.

Finally I was able to ring Tara. 'Martin,' she said. 'Tom has tried to kill himself.'

CHAPTER 16

The journey out of London was torturous, the traffic unrelenting. Tara had given me the bare details; my mind extrapolated the worst. The drive to Tom's house took an age.

Tom was four years younger than me. As children, we had played together, fought together, gone on adventures. When I was ten and Tom six, we went exploring a forbidden building site. There were a dozen of us, but the policeman who caught us picked on the littlest. 'What's your name, son?' Tom looked at me and said, 'Ask him.' That's how things were. I was good at coping; sweet, innocent Tom could never quite get to grips with the world.

What he lacked in practical skills, he made up for in good nature. His imagination was sparky; his humour made you smile and groan. For years he worked as a printer, but his passion was sculpture, bending metal into original, unexpected creations. He wrote quirky, striking stories. But he didn't recognise his own gifts. I think Tom found people intimidating, the natural world and animals more straightforward to deal with. He loved his children but had himself remained a naïf, wandering through life with eyes wide. He put on a brave face, but the world scared him.

Tara's message had shaken me. Tom had always needed someone to look after him. Our parents had done it while they were alive. Then Tara took on the task. I wondered if she was regretting it.

When I pulled into the drive the house was in darkness. Tara came to the door and switched on the light. She had been a nurse for twenty years and she rarely lost her outer calm.

'I came home from work last night and I couldn't find him. That wasn't too unusual. Since he lost his printing job, he's been acting quite strange. And drinking. I texted him and he said he was okay. He came home at midnight and went straight to bed. When I went to work this morning he still hadn't woken up. Then this afternoon I got a text from him and it said something like "Goodbye". I was worried, so I came back to the house and he wasn't here. I looked in the garden and found him in the shed. He had blocked up the windows and the door and lit a barbecue . . .'

'Oh, Christ. How was he?'

'Alive. The shed was full of fumes and he'd obviously drunk quite a lot; probably taken pills as well.'

'Could he talk?'

'Yes. He was woozy. He said he wanted to kill himself and told me to leave him alone . . .'

'And do you think he was serious? About wanting to kill himself, I mean?'

'Who knows, Martin? I've been dealing with cases like his all my life and I'd still struggle to tell you which are the serious ones and which aren't.'

'But was it out of the blue? Or have there been warning signs? He told me about the Prozac and getting lost, but I had no idea it was as bad as that.'

'He's been very unhappy. At first he kept busy, cutting the grass and keeping the garden tidy. And he was making his sculptures. But he gradually stopped doing all that and he started drinking earlier and earlier in the day. When I'd get home from work he was usually sitting in the garage smoking or he was asleep. It has been really tough for us all.'

'But what happened this afternoon was much worse than anything he'd done before, wasn't it? What did you do when he told you to go away and leave him?'

'I wasn't going to leave him to die. I rang 999 and the police came with an ambulance. There were four or five of them, big blokes. They wanted to take him to hospital, but Tom kept arguing and saying he wouldn't go. So they ended up having to wrestle him to the ground and force him into the ambulance.'

I pictured my brother being manhandled, a scared little boy maltreated and humiliated because he was unhappy with his life, because he had no one to soothe his hurt.

'They took him to A&E and pumped his stomach,' Tara said. 'He'd taken sleeping pills, right enough. But he kept trying to leave, insisting on discharging himself. They're holding him under the Mental Health Act.'

I was taken aback.

'God almighty. I saw him for lunch just a few weeks ago and he didn't mention anything like that. He spoke about some stuff that was worrying him, but nothing serious . . .'

'Well, you know Tom. He doesn't open up. He's always been good at disguising when things are wrong – in public, I mean. He can seem so lovely and so normal to everyone else, but at home he's a complete nightmare. His behaviour has been so extreme.'

I wanted to see Tom but it was late and Tara said there was no chance of visiting until the morning.

'But couldn't we try and ring to see how he is?' I said. 'I need to know he's all right, at least . . .'

'The problem with mobile phones is that they confiscate the chargers in case the patients use the electrical cord to hang themselves. So I don't know . . .'

'But if he has his mobile on him, surely there will be enough battery for us to talk to him, won't there?'

I rang Tom's number, not really expecting a reply. He answered after a dozen rings. His voice sounded tired and distant, but his manner was disconcertingly normal.

'Oh, hiya. Are you ringing me? I'm not at home, you know . . .'

I slept in the spare bedroom of my brother's house. Before I switched out the light I looked around the room, which doubled as Tom's study. The walls were lined with his paintings and with photographs of our parents. One showed Dad in his khaki uniform somewhere in the Middle East and there was a display case with his dog tags and medals. I loved my father and mother and I was sad when they died five years ago; but it struck me that Tom's sense of loss was a continuing one, an ongoing absence in his life. I dreamed of my brother that night and in my dream I resolved to hold him close, to see him more and to hug him to me.

In the morning there was a text from Ayesha on my phone, apologising for her behaviour after the meeting at the Foreign Office. 'I was ill-mannered,' she wrote. 'It wasn't your fault and I shouldn't have burdened you with all my problems. I think it's because I miss my father and I'm finding it hard to come to terms with him being dead. In any event I've decided you are right. We need to go to Pakistan.'

CHAPTER 17

Tara gave me directions to the hospital and I drove through the rain-spattered countryside. The thought of my brother confined against his will stirred memories of our dying father in hospital, vainly pleading to go home. I thought of what Ayesha had been through since the death of hers. I resolved to be more understanding of her concerns and her volatile behaviour.

The psychiatric unit was NHS modern; functional and depressing. I pressed the bell, glanced at the CCTV camera. A voice asked who I was and I gave my name.

'Thomas is here,' said the voice. 'Come in, walk straight down the corridor and wait in the day room.'

The door buzzed open; I was enveloped by a smell of detergent, stale cooking and sweat. A male nurse showed me into a linoleum-floored common room with Formica tables and plastic chairs, a drinks machine and a payphone. A few couples were already chatting, a mother visiting a son, a daughter come to see her father. A young man came in, picked up the receiver of the payphone and listened intently for thirty seconds before replacing it. He left the room disappointed, then returned and repeated the same ritual. A large, muscular patient with tattoos on his arms and neck peered in at the door, making the sign of the cross over us. An orderly watching through an observation window met my eye with a smile.

Tom came in. I embraced him, felt him return my hug then pull away and glance around the room.

'Hiya, Martin,' he said. 'You didn't need to come, you know . . .'

'Fucking hell, Tom. What are you doing in this place?'

Tom shrugged.

He saw the tears in my eyes, hastened to reassure me.

'It's all right, you know. It's all right in here. I'm all right.'

I nodded. He seemed a little slower, more deliberate in his speech; but he wasn't noticeably distressed.

'Are you sure? Are you sure you're all right? What the hell were you doing trying to kill yourself?'

He smiled. 'I wasn't. I was just in the shed having a ciggie.'

'You'd lit a barbecue. You were breathing in toxic fumes. And you'd taken pills.'

'Yes, but . . .'

'You have a wife. And the children. You can't do things like that to them.'

'Things like what? I haven't been feeling well; I've been unhappy. Why am I locked up here? I'm not a dangerous lunatic.'

'No. True. But you might be dangerous to yourself . . .'

'I'm not. I told you, I was just unhappy. And now the police are going to charge me with assault and affray because I didn't want them to take me away.'

'I don't think they are, Tom. The police know what you've been through and Tara says they aren't going to take any action. But the main thing is to get you well and get you out of here. What have the doctors said?'

'They're all very nice. I saw the main doctor this morning and he says they've given me a mild sedative. I don't think he's too worried; I'm an easy case compared to most of them in here.'

Tom could be moody, but it was true that he didn't have a violent or aggressive side.

'The doctor said they'll have to observe me and assess me before they decide if I can go home. They want to figure out if I'm suicidal. But it's not hard to know what answers they want you to give them; if you want to get out, you just give them the answers they want to hear.'

'Yes, of course. But the doctors want to help you, Tom. You want to get out of here and I don't blame you. But will you promise me at least that you won't do anything stupid when you get out . . . or that you'll talk to me if you're thinking about doing anything?'

Tom shrugged. 'I suppose so. In any event I won't be getting out for a while. They have to do all their enquiries before they can let me go.'

I drove back to London feeling sad, reassured and alarmed by turns.

CHAPTER 18

Tom remained in the psychiatric ward. The doctors were worried about discharging him and their assessments dragged on. I went to visit half a dozen times, driving up and down from London, and found my brother generally in good spirits. He had made a lot of friends among the nurses and patients and he told me about them with a glint of amusement in his eye. I asked him if he would be okay if I went away to Pakistan and he said of course he would.

Preparations for the trip were protracted. Ayesha kept adding and removing names from the list of people we were planning to interview, to the point that I wondered if she was serious about going. She agreed we should talk to the local police in Kahin Nahi and to Inspector Iqbal, the man she suspected of leading the cover-up of her father's murder. She said her great-uncle Guddu would be the best source of information, and she thought that Masood Jilani, the private detective who was making a painfully slow recovery from the bullet that had damaged his spine, might be willing to meet us if we promised him complete confidentiality.

I suggested we should also try to speak to her uncle Ahmed and to the men Ayesha believed to be behind the murder – the crime boss Javed Shafik and his two brothers. At first she agreed but then changed her mind, saying to do so would be too dangerous. I argued that there was little point in flying all the way to Pakistan if we weren't going to pursue the investigation to its logical conclusion. She was unconvinced. I set out to find a way round her objections.

In my days covering politics in London I had reported on several stories involving Pakistani exiles, ranging from human rights campaigners and billionaires to benefit fraudsters and criminals. One of the men I had interviewed was a politician called Mohammed Asif, who had been forced to flee Pakistan when his party, the United Front, was defeated and banned by the new government. Granted political asylum in Britain, Mohammed Asif had lived for ten years in north London, until the UF's fortunes revived and he returned to Pakistan in triumph. He had become the Governor of Sindh Province, with a palatial residence in the capital Karachi and considerable influence over the province's affairs. I wrote to him and he replied that he would be happy to put his authority at our service; he would provide us with the security we needed to visit and interview whomever we wished.

But when I told Ayesha, she frowned and shook her head.

'There's no way we can accept this, Martin. You need to write back to him and turn him down. I'm disappointed you did this without consulting me; I would have told you straight away not to do it.'

'What do you mean? You asked me to help you find out what happened to your father, and that's what I'm doing.'

'Well, I'm not prepared to go along with it.'

Tensions that had grown silently between us were crystallising; our personal dramas had left us both on edge. I should have held my tongue, but I didn't.

'So is this about control? Are you vetoing this because it was me who came up with it?'

'Not at all . . .'

'Then what reason can you possibly have for turning down an offer that'll help us get to the men who might have killed your dad? I can't understand that for one minute.'

'Okay, I'll tell you why. Pakistanis who offer help like that are all the same – they make promises, they're as friendly and as helpful as can be, but they're all devious. They always end up demanding money or asking for favours. They don't do anything for nothing. They're out for themselves.'

'Hang on. Who are "they"? Are you saying all Pakistanis are devious and out for money?'

'Pretty much. I wouldn't trust any of them.'

'Well, I'm astonished, Ayesha. If I had said that, I'd be in court on a charge of inciting racial intolerance. Yet you say these things about the very country your family comes from . . .'

'I say it because it's true. Pakistanis in Pakistan see us Brits as a source of money. That's all. So don't believe their promises; they'll end up fleecing you . . .'

If Ayesha really didn't want to accept the Governor's help, there was little I could do about it. Part of me suspected she was right about the money-grabbing; part of me wondered if there were other, more complex reasons for her anger.

I went to see Aled Parry-Jones. He had recently returned from Islamabad and was making a documentary on the Pakistani Taliban for the BBC World Service. We met in a café close to Broadcasting House.

'So how did your joust with the Foreign Office go?' he asked as we sat down.

I told him the story of our meeting with the minister and he laughed.

'Oh, so just the tea and sympathy, then? No practical help? Par for the course, I'd say. What's your next step?'

'That's what I wanted to ask you about. Ayesha has finally agreed to come to Pakistan, but there are all sorts of things bothering me. On the most practical level, what should I do about a visa? If I get a journalist visa, do you think they'll start asking what story I'm working on? Ayesha doesn't want the authorities to know we are digging into things like police corruption and cover-ups.'

'She's probably right. You'd be better off going as a tourist. If you get a journalist visa, you'll have the ISI tailing you day and night . . .'

'The ISI?'

'Military intelligence – they run the country. People forget that Pakistan exists in a constant state of emergency. The terrorist threat is so huge that the place has become a police state.'

'But why would military intelligence be interested in someone investigating a family murder?'

'Because you're foreign. Because all murders are suspect.

Can you be sure Ibrahim's death wasn't linked to terrorism? Organised crime, if that's what he was involved in, has close links with the terrorists over there. It's just like Northern Ireland, where the IRA and the UVF run the smuggling and extortion rackets.'

'Well, I can't be certain. I don't know what Ibrahim was up to, if anything. But when I mentioned terrorism to Ayesha she was furious.'

'Okay. So look out for the intelligence wallahs. They're hot as mustard and they're leery of any foreigner who doesn't have a transparent reason for being there. The ISI and the army are the only organisations that function properly in Pakistan. All the rest – politicians, businessmen, judges, police – are riddled with crime and corruption. Talking of which, did you check out the taxi driver connection I mentioned to you? Could Ibrahim have been mixed up in any of that stuff?'

'I'm not sure. But Ayesha seems pretty worried what we might discover. I came up with a way for us to get to the crooks Ibrahim may have been involved with, but she told me to forget it.'

'Well, again, she might be right. You don't want to be poking these guys – they can bite!'

'Sure. But I got a promise from the Governor of Sindh that he'd provide us with security, that we'd have full protection . . .'

Aled shook his head.

'You mean you've been in touch with Mohammed Asif? Can I ask what you know about the guy; about his reputation, I mean?'

'Only that I interviewed him once back in the day, when he was living in London. He was meant to be a political exile, but it seems he was claiming housing benefit for a house in Edgware that was owned by his brother. I never really got to the bottom of his politics.'

'I think you might have made a blunder there, Martin. Mohammed Asif is one of the biggest beasts in the United Front party and they're definitely not people you should fool around with. The UF are a real power in Karachi – Amnesty says they're up to their necks in summary killings and torture and abuse. But the biggest problem for you is that you've probably just tipped off the guys who are the political patrons of the thugs you suspect of murdering Ibrahim . . .'

'What? The UF and organised crime?'

'Sure. The phoney public works schemes that Javed Shafik and mafiosi like him are awarded are all set up by the UF. They'll be helping Javed cream off public funds and taking their cut, too. If you've told them what you're going over there to investigate, I think you might have put yourself in serious danger . . .'

CHAPTER 19

I had researched the death of Kelly Stafford in Burnley, scouring the records for any mention of local taxi driver Ibrahim Rahman. But it was a historical case and beyond the newspaper reports there was little to go on. I rang the Burnley police, who wouldn't or couldn't comment. The officers who worked on the investigation had left the force and I didn't have enough time to go looking for them in their bungalows and retirement homes. I thought about raising it again with Ayesha – I wondered if she too harboured suspicions of her father and if this were the reason for her fear of what our probing might unearth. But I decided against it. We were about to spend a lot of time in each other's company and I didn't want the atmosphere to be any more difficult than it already was.

I didn't tell her what Aled had said about Mohammed Asif and the UF. There seemed little point in further inflaming matters. I went to the Pakistani High Commission in Lowndes Square and got my tourist visa. We booked flights to Karachi with an open return and made a hotel reservation for the first ten days of our stay. We agreed we would see how events played out before deciding how long we would need to be there.

Our flight was booked for 9 a.m. on Thursday. On Tuesday evening Tom emailed to say that his mental health tribunal, the psychiatric assessment that would determine his fate, had been fixed for the following afternoon, Wednesday. But there was a lot to do in the day and a half before I left for Pakistan; I emailed to ask if he would be okay without me. His reply was reassuringly unequivocal.

Thanks, Martin. You definitely do not need to come tomorrow. I am certain the tribunal will go in my favour and they will let me out. I have spoken to all the doctors and they confirm I am completely safe. I have a good Mental Health Advocate who says he cannot see anything going wrong. I am so looking forward to getting back to my own home.

I am really grateful to you for all your help, for supporting me and for liaising with Tara and the children. I just want to tell you that the hug you gave me before you left last time meant a very great deal to me xx

Relieved, I wrote back:

Thank you, Tom. I haven't done much except to keep the conversation going between you and Tara, but I think that is the most important thing at the moment, yes?

I love you, bro, and I want things to be good for you. Martin xxx

I packed for the flight with a fretful heart, waiting for the news that would stop me going. On Wednesday evening a text pinged on my phone. I knew it would be Tom telling me his application had been refused.

'I am out! Hooray! Love, Tom xxx'

On Thursday morning I woke refreshed.

Ayesha and I had agreed to meet at check-in so we could get seats together, but I was early and went to get a coffee in the airport terminal. I was at the cash register when my phone rang.

'Martin, I can't go home.'

'What do you mean, Tom? Of course you can go home.'

'I can't. I'm not allowed within 500 yards of the house . . .'

The options flashed before me. I knew the right thing to do; I should cancel my trip and go to rescue my brother. But other thoughts crowded in.

'Okay. Where are you now, Tom? Can you find a café and sit there until I ring you back?'

I called Tara but there was no reply. Tom picked up as soon as I rang his number.

'Listen, Tom. This is some cock-up. I have to get on a plane to Karachi. Could you go and stay with Rick Taylor tonight? You've probably got no money, right? So here are the Internet codes for my bank account.' I read them out to him. 'Take as much cash as you need. If this isn't sorted by the weekend and you can't carry on imposing on Rick, you should go and see Rob Butcher, the estate agent who sold Mum and Dad's house. I'll ring him and say you might need a short-term let. You can use my bank account for the deposit and the rent.

When I get back from Pakistan we can figure out what to do about a longer-term solution. In the meantime, don't drink, Tom. And please don't do anything foolish, okay?'

Guilty and anxious, I rang Tara again but there was still no answer and the flight was closing. At the desk I asked if Ayesha Rahman had checked in and if I could sit beside her, but the Pakistani Airlines clerk shook his head. 'You're the last passenger, sir; there's one seat left and it's in the last row.'

I looked for Ayesha in the departure lounge. The boarding process was chaotic. I couldn't spot her. The gate was manned by PIA staff, I was the only white face and 450 Pakistani travellers were besieging the exit. Precedence seemed to go not by row number but by subtle gradations of social rank that are invisible to non-Pakistanis. People pushed and shoved; all struggled to board first, but there were fiercely proclaimed levels of self-perceived importance. Elderly gentlemen of military bearing and smartly dressed businessmen harangued the ground staff demanding to be let on first, demands that were usually complied with. Once on board, families manifested their standing by displays of gold jewellery, by shouting, argumentative children and by the loudness and rudeness of their complaints to the air stewardesses. One man berated a steward because someone's case was in the luggage bin above his seat. The steward offered to place the gentleman's bag in an adjacent locker but was rebuffed. The dressing-down continued, imperious and audible to the whole cabin, until the steward pleaded with the owner of the offending case to be allowed to move it.

The seats next to mine were occupied by two young Asian men. They were in jeans and T-shirts and addressed each other in what I took to be Sindhi; when they spoke English it was the slangy, dismissive argot of young British Pakistanis parodied by Ali G. They looked at me, I thought, with suspicion; there was no attempt at conversation.

After take-off I went looking for Ayesha, who was seated further forward on the other side of the plane. Judging by her smile I evidently looked relieved to find her. When I got back to my seat lunch was being served. The two young men had lamb curry on their trays, but the stewardess offered me the choice of Pakistani or English food. I asked what the English dish was and she said 'Chicken Forestière'. One of the young men sniffed. 'That's a bit racialist, isn't it? She didn't ask us!' It was unclear if he was joking or serious, or to whom the remark was addressed, but I tried to lighten the mood. 'You're right. And what's worse is that the English food is actually French . . .' They didn't smile. I decided we weren't going to have much in common.

An hour into the flight an announcement came over the Tannoy, in Urdu then in English. 'If there is a doctor on board, please would you make your way to row fifteen.'

I looked to see if anyone was responding and was surprised when the man on my right tapped my shoulder.

'Excuse me – can I get out?'

I let him past and was about to sit down when the other man raised a hand.

'Sorry. Me, too.'

When they returned they told me an elderly woman had

fainted but been revived with a glass of water and some deep breathing.

'We weren't even needed; there were four doctors there already. That's Pakistan for you – endless supplies of qualified medics . . .'

My preconceptions were confounded. Conversation flowed. The men were brothers and both were doctors, the elder a GP in Bradford, the younger a surgeon at Leeds General.

They had been born in Yorkshire and were thinking of emigrating to Australia, where there was a shortage of young doctors and pay and climate were considerably better.

I asked where they were travelling to and they said they were going to visit their parents. Their father had decided to sell up in England and return to his roots by building a house to retire to in the Orangi district of Karachi.

'But isn't Orangi meant to be dangerous?' I asked. 'I mean, I've heard a lot of bad things about it . . .'

'Karachi's the most dangerous city in Pakistan, and Orangi's the most dangerous part of Karachi,' the brothers said, laughing. 'At least it is if you don't come from there. It's overrun with criminals, Taliban and terrorists. But we know the place and our parents live there, so we're okay. Where are you heading for?'

'Well, eventually I have to go to a place called Kahin Nahi. Do you know it?'

The brothers grimaced.

'Yeah, sure. And you were calling Orangi dangerous! Good luck in Kahin Nahi, mate!'

Four hours into the flight, the older brother asked again if he could get past me. I expected him to go to the toilet, but he took out a mat from his rucksack and laid it on the floor. With the aid of a pocket compass he aligned himself with Mecca and prostrated himself to pray.

In the passport queue at Karachi, the brothers complained about the squalor, the smell and the chaos.

'It's so third world. God knows what Westerners must think when they come here for the first time. This country could have a massive tourist industry – there's so much to see and so much history – but the Pakistanis can't get their act together. Wait 'til we get to customs. There are queues for everything, the luggage always gets lost and nothing works.'

Ayesha appeared as we were waiting for the bags, spoke to the brothers in stumbling Urdu then laughed and switched to English as we said goodbye. In the crowded arrivals hall we found our driver and set off into the smothering heat of Karachi's fieriest summer for twenty years.

CHAPTER 20

Karachi is a city of havoc, misruled by violence, patronage and greed. It holds impressive, unenviable records – for murder, kidnapping, corruption and torture. Three decades of political civil war have left its inhabitants looking over their shoulders and its streets littered with bodies.

It wasn't always so. Karachi was once the pearl of Sindh, a southern paradise of fruit trees and butterflies, where children played safely and doors were left unlocked. A guidebook for US troops posted there in 1943 called it 'the Paris of the East . . . the cleanest city in the whole of India . . . with beautiful beaches and bathing places'. The 1950s and '60s were Karachi's *pur sakoon dor*, the era of serenity, when restaurants, nightclubs and cinemas flourished and no one questioned the right of women to visit them unchaperoned. A catchy Urdu rock number with electric guitars from the 1964 film *Chingari* gave Karachi its enduring sobriquet *Ae Roshniyon ke Shehar Bata*, City of Lights, evoked with wry irony in today's era of power cuts and darkened streets.

The seeds of future conflict had been sown in 1947 when partition sent millions of Muslims scurrying into the city, tripling its population, and hundreds of thousands of Hindus, Karachi's traditional administrators, managers and businessmen, fleeing from it. The incomers, the *Mohajirs,* vied with established communities to fill the economic and political vacuum. Arguments flared over property ownership and land rights, electoral representation and community identity. Seared by the horrors of partition, fearing discrimination, the Mohajirs mobilised and organised. Their political party, the MQM, fought for power with such ruthless tenacity that it became respected and feared in equal measure.

The British settlement had left Pakistan with democracy, but it developed in its own way. Votes were something to be bought, extorted or wheedled out of a population that went for the highest bidder. All political parties took and offered *bhatta*, bribes and protection money. Rival factions competed for jobs, land, water and public funds; many of them acquired a militant wing with knives, guns and grenades. Karachi became a battleground, whose spoils were control of the state and city governments, the police, the courts, rents and revenues. The MQM proved the most efficient manipulator of people and of the system. Maintained in power by Karachi's preponderant Mohajir population, it ruled with impunity. The party distributed largesse to its influential supporters, political and criminal, in the form of contracts for grandiose public schemes – roads, housing, power stations and dams – that existed largely on paper and whose purpose was to enrich grantors and grantees alike from public coffers.

People came to dread the MQM's wrath. The party's thugs kidnapped, tortured and murdered with a growing sense of entitlement. Most of the city's police were in their pockets and those who tried to curb their activities met grisly ends. By the mid-1990s armed clashes were an everyday event, a rumbling civil war between the MQM and its rivals that caused thousands of deaths. Political factions and criminal gangs maintained secret facilities where skilful torturers would mutilate opponents before dumping their corpses on the street. Body bags were a ubiquitous, reliable barometer of the violence.

But Karachi remained Pakistan's economic powerhouse, generating two-thirds of the nation's income and over half of national tax revenues. In the 1990s, war in Afghanistan turned it into the hub of Pakistan's trade in heroin and smuggled arms, boosting the black economy and the city's murder rate. The prizes are extravagant, the incentive for politicians to retain power massive. Karachi's wealthy elite now live in barricaded security, armed guards every ten yards, high walls and barbed wire. The state has been displaced by informal power structures that people recognise, despise and obey. No other city in the world can match its unique, flaming, depressing energy.

On the way from the airport we passed a dozen checkpoints, manned by machine guns of the Pakistan Rangers. The road, which in British times had been wide and smooth, was potholed now, clogged by brightly painted buses and lorries with passengers clinging precariously to roofs and rails like bees swarming on a honeycomb. In the scrubby wasteland to either side, the needy teemed. The air conditioning in the car was at full blast but still the heat clung to us.

Entering the hotel was to pass from one world to another. Security guards directed the car into a steel cage, where hydraulic barriers pinned us in place while doors, bonnet and boot were opened and searched. Mirrors on poles were rolled beneath us looking for bombs; our luggage lifted, taken for x-ray then returned by scurrying attendants. Cleared for entry, we emerged into flowering gardens where water sprinklers irrigated immaculate lawns; billowing marquees with tables covered in white linen were presided over by khaki-clad guards in watchtowers, idly flicking the safety catches of their Kalashnikovs.

In the marble reception hall, men in suits with bulging breast pockets spoke into walkie-talkies. A tall, distinguished commissionaire with the high plumed headdress of the Frontier Corps greeted us with a bow, snapping his fingers at two bellboys who ran to take our cases. It was an island of unlikely civilisation in a ravaged landscape.

Ayesha said she needed a shower and a change of clothes, but suggested we meet in a couple of hours for a drink. I had just begun unpacking when the phone in my room rang.

'Martin, I need a favour. I need you to ring room service and order me a bottle of wine. I just tried them and they say only non-Muslim guests can have alcohol. I gave them an earful, but they won't budge. See what they've got, will you? I don't want anything rough.'

I made the call, but the service wallah said the hotel's policy was not to serve wine; they had Murree Beer, which he described as tasty and nutritious. I ordered three bottles and dropped them off at Ayesha's room. When we met an hour or so later, I had the impression she had drunk them.

'So, finally . . . we're here,' she said as we sat in the hotel lobby. 'I hope you've got our plans worked out. I don't want to spend more time in this place than I absolutely have to.'

'Of course,' I said. 'Neither do I. But I do think we need to see all the players in this drama . . . suspects as well as witnesses.'

'Oh God, Martin; don't start that again. You know what I think about all that . . .'

Ayesha wasn't slurring her words, but her voice had the emphatic edge to it that comes with drink.

'Yes, I do. And I don't want to do anything dangerous, any more than you do. Imran will be here in half an hour and he'll be able to tell us who we should be talking to . . . and who will agree to talk to us.'

Imran Hayat was a young Pakistani academic, an expert in the history of his country's chaotic legal system and a supporter of liberal politics in an increasingly Islamic state. I had been put in touch with him by a friend at London University and Imran had spent a month working on my behalf, trying to find addresses, fix meetings and arrange interviews. Ayesha was in a mood to find fault with everything.

'Oh, bloody Imran! You keep talking about him as if he's going to solve everything. I thought *you* were meant to be the great journalist. How come it's Imran and not you doing all the research?'

The animosity in her words demanded to be taken

seriously. She asked me to order her a drink and I hesitated. She insisted. Her voice was raised. We were beginning to attract the interest of people at other tables. I ordered the drink.

Imran arrived late. Hotel security had been reluctant to admit him and phone calls to our rooms had gone unanswered. I apologised, but Imran was gracious.

'Oh, no. It is much better for them to be over-vigilant. There was a suicide bombing at this hotel three years ago that caused fifty casualties. Lashkar-e-Jhangvi claimed it . . . Al Qaeda people, you know . . .'

Imran was polite and intelligent, his English unaccented to the point of sounding almost too perfect. I liked him at once.

'Thank you, Imran. I'm drinking coffee, but Ayesha has a beer. Would you like one?'

Imran shook his head and asked for a mint tea. He was wearing traditional Pakistani clothes, a light-coloured shalwar kameez with leather sandals. He seemed at ease in the Western plush of the hotel, but at the same time keeping his distance. Ayesha had been weighing him up since he arrived.

'So, Imran. Martin has been singing your praises. He says you'll be taking us to see everyone who's anyone in this country. He thinks you're the Pakistani answer to Sherlock Holmes, the great bloody Imran with all the answers at his fingertips . . .'

Ayesha caught my glance and raised her hands theatrically. 'What? Have I said something? What are you giving me that look for?'

I was about to apologise to Imran, but he smiled and gestured towards Ayesha's beer.

'A brewery in an Islamic country; quite an anomaly, don't you think? The British founded the Murree distillery in the nineteenth century; its slogans used to be "Have a Murree with your curry" or "Eat, drink and be Murree", which is rather amusing. But things are trickier now. Most of our politicians and our English-speaking elite enjoy a tipple, but the religious right are getting angry about it . . . and quite violent. They posted photographs on the Internet of the Governor of Punjab taking a drink and accused him of being *haram*, unclean and un-Islamic. That stirred up a lot of fury among the common people; then the Governor was murdered.'

Ayesha sensed that Imran's message was intended for her; his words sounded disapproving, but his tone was even and friendly. There was a moment of awkward silence.

'I think we should talk about our plans,' I said. 'Imran, can you tell us what you've been able to find out?'

Imran nodded. 'I have been trying to arrange several interviews, with mixed fortunes I am afraid. I have been telephoning Masood Jilani, the private detective you told me about, but so far he is refusing to see us. He was, of course, shot in the course of his investigations, so this is understandable; but I will keep working on him. Inspector Iqbal is refusing to answer my calls, almost certainly because he has been taking bribes in this case. I have made some enquiries about Javed Shafik, our principal suspect, and it is true that he has been linked with criminal goings-on. He has been involved in illegal alcohol distribution, probably in the drugs trade and possibly in human sex trafficking, forcing young girls into prostitution. Perhaps of most interest as far as Ibrahim Rahman is concerned are Javed Shafik's activities involving government contracts . . .'

Ayesha hit the table with the flat of her hand.

'Stop! I've already said this is wrong! I don't want to hear any more about my father being involved with Javed Shafik and his bloody gangsters . . .'

'Ayesha, wait a moment.' I tried to calm things. 'We need at the very least to hear what Imran has found out. This is important.'

Imran lowered his eyes. 'Well, I was saying that Shafik is undoubtedly involved in organised crime, but, as with so much in Pakistan, there is a nuance. Shafik is a protégé of the UF, the United Front party that is very powerful here. Politicians and gangsters look after each other and make each other rich. But they are both part of the parallel structures of authority that have displaced the state in this city. Men like Shafik provide services to the population – they offer the people protection, find them accommodation, guarantee their water and electricity supplies, moderate their rents and arbitrate in disputes. Shafik does all of this. And he sponsors local youth clubs and cricket teams. So while he is certainly a mafia boss, to many people he is also a legitimate operator, a social activist, a protector of the weak.'

Ayesha snorted. Imran pressed on.

'This does not mean I wish to exonerate Javed Shafik. But it does mean there may be a way for us to get to him. I have told his people that Martin is a British journalist who wants to write about Shafik's philanthropic activities. They have relayed the message to their boss and he is interested. I say "interested" because he is not stupid: he would be flattered to have a positive article written about him, but I sense he is suspicious of our motives. We need to be very careful. Shafik is a ruthless man.'

Ayesha leaned forward.

'So, what exactly are you saying? That my dad was a crook? That you're going to take us to see his boss? You think you're going to stitch my father up . . .'

Imran looked at us then resumed with the same unruffled civility.

'Actually, Miss Ayesha, I have some evidence that might contradict that theory. I believe Masood Jilani told you about Mr Rahman's activities during his visits to Pakistan, in particular his purchasing of land and the building of a rather luxurious house . . .'

'You know full well he told me about that! And you know Masood thinks it proves my dad was in cahoots with Shafik . . .'

'Well, that may of course be true. But there could also be other explanations. It is a fact that Mr Rahman – Ibrahim – was buying land around Kahin Nahi. I have traced several of his purchases and most of them involve plots adjoining or close to the property of the Rahman family, the lands farmed by Mr Rahman's father and his father before him. So it could be that Ibrahim started buying the land for entirely innocent purposes. But then I think something happened, something – or someone – that drew him into buying more and more until he was in it way over his head . . .'

For the first time, the hostility disappeared from Ayesha's expression.

'But how could Dad have afforded to buy all that if he wasn't getting money from somewhere dodgy?'

Imran shrugged. 'That is something we will have to find out. We'll need to speak to the patwari who dealt with the transactions. All I am saying is that there may have been a less sinister explanation for the land purchases than we have been assuming. But I have the strong impression that they played a part in Mr Rahman's tragic end . . .'

CHAPTER 21

We had arranged to meet for breakfast, but Ayesha did not appear. The heat seemed to have moved up a notch; even the hotel's powerfully cooled interior was beginning to turn sticky. I had finished eating and was about to ring Ayesha's room when she walked up to the table and slumped in a chair. She was wearing dark glasses.

'Sorry. Sorry for keeping you waiting. I see you've finished. Anyway, I only want a coffee.'

She clicked her fingers to the waiter, who bowed and went to fetch her order.

'I'm fine. You don't need to say anything. What's Imran got fixed for us?'

She appeared less resentful now, less angry. The suggestion of a possible exoneration for her dead father had attenuated her indignation.

'"Good morning, Ayesha . . ." Isn't that what people usually say when they meet? Don't they usually ask how we slept and stuff like that?'

'Very funny. Thanks for reminding me. Why don't you just answer the question . . .'

Her words were spiked, but there was a hint of a smile.

'Well, Imran's already rung,' I said. 'He's arranged for us to meet a senior commander in the Karachi Police Department. Apparently he and Imran were at university in London together. Imran thinks this fellow will be able to persuade – or order – our friend Inspector Iqbal to talk to us.'

Ayesha nodded. 'Okay. That sounds helpful. And what do you make of the things Imran was saying last night – about my dad's land purchases? Who is this patwari person he was talking about?'

'I asked Imran about that when he rang this morning. The patwari is the local official who records land sales. Like a land registrar in the UK, I suppose; but Imran says it's more complicated here and we need to be on our guard when we're dealing with him. He'll explain when he sees us.'

Imran arrived as Ayesha was finishing her coffee. He bade her good morning, asked if she had slept well and looked surprised when I laughed. Imran said his friend, Commander Zaid Alam, would be joining us shortly, but he wanted to explain a few things before we met him.

'Zaid is a top policeman and I can vouch for his honesty. He is highly educated; he runs a tight ship, but he is beholden to the system of policing that pertains in Pakistan. This is not the UK. Police and politicians work closely here. And this can lead to corruption. Zaid knows full well that cops like Iqbal Hafiz take bribes. It is not ideal, but it has been like that for centuries.'

'Thank you, Imran,' Ayesha said. 'We understand. And we're grateful to your friend for helping us get to see Inspector Iqbal. Can I just ask about what you were saying last night concerning my father's land purchases? You said the patwari might be able to help us . . .'

'I hope so; but again I think it will depend on how we approach things. Like the police, patwaris exercise unchecked power. They alone draw up the records of land sales and transfers, boundaries and legal titles. Civil servants are rarely monitored by the centre, so they are masters in their own kingdoms. Tampering with the records is rampant. Land-grabbing crooks pay patwaris billions of rupees to get property illegally transferred to their names, leaving the real owners bereft. Even feudal lords seek their favour and they escape punishment because of their political connections. The patwari who dealt with your father had great power over him; he could register the land to whomever he wished, and could be bribed or threatened into favouring the most persuasive party. That sort of thing has caused countless feuds and murders. So my first thought was that something of this ilk may be at the root of your father's troubles. When we go to see the patwari, we need to be very aware of this . . .'

Imran stood up and waved across the lobby. A tall, athletic man in a white shirt with epaulettes was striding towards us accompanied by a retinue of uniformed policemen.

'Zaid!' Imran thrust out his hand and the two men embraced. 'It is good to see you. Thank you for coming . . .'

'Not a problem, my friend. I am here officially to check

on the security of this hotel and its many distinguished Western visitors.' He smiled in our direction and Imran made the introductions. A representative of the hotel management arrived with two waiters, inviting us to sit at a fresh table on which they spread a selection of snacks and drinks, while the uniformed officers stood guard. Zaid was patently a man of influence.

'How can I help?' he said as the waiters fussed. 'Imran has told me the essentials of your inquiry. I know you have concerns about the conduct of some of my men. Please tell me what I can do.'

I began to explain about Ibrahim Rahman's murder and our suspicions that the Kahin Nahi police had been bribed to let his killers go free. Zaid listened politely; when he spoke it was clear that he had read the file.

'Let me say this: Kahin Nahi is probably the most dangerous and crime-ridden neighbourhood of the dangerous, crime-ridden city we call home. Inspector Iqbal Hafiz is a difficult man; he is rude and ruthless, and he is almost certainly corrupt. But his methods keep a lid on the violence, which is an achievement. It is a terrible thing when evil men get away with evil deeds; but sometimes policemen must choose between two evils. In Karachi compromise is a way of life, and the noblest of us are flawed. We are forced to make backroom deals and trade-offs between principle and power—'

'But this is my father we are talking about!' Ayesha's anger had returned. 'How can you sit there and talk about compromise? How can you defend men like Iqbal who have taken money to cover up for criminals?'

'I do not defend them,' Zaid said. 'I am explaining to you the background against which these events took place. I am aware that corruption happens. If it goes too far, then I intervene. But this is how the system functions; you cannot eradicate it without everything breaking down. I will tell Iqbal that he must speak to you. Then it is up to you to decide where the truth lies.'

Zaid tapped in a number on his mobile phone and was answered immediately. He spoke briefly in Urdu and clicked the phone off.

'I have told Iqbal. He is expecting you . . .'

Imran laughed. 'Zaid-ji, how do you do that? I called Iqbal for days and he never answered!'

'Are you naïve, Imran-ji? All police have two phones – one for the public that they never pick up and one for important calls; I got the second one. Now, how are you planning to get to Kahin Nahi?'

Imran said he would drive us in his car, but Zaid looked dubious.

'For you and for Ms Rahman, of course, that is fine. The problem is Martin. We are experiencing a spike in car-jackings, in which Westerners are prize targets. On that score Martin sahib sticks out like a sore finger . . .'

I began to say I was willing to take the risk, but Zaid raised a hand.

'I cannot allow you to go unaccompanied. Daniel Pearl was abducted in broad daylight in this city right outside the Metropole Hotel and ended up with his throat being slit on camera. I shall provide a detail of my men to take you to Kahin Nahi.'

CHAPTER 22

Karachi was suffering in the heatwave. Temperatures were nudging into the mid-forties. On television spokesmen for the National Disaster Management Authority gave updates of deaths and prognoses for the city's water supply. The chronic power cuts, normally accepted with wry humour, had turned deadly as whole districts were left with dry taps and standpipes. The rich ordered deliveries from water tankers; the poor slipped into dehydrated decline. On the streets volunteers handed out dates and drinks for *Iftar* meals to break the Ramadan fast. In the hospitals dying patients lay in corridors. Thousands fled from homes that had become unbearably hot, sleeping in the open, staggering down highways in search of shelter. City services were overwhelmed; the morgues ran out of space, bodies were stacked in meat storage facilities and gravediggers quadrupled their fees.

The hotel reception rang in mid-afternoon to say that our escort had arrived. In the lobby three policemen in body armour were waiting for us, machine guns across their chests. Karachiites, long inured to the city's trappings of violence, barely gave them a second glance. We set off northwards in an armoured jeep, passing through the middle-class suburb of Nazimabad with its 1950s apartment blocks built for the influx of Mohajir refugees, then on into Liaquatabad and Buffer Zone. The roads became rougher, the streets more frequently scarred by open sewers. The jeep had no air conditioning; all of us, not least the policemen in their flak jackets, were suffering. In the *katchi abadis*, the slums of Karachi's Orangi Town where a million people scrape out a fragile existence, our guardians flicked the safety catches of their weapons. Imran spoke to them in Urdu but their reply was terse. He whispered to me that we were 'in a place where police are regularly strafed'.

We turned into a narrow one-way street. Crowds filled it, slowing our progress. People were looking in at the windows. The policeman in the back of the jeep put his hand on my head and pushed me down. It was cramped and hot; I could see nothing beyond a row of feet. Outside, voices were raised; the jeep seemed to sway as if rocked by unseen hands. Memories of the two British soldiers dragged from their car and murdered by an angry Belfast crowd in 1988 flashed into my mind. Then the jeep accelerated, bouncing precariously down the uneven road. The policeman laughed and pulled me upright.

After a moment Imran nudged me. 'They were feeling edgy,' he said, 'because that is where a police patrol was shot dead last month. They'd set up a sting on a gang of car thieves, but someone had been tipped off and they were fired on from all sides. A crew from SAMAA TV who'd gone along to cover the operation got caught in the crossfire.'

Kahin Nahi was beyond Orangi Town, at the very limit of the city. A scruffy main street was lined by shacks, with a garish marriage hall rising above them. In lay-bys at the side of the road, men congregated around parked trucks and trailers, smoking, talking and arguing. Piles of rubbish were everywhere; dogs pulled at the carcass of a dead donkey.

We made a sharp left turn and came to a halt in front of an armoured gate set in a wall of umber brick. The police station guard waved the barrel of his rifle at us, indicating that we should park further away. Regarding it as a slight, our driver switched off the engine. There was a stand-off until the driver produced a document and thrust it at the sentry. He weighed it up quizzically before disappearing inside.

The gate reopened and we were ushered out of the car. Behind the wall was a quadrangle of scrubby grass with chickens scratching at the baked earth; at its centre, set back from the outer defences, a single-storey building flying the Pakistani flag proclaimed itself to be 'Police Station No. 211; Kahin Nahi District, Karachi'. The sentry pointed to a door.

Stepping from blinding sunlight into the dark interior was disorienting. I sensed that the room was small – around twelve feet by twelve – and I heard a voice speaking in Urdu. A stocky, moustachioed man was sitting behind a desk, dressed in the grey-blue uniform of a Deputy

Superintendent of Police, with a mobile phone clamped to his ear. He took no notice of us. Ayesha, Imran and I stood uncertainly then settled on a row of hard-backed chairs ranged against the wall. Inspector Iqbal did not look in our direction; it was hard to tell if he was genuinely busy or just making us wait. Imran sat impassively, but I knew Ayesha was seething.

An ancient air conditioning unit set high on the wall rumbled noisily, dripping water onto the floor. When a puddle formed an elderly man in grubby pantaloons ran in and mopped it up with a towel. I watched the ceremony repeated several times, fascinated by its Sisyphean precision. The plaster on the wall behind Iqbal's head was peeling. A portrait of Muhammad Ali Jinnah looked down on the servant of the state he had founded. A carved wooden panel immortalised the names of the DSPs who had served before.

When Iqbal ended his call and put down the phone, Ayesha began to speak but Iqbal snubbed her.

'Imran-ji,' he said in accented, fluent English. 'The Commander is your classmate? He wants me to talk to you? But I don't know what about. There is nothing to tell about this stupid case!'

I tried to object; Iqbal ignored me and switched pointedly to Urdu. A game of status was being played and I was losing it. I motioned to Imran, but he shook his head. When Iqbal paused, Imran spoke.

'DSP Iqbal, sir; thank you for receiving us. We know you are busy . . .'

The phone on Iqbal's desk rang and he picked it up at

once, speaking in English so we could understand that the most trivial matters took precedence over us. He spoke about a dinner he had attended, about vacation plans, about acquaintances in the UK, their medical problems and the deficiencies of the British health care system. 'British Pakistanis!' he concluded, with a glance towards Ayesha. 'They claim benefits over there; then come here in their gold bracelets and chains!'

Iqbal was playing the maharaja; Imran said later that I reminded him of 'Sir Clive at the court of the Great Mughal', impotently waiting to speak. After fifteen minutes, I got up and went to the door from which the floor-mopping flunkey had entered. I motioned to Iqbal that I wished to wash my hands. I found the bathroom, but instead of using it I loaded a cassette into my pocket tape recorder. I made to flush the toilet, but discovered the building had no running water. As I returned to the audience room, Iqbal plucked a tissue from a gold-plated box on his desk and handed it to me without interrupting his phone call. The recorder in my pocket was turning.

When Iqbal deigned finally to address us, he gave no indication of being on the defensive. He was a man used to giving orders, used to the deference of petitioners forced to hang on his whim.

'So here is Miss Ayesha, back with us again,' he said with a hint of a sneer, 'still not satisfied with Pakistani justice.' Iqbal addressed himself to Imran to show that Ayesha and I were beneath his dignity. It was a gesture of contempt, but I wondered if there was weakness in it.

'You know that I am talking to you only because

Commander Zaid has requested it. What is it that you wish to ask?'

'We wish to benefit from your expertise, DSP Iqbal,' Imran said carefully. 'We understand that the first set of miscreants arrested for the murder of Ibrahim Rahman have proved to be innocent of the crime.'

Iqbal sat impassively, his head slightly cocked.

'So we wish to explore what further facts we might discover with your assistance. We know that prior to his death Ibrahim was buying land in the Kahin Nahi district. And since land is a sensitive issue, it struck me that Mr Rahman might have been killed in a land dispute. Perhaps there was someone competing with him for the property and the competition got out of hand . . .'

Iqbal snorted. 'Then you know nothing about Kahin Nahi. The land here is worthless. There is so much of it, millions of acres. It is never going to be developed for building and it is the worst agricultural soil in Pakistan. You can forget that theory!'

Imran looked pensive.

'Iqbal sahib, I bow to your knowledge. I do not know why someone would want this worthless land. I do not know why Ibrahim himself would want it. But it seems that he did do. And this is what puzzles me: he was so attached to the land that he was willing to defend it . . .'

I saw Iqbal's eyes dart to Ayesha. Imran's account had taken an unexpected turn.

'Masood Jilani, the unfortunate detective fellow who worked for Ms Rahman, informs me that Ibrahim called a meeting of landowners in Kahin Nahi. These were small farmers, mainly families with inherited property – worthless property as you say, DSP; but Ibrahim was organising people to protect it . . .'

Iqbal shifted in his chair.

'. . . I understand that there was a confrontation involving a certain amount of violence, in which the Kahin Nahi police had to intervene. I am sure this will be logged in your records, Iqbal-ji . . .'

Iqbal's fingers tapped on the desktop.

'Perhaps I remember something,' he said. 'We have endless problems with land disputes. I can't be expected to remember them all.'

'No. Of course not. But I think you might remember this one; because it involved someone you know personally. I believe that Ibrahim Rahman's quarrel was with Mr Javed Shafik . . .'

For the first time since we arrived Iqbal wavered.

'Imran-ji,' he said hurriedly. 'I can tell you that this is not the case. Shafik has nothing to do with this affair.'

'Oh, for God's sake!' Ayesha leapt to her feet. 'You say that . . . because Shafik has bribed you to cover up for whoever killed my dad!'

Iqbal's fist clenched.

'You silly English girl! You need to watch your tongue. This is not England. You come here and you think you can tell us what to do. You think things will be like they are in England. Well, this is Pakistan. You don't know the first thing about this place!'

Iqbal realised he had let his anger get the better of him. His eyes narrowed.

'My strong advice to you, Miss Rahman, is to drop all these accusations and go home to England. In England perhaps crimes get solved. But here people get killed by powerful men and the murderers are never found. I advise you in your own interest, in your dead father's interest and in your family's interest: go home at once!'

Ayesha's hands were shaking; she leaned on the chair to steady herself, but she did not back down.

'So . . . you're threatening me . . . you're warning me . . . But you're not denying that you know Javed Shafik . . . that you took a bribe from him . . . that Shafik killed my father and you're protecting him!'

Iqbal was calm now. He spoke with the assurance of a man who makes the rules and has little to fear from them.

'I am sorry to disappoint you, but your father was no hero. He didn't quarrel with Shafik; far from it – *he worked for him!* Ibrahim Rahman was a partner in Shafik's business; he was Javed Shafik's accomplice. And you are very foolish indeed if you believe otherwise.'

'You're lying!' Ayesha groaned. 'My father would never work for a criminal like Shafik!'

'Really? And what about all the other things you don't know about your father? Like his fondness for young girls, for instance . . . Rahman was far from the lovely, inno-cent father you think he was – or pretend he was, or have convinced yourself he was – he was a lecher, a dirty old man who liked little girls!'

'No! That's a lie! You have no evidence of that . . .'

Iqbal was enjoying his triumph.

'Do you think we're stupid? Do you really think we don't

know about the traffickers sending girls back and forth to the UK, pretending they're child brides? Why do you think your father was always coming here? Do you think we don't know about your father's shady past? About the girl he abused and murdered in Burnley? You would do well to think about that. And you would do well to get out of Pakistan while you still can!'

CHAPTER 23

The journey back to the hotel passed in hot, angry silence. Ayesha said she was tired and went to bed. Imran and I sat for a while over a coffee, but Inspector Iqbal's outburst had unsettled us. His accusations had rekindled my doubts about Ibrahim, while for Imran there seemed to be an undertone of perceived national shame. It is easy to say that evil exists in all races and nations, but the peculiarly Pakistani character of the alleged crimes was harder for him to swallow.

Imran asked me what weight I gave to the story of the dead girl in Burnley, but I had no answer. We both wanted to dismiss Iqbal's accusations as clumsy smears designed to humiliate Ayesha, but we both feared they might be true. I asked Imran what else Masood Jilani had told him about Ibrahim's land acquisitions and about his reasons for convening the meeting of local landowners. Imran shrugged: he didn't know anything more than what he had said to Inspector Iqbal, and much of that had been based on speculation. We parted with a tremor of apprehension.

When the three of us met for breakfast the following morning, Ayesha seemed reinvigorated. Having phoned her great-uncle Guddu she told us that Guddu remembered Ibrahim's attempts to rally the landowners of Kahin Nahi. He could not recall exactly what the bone of contention had been, but he confirmed that there had been a public meeting and that it was broken up by the police.

'So don't you see?' Ayesha said. 'This proves what I've been telling you. My dad was trying to protect people; he was getting the small landowners together to fight off crooks and land-grabbers like Javed Shafik and his gang. He was murdered because he was standing up for what was right. He was never in league with Shafik – that was all lies by Iqbal. My dad was never an abuser or a murderer . . . he was a hero!'

'Just like Yul Brynner against the Mexican bandits in *The Magnificent Seven*, you mean?'

'My God, Martin!' Ayesha gave me a withering look. 'How can you be so cynical? I thought you wanted to help me. I thought you cared. And you come out with something like that . . .'

I had spoken the words before I could stop myself, but they captured the instinctive mistrust I felt about Ayesha's determination to exonerate her father.

'Perhaps I am cynical. It would be great if your dad turns out to be a hero – we would all prefer Yul Brynner to a . . . to a child abuser. But we have to be realistic; we need evidence before we start drawing conclusions.'

'You don't want *anything* good to come out of this, do you? I find something positive for a change, something encouraging after all the awful things I've had to go through since Dad died, and you pour cold water on it! I can't believe you said that about *The Magnificent Seven*. That is so disrespectful! I think you'd be happier if this whole thing turns out to be a complete disaster . . . so you can write a really horrible book damning me and my father and Pakistan and everything and everyone you come across!'

Imran stepped in.

'Ayesha, Martin – why don't we think about how we get clarification of these matters? Why don't I ring the patwari and ask if we can see him? At least that would give us some first-hand information . . .'

'Maybe. Or maybe we should go and see Javed Shafik . . .' I was angry; and this felt like a turning point in our search for answers. 'Now we know Shafik is up to his neck in human trafficking and scams and violence . . . why don't we go and ask him if Ibrahim was in it with him? That would be the best clarification by a mile!'

Imran lifted his hands in a gesture of calm.

'I am working on Javed Shafik, Martin. I told you I'm waiting for him to decide if he wants to be interviewed by you. So in the meantime I am going to call the patwari, okay? At least it will give us something concrete to do instead of sitting here getting angry with each other.'

Imran went into the hotel garden to make the phone call and escape the acrimony. Ayesha and I sat brooding. I yielded first.

'I'm sorry. I was wrong to mock you. But you know we've always said we need to be honest with each other. It's no good constructing some idealised picture of Ibrahim just because that's how you would like him to be . . .'

'That's not what I'm doing! It's you who keeps twisting things. You ignore the positive evidence and insist on the worst possible interpretation of everything. Don't you believe me when I say my dad was fighting for the people's rights? Don't you trust me?'

'If we're being completely honest, Ayesha, I'm not sure that I do. You remember when we spoke about the Governor of Sindh and you said that stuff about Pakistanis being driven by self-interest? Well, sometimes I can't help wondering if that applies to you, too.'

'What's that supposed to mean?'

'It means you've always tried to bully me into writing what you want me to write; that you've always—'

'Well, poor little Martin! The big journalist bullied by a little Pakistani girl. Don't make me laugh!'

'Come on, Ayesha. You know there are different sorts of bullying. You can do it in more subtle ways . . .'

'Well, you know what? You say you can't trust me, but I honestly don't know if I can trust you. You say I want to whitewash my father, but I think you're desperate for some lurid, horrid scandal . . . so you can sell more books!'

Imran reappeared and an ingrained English horror of making a scene made us fall silent. Nothing had been resolved; it was just easier to allow Imran to take charge.

'So. Good news. The patwari is available. He made a point of saying he will clear his diary for us, which means he is expecting a present. We shouldn't take anything too valuable; we don't want him to think we are desperate . . .

or made of money. Martin, do you have something like a BBC pen or a tie? That would be a good level to begin with; we can up the stakes later on.'

I gave Imran a couple of BBC T-shirts that I had brought for this purpose and we picked up a driver from the hotel. As we drove through the midday traffic Imran spoke about the man we were going to see. Asif Chaudhry had been a patwari for over thirty years and his father and grandfather had held the post for similar terms.

'If you have these people on your side, you have a useful ally,' Imran said. 'If they are against you, you have a problem. It may seem strange to English people that we must kowtow to a bureaucrat, but I urge you to show respect. This fellow is very influential; he may hold some keys to our investigation.'

After what Imran had said about the patwaris' wealth and power, I was surprised when we pulled up outside a rundown building with boarded windows. A nameplate in Urdu and English dating from the days of the Raj announced that this was the Office of Divisional Surveyor and Land Registrar, Patwari Chaudhry. In the course of our journey the weather had shifted from dry heat to oppressive humidity; steamy sunshine and dark clouds were now vying for possession of the sky. Imran knocked.

'Patwari sahib? Chaudhry sahib?'

He pushed gently at the door, which opened. We found ourselves in a sort of waiting room. It seemed deserted. Shelves lined the walls, stuffed with official papers in fraying cardboard folders. A fine dust flecked the sunlight that crept through the cracks in the boarded windows.

'I thought you said these documents were precious,' I whispered to Imran. 'That people kill and bribe to get their hands on them. How come they're just left lying where anyone can take them?'

'Ah, but these are not the precious ones!' The politely mocking voice came from a door at the far end of the room. A stooped figure in a cream waistcoat was peering at us through half-moon spectacles.

'Welcome, welcome, gentlemen and lady. Patwari Chaudhry is pleased to meet you. Do come into my parlour.'

The inner room was darker; a lamp burned on a desk piled with documents. The place was improbably cramped, submerged under fathoms of paper. My shoulder brushed against the door jamb and a piece of the wooden frame fell to the floor. I made to apologise, but Chaudhry raised his hand.

'You see the squalor to which the Pakistani state condemns its servants. Our offices were built by the British and no funds have been provided for maintenance since then. Such are the conditions in which we patwaris work; we labour from dawn until dusk, yet we remain on the receiving end of criticism that we are corrupt!'

'Not from us, patwari sahib!' Imran hastened to reply. 'Allow me to introduce Mr Martin and Miss Ayesha. Both have come here from England to meet you.'

Chaudhry smiled. 'Ah, yes, England. Blighty. Have you brought anything with you from England?'

Imran handed over the two T-shirts with a slight bow. Patwari Chaudhry felt them between his fingers. 'Thank you,' he said. 'I shall give these to my nephews. Is there something else? I mean, something for which you require my assistance?'

Imran nodded. 'Chaudhry sahib, Mr Martin is a journalist. He is researching about our notorious land-grabbing practices and mafia gangs that are involved in this—'

Chaudhry laughed. 'Yes, of course – land mafias are us. Or that is how the world thinks of us, a lawless state where property is not safe and life is gravely at risk. What do you want from me?'

'We would like you to tell us what you know, Chaudhry sahib. We will be grateful for your help.'

Chaudhry leaned back in his chair and folded his arms with the air of a man who has been asked about his favourite subject.

'There are many tales of this practice. I have seen it at first hand and can tell you things that others cannot. This information is valuable.'

He directed his eyes to the ceiling. Imran placed a bundle of rupee notes on the desk. With a quick glance Chaudhry pushed it under a leather-bound blotter.

Imran had said we should not disclose our specific interest in Ibrahim's land dealings, as the patwari would demand a bigger bribe. The aim was to extract the information tangentially, through the general questions of a Western journalist pursuing a story.

'Mr Chaudhry,' I said. 'Is it true that the land mafia is as powerful as the Pakistani media make out?'

'Much more powerful!' His reply sounded like a boast. 'In Karachi the land mafia is involved in drugs, kidnappings, bank robberies and many other crimes. They are well connected. They get tipped off about uninhabited plots and buildings in prime areas. Then they move in with fake documentation to take possession, leaving the real owners, often living abroad, to pursue their case vainly through the courts. Millions of acres are seized every year.'

'And why does the government not do anything about it, if it affects so many people?'

'My boy, you are naïve! The government is involved in it. The land mafia is a conspiracy of criminals, politicians, property dealers and – it has to be said – corrupt patwaris who provide the forged documents. There is a case at the moment where the relatives of one of our leading parliamentarians have helped themselves to a huge slice of land on the Lyari River outside the city. They have started cutting down trees, erecting buildings and dumping their waste into streams that supply drinking water to thousands of people. This is valuable land, yet these crooks have come in and started building homes. They are so powerful that they have got electricity piped in from the national grid. Who can even think of challenging such people?'

'And what about individual families who fall foul of the land mafia?'

'My God, they are legion! You need only look at the suburbs around Karachi where land has been occupied since time immemorial by natives of the place. They are poor and ignorant; they don't have the means to secure the proper *fards* and *pertt sarkars* – the land documents that would prove their ownership. So as the city's boundaries expand and these places become valuable, the land-grabbers move in. I dealt with one couple who went away for a week and returned to find a wall had been built round their land, watched over by armed guards. When they went to lodge a complaint, it turned out the police were part of the conspiracy and refused to file the report.'

'Does no one do anything to defend their rights?'

'Last autumn property owners from Shabrati Goth in Karachi Federal Area B tried to stage a rally against land-grabbers who were threatening to kill them if they didn't vacate their homes. But the land-grabbers had bribed the local officials so the rally was broken up by armed police. The state has no interest in protecting people who dare to raise their voice against the land mafia.'

'And yet you are saying that people do actually stand up to them?'

'There was a case right here on our own doorstep. The Orangi Pilot Project director, Perween Raja, had worked for years to help people in places like Orangi and Kahin Nahi. She fought to get them proper sanitation and a clean water supply. Water has become the monopoly of criminals who get funds from the government to build water schemes then pocket the money. So Perween drew up a map of illegally occupied land that had been taken over with the help of corrupt political parties, and that is what got her killed. Four gunmen opened fire on her car near Pirabad Police Station. Karachi is full of criminal gangs and political and religious militants. Land-grabbing is big business for them, and people like Perween who have the courage to speak out put their life in danger.'

'May I ask if one of these criminals, a man called Javed Shafik, has ever come across your path?'

Chaudhry looked at me carefully. 'Yes. But this is not surprising. Javed Shafik is a big figure in the property business. It is inevitable that he would come to a patwari to get the certificates he needs.'

'I am not implying any wrongdoing on your part, Mr Chaudhry. But I would like to hear your views of Mr Shafik. Some police officers have told us that he is influential in the organised crime world.'

'This is true. Shafik is a drug-dealer, a blackmailer, a people-trafficker. He has more illegally occupied land than anyone in north-west Karachi. But he has the backing of some powerful politicians, men who control this city. I cannot refuse to work with him or I would suffer the same fate as Perween Raja.'

Imran took over. 'You mentioned a rally against the land-grabbers in Shabrati Goth. Do you recall something similar in Kahin Nahi? It was led by a fellow called Ibrahim Rahman, who I think came to see you about his own land deals. Do you remember him, Chaudhry sahib?'

The patwari squinted at Imran. 'Perhaps I remember this Rahman. What would be your interest in him?'

'We just happen to be interested in the case. Can you tell us what Mr Rahman said when he came to you?'

The patwari thought for a moment, suspicion in his eyes. 'I remember one thing. Rahman talked to me about his daughter—'

'Really! He mentioned me?' Ayesha looked startled.

'Ah!' said the patwari. 'So this daughter is you? It seems this is not just another case you happen to have read about . . .'

Imran mumbled a few words in Urdu and Chaudhry nodded. Imran placed more banknotes on the table. Chaudhry smiled.

'I see we shall have to consult those documents that Martin sahib was mentioning when you first came in here, the ones that hold the secrets . . .'

In a third room deep within the building he took a series of keys from a locked cabinet, inserted them into a heavy iron door and disappeared from view. Five minutes later he reappeared with a bundle of papers, relocked the safe room and sat down at a table.

'We are interested in what land Ibrahim bought,' Imran said. 'We also wish to know if anyone was competing with him over ownership of this land, anyone who might have quarrelled with him because of it . . .'

Chaudhry motioned us to sit opposite him.

'Let me consult the documents. I have some recollections of Miss Ayesha's father, but this was a complicated case. I wish first to refresh my memory.'

Chaudhry leafed through the papers, nodding to himself as he opened then re-sealed one file after another.

'Yes,' he said. 'My memory was not deceiving me. There was someone else interested in these parcels of land—'

'I knew it!' Ayesha could not restrain herself. 'It was Shafik! He was the one who wanted my father's land. It was Shafik who killed him!'

Chaudhry shook his head. 'No, miss. It was not Shafik. The person who was also interested in the land your father bought was much closer to home . . . it was his brother Ahmed.'

Ayesha looked deflated. 'Ahmed? But Ahmed's interest could have been completely innocent. It could have been two brothers trying to secure the ancestral family lands . . .'

Chaudhry said nothing, but I had a sense that he was puzzled by Ayesha's response.

'Can I ask you something, Chaudhry sahib?' Ayesha was following her own train of thought. 'Did my father mention me by name?'

'Yes, young lady, he did. And he also mentioned one of your brothers – with the name of Tariq, if I remember correctly.'

'Yes, that's right, Tariq. And what did he say about us? Can you remember?'

'It was some time ago and I have a lot of people coming through these doors. Your father did not speak very much, but I sensed he was anxious, perhaps even scared about the business he was engaged in. I had the impression that he was involved in a task of considerable importance; and that it had your safety and your brother's safety at the heart of it.'

Ayesha blinked. 'Our safety? How could buying land out here in Karachi have anything to do with our safety? I live in London and Tariq lives in Burnley. That doesn't make sense . . .'

'I told you, young lady, my memory is not clear. I can recall nothing more from the conversations I had with Mr Rahman; but one thing that does not fade is the written evidence. I have checked these files and I was not mistaken. Look, here are the fards relating to your father's land purchases and here are the signatures on them. The land is owned jointly, by your father . . . and Javed Shafik.'

'But that can't be true!' There was pain in Ayesha's voice. 'There's no way my father and Shafik could have been working together! . . . Did you forge the fards because Shafik told you to? Did he bribe you, or blackmail you into putting his name on my father's land?'

The patwari smiled. 'Oh no, Ms Rahman; far from it. I fear your explanation that Shafik quarrelled with your father is mistaken. Javed Shafik and your father came in here together; they were the best of friends . . .'

High above Karachi, storm clouds unleashed the restive energy that had been stirring within them; the current crackled in thunder claps that shook the walls and rain that lashed the zinc of the patwari's roof.

CHAPTER 24

Karachi stumbled. Street drains, clogged with the ubiquitous rubbish that disfigures Pakistani cities, blocked within
minutes. Water filled the carriageways and spilled onto the
pavements. Buses, rickshaws, cars snarled into citywide
gridlock as exhausts filled with moisture and motorcycles
backfired. Outside the patwari's office a stalled yellow
Toyota had halted the traffic; the driver was kicking the
car, trying to push it aside as lorry-drivers yelled abuse.
Pedestrians leapt precariously from one island to the next,
seeking to avoid the snakes in the ankle-deep water. A cow
wandered disconsolately amid the traffic.

We crawled through the rainstorm. The driver took
shortcuts and diversions, threading down alleyways, driving through gardens. But a mile from our hotel, the traffic
congealed. Dusk was falling. Ayesha, who had said little
since we left the patwari's office, lost patience.

'Can you ask the driver where the nearest bar is?' she said
to Imran. 'And I don't mean some side of the road tea and
Pepsi place. I need a drink.'

'I'm not sure that would be very safe, Ayesha. This is not a lovely neighbourhood. And all the bars with alcohol are run by bootleggers, inevitably connected to criminal elements. They can spot you are from abroad . . .'

'For God's sake, Imran, just do what I say! We aren't your mates, or little children you have to look after; we are paying you to do what we tell you to do!'

Imran lowered his eyes and addressed the driver in Urdu. After a brief conversation he reported that there was a bar with alcohol two blocks off the main road; we would need a password, which the driver provided, and prices would be steep.

'At last! Thank you!' Ayesha gathered up her belongings and turned to me. 'I don't suppose Mr Teetotal Imran is going to join us, but what about you, Martin? Are you going to come and keep an eye on me?'

Illicit alcohol in a rain-soaked Karachi bar was a meagre attraction; but I was concerned for Ayesha's safety and I knew that abandoning her would deepen the friction between us.

'I suppose so. But can we agree that we aren't going to stay all evening? A couple of drinks and then back to the hotel, okay?'

Ayesha shrugged and opened the car door. I told Imran to go home; we would meet as usual for breakfast in the morning.

We found the bar easily enough. It resembled most Pakistani cafés, with billboards advertising Coke and Fanta and crates of indeterminate liquid in plastic bottles stacked around a few folding tables and chairs. The owner seemed surprised when Ayesha spoke the password the driver had given us, but we didn't look like policemen so he waved us through to a room behind the counter. There were half a dozen customers, all men, with glasses in their hand, puffing on the dark Morven cigarettes that give public places in Pakistan their indelible aroma. The looks we received told us we were interlopers.

Ayesha ordered without asking me what I wanted; a boy brought us two tumblers with cheap whisky. She downed hers in a gulp and motioned me to do the same, a ritual repeated once then once again. The alcohol infused us with a warmth we hadn't shared since the days of our first meetings; the other's opinions no longer seemed so offensive, so unpardonably wrong. But we remained wary. We spoke of the rain, the traffic, the hotel, the dirt and smells, avoiding the issues that divided us. Gradually Ayesha relaxed. She mentioned Peter, fleetingly, but I knew she wanted me to pick up on a topic she had avoided since our vexed discussion weeks ago. She was pressing ahead with wedding plans. There would be autumn ceremonies in both church and mosque to cater to each of the happy families.

'So how do you like that?' she said.

'Very much. I'm pleased for you.'

'I can't invite you, of course.'

She was teasing now, confiding but prickly, looking to provoke a response. She did.

'Oh, really? Why can't you invite me?'

'Because people would talk. They'd think we'd been having an affair.'

Ayesha had placed her hand on my wrist. I should have pushed it away.

'I hardly think people would say that,' I said. 'We are working together.'

'Yes, but we have been spending a lot of time together. That's unusual for my community, at least without a chaperone . . .'

Ayesha laughed then grew serious.

'I have been lonely, you know. And scared. There haven't been many people who've understood that. To the world I appear so . . . self-sufficient. I know we've argued, but at least you have thought about me as a person. And you've engaged with all this . . . instead of just sweeping it under the carpet.'

'Well, I'm doing my job. I can't write your story if I don't try to understand you. Although it hasn't been easy.'

Ayesha smiled. 'At first I didn't like you; you seemed so arrogant. But I've got to know you now. And I think you have taken a genuine interest in me. It's the first time I've had that since my dad died.'

A show of empathy can be a powerful tool. So many people are starved of it that even a little compassion unblocks many things. I pushed her hand away.

'Come on; let's go. I think the rain's easing. And you're getting drunk. We need to eat something.'

'Oh, okay . . .' She looked surprised. 'Can I just ask why you are saying that? Why don't you want to have a drink with me?'

'We've had a drink, Ayesha. And it's getting late.'

She shook her head. 'Is it because you believe what DSP Iqbal and patwari Chaudhry have been saying?'

'No, it's not that . . .'

'I think it is . . . I think it's because you've decided my dad's guilty, so I must be guilty too . . .'

'That's nonsense, Ayesha. Even if all those things were true about your father, how could that make you—?'

'I think you hate me, Martin. I think you've decided I'm a liar.'

'No, it's not that—'

'I think you only signed up for this because you want to make money out of me!'

Ayesha's eyes had glazed; her voice was raised. The men in the bar were looking at us.

'You want to write some crap book and make a lot of money! Well, if you want my help you'll need to pay me a fee. You'll need to pay me for all the help that I'll be giving you in your research . . .'

I wanted to point out that she had been insisting on paying *me* a fee. I tried in vain to calm her.

'Otherwise, don't count on me to carry on "working with you", as you so dismissively put it. I'm not "working" like you are, Martin . . . This is my bloody life we're talking about!'

The men in the bar were transfixed by the foreigners fighting in their space. Two of them stood up and walked towards us. I thought they were offering to intervene, but one asked for a light while the other leaned over the table between me and Ayesha. Almost too late I realised he had picked up her handbag. As I rose to my feet the man with the cigarette pushed me, but I avoided him and set off after the fellow with the bag. He too was clearly worse for drink, because I caught him and he didn't resist. I grabbed the handbag, went back to the bar.

Ayesha looked bewildered. I pulled her to her feet then out into the street. The rain had stopped. We flagged down a tuk-tuk for the mile or so back to the hotel. In the cramped seat behind the driver I felt Ayesha's shoulder nestle into mine. She mumbled a thank you.

'But I think you don't understand what I've been through since my father died. For me it's not just a detective story. You want to find out who killed him, like Sherlock Holmes or something. But I need to know why . . . and who he was. Because that changes everything – the way I look at him, at my life, at myself. Right now I don't know who I am or where I'm coming from, Martin . . . You don't understand, because nothing like that – nothing so massive that it shakes you right to the core – has ever happened to you. You've been lucky . . .'

When I got back to my room I found an envelope pushed under the door. The handwritten message from the hotel reception was timed at 12.32, when we were on our way to the patwari's:

Mrs Tara has telephoned. Tom has killed himself.

PART THREE

CHAPTER 25

After Tom's death I stopped work on Ayesha's book. The hours spent in Karachi waiting for a flight home had been interminably lonely. Watching the sun rise then set through the drawn curtains of my hotel room I had felt life crowding in on me with fears and reproaches. I tried to put my brain into sleep mode; I had been trying to do so ever since. But the mind turns willy-nilly, churning over what has been and what is to come. Reminders of the past said 'it wasn't too late then; you still could have done something'. On the plane home I found the seat I'd sat in for the outward journey; I remembered who was sitting near me, what I'd eaten, what film I'd watched, and the wrenching, tearing in my gut said, 'Tom was alive; it still wasn't too late.'

Back in England I devoted myself to the feverish, nagging imperative of uncovering what had happened. Perhaps knowing would help explain. Or perhaps I just needed to be doing something, anything to escape the circling, self-embedding regrets.

I heard intermittently from Ayesha – texts, emails,

voicemails — with messages that swerved from sympathy to anger and rebukes. She wanted me to contact her; she wanted to tell me how sorry she was about Tom and about our quarrel in Karachi; she wanted to share some new, important facts she had discovered after I left Pakistan; she wanted me to promise I would write her father's story.

I didn't reply. But her voice was in my ears; in my dreams her story mingled with memories of Tom, her dead father shading disconcertingly into the image of my dead brother. I spent my days investigating my brother's death, my nights dreaming of Ibrahim's, until the narratives became entangled in my mind. I was looking for answers about two deaths, in two places, in two minds about resuming contact with Ayesha.

I learned that Tom had tried to see Tara. He had gone to the house and been arrested for breaching the restraining order against him. Tara had made a statement to the police and agreed to testify in court. Tom was facing a criminal record that would disqualify him from working in any job that meant mixing with people or, absurdly, with animals. He couldn't work in shops, in schools, in parks or even as a volunteer dog walker. It was this last one that upset him the most. When he was five he founded a society called the Be Kind to Animals Club, the BKTA, and went knocking on people's doors asking if they had any pets, checking they were being nice to them.

I know that all marriages are a mystery and rarely does fault lie solely on one side. But I found it hard to accept that Tara had had my brother arrested. I felt anger and sorrow. I couldn't bring myself to talk to her. I struggled to imagine

Tom's thoughts and feelings in the days that led up to his suicide. Tracing his movements, where he had been and whom he had met, seemed a way to scratch at the conundrum. Tom had left the solicitor a contact address that I didn't recognise. I checked with Rob Butcher the estate agent and discovered that it was a rental property, a small furnished house whose owners were away and wanted a short-term let. Tom had taken it on a rolling contract with a four-week notice period. Rob gave me the keys.

I braced myself for the company of death – no one had said how long it had been before Tom's body was found – but the odour in the hall was not of decay. It was a stinging, oily presence and it hung heavy in the air. I opened the curtains; the lounge was littered with papers. In the kitchen a sleeping bag was crumpled on the tiles; beside it, a whisky bottle and a charred disposable barbecue. Tom had lain in this kitchen; his parents gone, his brother continents away, his wife lost; and this is what remained. Out in the street a dog barked; a baby cried; the sun poked in.

I sat in Tom's chair and arranged his bank statements and bills in date order. I counted receipts for beer, for cigarettes, for whisky. I found the chit from the Co-op for two disposable barbecues and wondered where the other one had gone.

In Tom's bedroom the shirts on the rail, the shoes by the bed, the old Soviet propaganda posters on the wall were unnervingly familiar. I picked up a faded black jacket and found it fitted. In a drawer were sleeping pills, some opened, some intact, with names that sounded like characters from a Tolkien fantasy – Lunesta, Zolpidem, Ambien,

Rozerem. There were receipts from unregulated Internet websites accompanied by advertisements for painkillers and antidepressants. It jarred that Tom, depressed and a risk to himself, was able to buy such quantities of pills when high-street chemists refuse to sell customers a second jar of mini aspirins.

A half-unpacked rucksack lay in the corner, filled with his camping gear – waterproofs, woollen socks and shirts, well-worn hiking boots. It looked as if he had been rummaging in it, perhaps pulling out the sleeping bag that he'd taken to the kitchen and drawn tight over his head to trap the fumes. But if he was unpacking the rucksack, wouldn't that mean he had been using it? Had he returned from a trip? I unzipped a pocket and found an Ordnance Survey map of the Llyn Peninsula. As children we had spent summer holidays there, in remote cottages outside Llanbedrog or Bodwi Bach, hiking in the mountains with our parents, swimming in the sea, shopping in the market at Pwllheli. Had Tom been looking for the memories of our childhood, seeking solace in the past?

I found his car outside. In the glove compartment was a petrol receipt from Abersoch and a postcard of the church on the beach at Aberdaron. A wave of memories swept over me like a rip tide drawing me back to a shared past that now I shared with no one. I sank into the driver's seat and it felt right; neither it nor the mirrors needed adjusting. I could smell him in the car – the aroma of his cigarettes, of his outdoors apparel, his tent and anorak. I remembered the last time he had driven down to see me, pictured the car turning into the drive. When he came in he smelled of fields and grass. We sat on the couch and spoke about what we should do with our parents' house; Tom asked if I would edit some short stories he had been writing. He was looking to the future. I gave him the dates I would be in Pakistan and he put them into his phone. Now I wonder if he took my absence into account when deciding when to kill himself. We spoke about the problems in his marriage and discussed what would happen if it fell apart. He sounded sanguine, but I should have pressed him. Looking back, I think his optimism was forced. He was still the scared six-year-old who told the policeman to 'ask him'.

I returned to the house. I wanted to take our father's medals that Tom had hung on the wall and I needed a bag to put them in. Tom was a Labour Party supporter who shopped at the Co-op, so I wasn't surprised when I found Co-op bags-for-life in the kitchen. He hadn't overtaxed them.

CHAPTER 26

'So how are you coping? How has it been?' There was something in Denise's tone; it took me a moment to realise she was addressing me not as a colleague but as a patient.

'Numbing,' I said. 'I talk to him a lot. There are things I don't understand. Things only he can explain.'

'Yes,' Denise said. 'The suicide of someone close raises questions we can rarely hope to answer. And that knocks us off balance. Can you tell me how your feelings have evolved? Is that something you're able to do?'

'Most of all I feel great sorrow and great pity for Tom. I feel deep sadness and loss for myself. Regret and guilt about the past. Anger with some people's behaviour. And terrible bewilderment about the whole thing. That's where I've got to.'

'I think we discussed this when you asked me about your friend whose father was killed. We spoke about the unanswered questions that make death so painful to cope with.'

'We did. And back then it seemed interesting in a detached sort of way. But it's different now . . .'

'Of course. Things are different when they happen to us rather than to other people. And how are you – in yourself, I mean?'

'Okay . . .'

'You can see why I'm asking about this. It's partly because suicide has a genetic component. Your mother and your brother both killed themselves.'

'I can't picture a dejection so awful that it would stop me wanting to see the spring, if that's what you mean. If my life fell apart I'd still want another go at things. I'd always want to see what life could bring.'

'Yes. And it's true that you haven't sunk into inertia. Far from it. I wonder if there's even a bit of the opposite going on . . .'

'Meaning what?'

'Meaning the way you've thrown yourself into all the chasing around, the compulsive pursuit of answers. It's about Tom now, but it struck me first in connection with Ibrahim. I just wonder if there's a bit of mania about it, a bit of obsession?'

'You mean, am I turning into Captain Ahab?'

'Yes, something like that. And if you are becoming Captain Ahab, perhaps you need to ask yourself if you understand – I mean really understand – why you are so driven . . .'

'Am I doing it to help Ayesha, or for some motive of my own?'

'Yes, I suppose so.'

'To do with Tom, you mean?'

'Maybe. But perhaps more even than that. I wonder if

you've been conflating the two deaths. I wonder if the answers you've been pursuing are not just about these individual deaths . . . but about death itself.'

'I'm not sure I follow.'

'Is your obsession directed not just at solving Tom's death and Ibrahim's death, but at solving death itself? Are you trying to pursue death, to pin it down? Talking to you and reading your notes, I have the impression that you're waging a one-man assault on mortality, trying to deconstruct it by unleashing the powers of reason upon it, trying to defuse it, draw its sting . . .'

'That sounds a little hubristic. How exactly do you see me conducting this assault?'

'Wasn't it Shakespeare who said that what we understand we tend to forgive? Maybe not Shakespeare. I sense that your mind is straining to understand death, to chronicle it and grind it down with your reason . . . So that when you finally understand it you will be able to forgive it; you will reconcile yourself to its purpose . . .'

'I can't say I've ever thought of it that forensically.'

'I'm not saying that you have. Powerful emotions can drive us to do things without us knowing why. All I would say, Martin, is that you aren't going to triumph over your own mortality by playing the detective in someone else's.'

CHAPTER 27

Immersing myself in the detective work was comforting. It gave me a purpose, channelled the pain into a process. And it brought me closer to my brother. The jacket that fitted, the car seat that didn't need adjusting seemed tokens of our togetherness.

I went back to the rented house and chose more reminders of him – the book he was reading and would never finish; the camera with the photos he'd taken in Wales; three of his witty, idiosyncratic wrought-iron statues. I searched carefully, haunted by the fear of missing a vital clue that might explain the unexplainable. Tom's mobile phone had slid under a cupboard beside the sleeping bag and the disposable barbecue. It was switched on, the battery low but serviceable. I clicked on Messages. His last texts had been late on the Tuesday evening.

Hi. Trying to die at the moment. Hope it works this time x

Is that it then, Tara? Xxx

I have been trying to ring you all afternoon xxxx

xx love you

Love and miss you all xx

I switched off the phone. I sat in my brother's chair. I heard his voice, I saw his face, and the weight of the soul's midnight descended. Questions were jostling. In the absence of answers I needed activity.

I rang the coroner. He said the autopsy had been completed. An inquest had been opened then immediately adjourned. Tom's body could now be released. I picked up Tom's death certificate – temporary because the cause of death had not been fixed – and made an appointment with the undertakers. I told the woman who met me that I would be making the arrangements, not Tom's wife. I told her I was in a hurry, with no time to chat. I caught her weighing me up and realised that she understood. Maureen had dealt with the bereaved. She knew who needed the baby talk and who didn't. Her manner was considerate but businesslike.

We ran through the formalities. We chose the coffin, ordered the flowers, booked the hearse. We agreed that Tom would wear my shirt and suit. Maureen said the earliest date for a funeral was not for another ten days, less than ideal given that Tom had been dead two weeks. When I asked about seeing him, Maureen frowned.

'Not all suicides are viewable. We are quite frank about these things. If when we bring him here we don't think it's advisable to see Tom, we will tell you so.'

I appreciated Maureen's honesty. I warmed to it, and unexpectedly to her. She was wearing a white blouse and dark tie, what undertakers must regard as a sober combination, though her legs in black tights as she swivelled on the chair in front of me were anything but. I allowed myself a smile at the incongruity of my thoughts. Maureen said Tom's body would arrive from the morgue in a couple of days; if I came back she would advise me whether or not I should see him.

The vicar had an earring. We drank tea in the rectory while the birds sang in the trees. He was good at his job. He let me pour out what had accumulated inside. The sun appeared from behind the clouds and I said I didn't understand why Tom hadn't wanted to stay and see this beauty in the world. Why didn't he stay to see the bluebells blossom and the oak tree grow? Who will tell Tom that the bluebells are coming through? Who will tell him that the leaves are out on the oak tree? Who will tell him? Oh God! Who will tell him!

The vicar said I mustn't feel guilty.

'We say we are not our brother's keeper,' I said slowly. 'But we are. And I didn't keep him . . .'

The vicar nodded.

'. . . If I could be sure this was an adult who took an adult decision to kill himself that would be easier. But Tom was a boy who couldn't cope. He was looking to me for help and I didn't give it to him. When I recall our conversations and reread our emails I can see that he wanted me to help him. But he was struggling to put it into words. The hardest thing is that I didn't understand what he was saying. And I didn't give him what he was asking for . . .'

The vicar pushed a box of tissues towards me. I pushed it away.

'Sorry . . . I'm trying to be rational. I know I showed concern and compassion towards him when he was in trouble. I know I helped him with practical things. I acted as go-between when he and Tara were trying to patch things up and I visited him in hospital. But did I show him enough love? That's the question that gnaws at me. I told him I loved him; I put kisses at the end of my emails; I hugged him, even though it embarrassed him. I sat with him and discussed his problems, discussed the future and discussed what I could do to help. *But did I show him enough love?*'

The vicar spoke about loss and the persistence of guilt and regret. I took a tissue from the box.

'I so, so want to speak to him. I want to show him what I'm writing about him in all these pages. And I want to tell him — again and again, although I really do think he knew it — that I love him and that I'm sorry for all the things I might have done to hurt him. But I can't. And that torments me terribly . . .'

He poured more tea; waited until I could continue. We chatted about our jobs. I said a vicar must encounter a lot of human suffering; he said he did, and I asked how he responded to it. He said you have to be good at listening. When I asked what else he could do for people in distress he mentioned tea and cake (he was from the Church of England) and said surprising numbers of people in our society are lonely; it was important to give them a shoulder to cry on. I waited to hear what else he might suggest; when he didn't, I asked if he'd forgotten something. 'Everything you've said sounds sensible, but all of that could be offered by a therapist. Why did you not mention that God will comfort those who mourn, that Christianity promises to reunite us in heaven?' He shrugged and smiled.

In the car my thoughts wandered. Humankind invented heaven for consolation, but also for unanswered questions. There are so many things I wanted to ask Tom, to share with him, to laugh about and hear his opinion on. It hurts me so much that I can't do that. So a heavenly reunion and a long chat would actually be quite nice, thank you.

Tom's friend Rick Taylor showed me how to access Tom's Facebook pages and I was struck by their wit and profundity. There were jokes lit by Tom's self-deprecating humour; there were acerbic notes on life, bantering exchanges with friends. And there were links to every newspaper article I had written, every interview I had done, every review of my work. Tom knew I would not see it and he never spoke to me about it. I wish he had. Because now it seemed a token of the love he had for me, evidence that he was interested in my life and rejoiced in my successes. I learned that Tom did not resent me, was not jealous of me, and I love him for that.

His Facebook pages brought me solace. But they made me wish I had listened more closely to him. It seems to me that we all want to be judged; we want to be told if we are good or bad, to know what we are worth. We can't make that call for ourselves and I think Tom was looking to me to be the judge of his life. I didn't realise it and perhaps I failed to offer him the validation he needed. When he told me with pride about renovating our parents' old house, about the commendation his work had won at a sculpture show or about striking a good bargain to buy a new car, he wanted my approbation. And he wanted to know if these minor triumphs were the sort of thing on which he could be judged: could he allow himself to be content on the basis of those things? Or did he need bigger, more difficult triumphs – possibly beyond his scope – to be considered a good person?

I found his last Facebook postings hard to read.

Friday 15:49 I have been walking in the Welsh mountains. I saw a cacophony of crows pecking at the carcass of a dead sheep. They had pecked the eyes out and were going through the sheep's ears into its brain. As I got closer I realised that the poor sheep was still alive.

Saturday 19.33 More long walks. Beautiful views. Dido has snuggled down and gone to sleep after her tea. It's comforting to watch a tired, fulfilled dog sleeping. She is running and giving little barks chasing a squirrel up a tree (in her dreams).

Sunday 14.51 I drove back here from Bodwi Bach in less than two hours. The AA route planner says it should take three. Does anyone know if the speed cameras are working?

Sunday 21.09 I just received this email from BT. Naturally I have sent them my bank details: *Dear Sir/Madam, BT is making integrity check on it customers, how customer use the account and if account still owned by customer. If account is not using for a longer period of time (2 month's) it being disabled and then remove in next two month inactivity.*

Monday 07.23 A sunny day here. When I left the mountains yesterday there was snow on them. The dog and I both agree where we would prefer to be.

Monday 18.07 I heard three words today that I haven't heard in ages. They were *palaver, malarkey* and *ne'er-do-well* (none of them was aimed at me!). I love these old expressions that our parents used to use when we were little.

Tuesday 04.56 It's nearly 5 o'clock in the morning and my next-door neighbours are still having a rowdy noisy party that started at 9 o'clock last night. Perfectly reasonable to have a bit of fun ... but don't you think they could have invited me? *From Dave: Hi Tom, Why don't you knock on the wall?* Tom: Pardon?

On the Tuesday afternoon Tom posts a cartoon of a gloomy-looking man with a thought bubble coming out of his head saying, 'At least the dog loves me' and a thought bubble coming out of his dog's head saying, 'Wanker'.

Tuesday 20.41 But if we walk in the Light as He Himself is in the Light, we have fellowship with one another, and the blood of Jesus His Son cleanses us from all sin. If we say that we have no sin, we are deceiving ourselves and the truth is not

in us. If we confess our sins, He is faithful and righteous to
forgive them and to cleanse us from all unrighteousness . . .

His final post is late that evening, shortly before the series
of texts that I found on his mobile phone:

Everyone I know thinks I am a good person, everyone I smile
at returns my smile. People who know me think that I am
funny, entertaining and good company. But I am so lonely.

I read Tom's Facebook postings then typed them out
myself, trying to enter the train of his thoughts. I wanted to
feel what he was feeling when he typed 'I am so lonely' and
'forgive me my sins'. It had always seemed that we had time
ahead of us, in which we would say the unsaid things. But
we were wrong. And we didn't say them. Recreating his
life fostered the impression that he was still in the world,
that I could rejoin him when my schedule allowed. When
the illusion faded the world seemed darker for the glimpses
of his presence.

I went to see Tom. Maureen said she was surprised by
how well and how handsome he looked. To me he seemed
snug and peaceful, like on those evenings long ago when
our mother tucked us up in bed. I stood by his coffin. I
told him I loved him and he said, 'I know.' I told him how
much I missed him and regretted not having done more to
keep him, but he said, 'It's not your fault, Martin.' When
I asked if he forgave me, he said of course he did. I could
see he didn't want to talk about such things, but I told him
I needed to and he said okay. I said I was sorry I hadn't told

him more often and more clearly that he was loved and valued; he told me not to be daft. I talked about the times I gave him a hug when I saw him in hospital and how he was embarrassed but I knew he was grateful; he laughed. I said I wished I had done it more often; but he said, 'Stop it, Martin. You know that's not how we do things. I know you love me. Everything's all right.'

CHAPTER 28

In the end, Ayesha knocked at my door. She came with a confectioner's box of gulab jamun and sugared chomchom. The sweets were a peace offering, she said, a token of her sympathy and friendship. She proffered her hand and I felt tears unexpectedly in my eyes. Her appearance on my doorstep seemed an acknowledgement of a shared sorrow that should outweigh our previous differences.

'Well . . . What's this you've brought? How did you find those in London? I'm surprised you're not wearing a sari.'

Ayesha laughed and invited herself in.

'I didn't find them, Martin; I made them. There are lots of things you don't know about me.'

'You can say that again. Who taught you Pakistani cooking, for instance? I thought you were such an Englishwoman.'

'Who do you think? My mother, of course. We Pakistani girls all learn cooking from our mothers; it's part of our DNA, all those spices and smells and flavours. It makes us who we are.'

'Yes. Part of your identity . . . I don't really associate you with your mother, though. The one time I saw you together you seemed so remote . . . as if you had nothing in common.'

Ayesha frowned. 'Why are you talking about my mother? It's got nothing to do with it.'

I apologised, but she was annoyed.

'I don't know why you said that, Martin. It's a stupid thing to say. And just when you and I were getting on together.'

'I know. I'm sorry. And I am happy to see you. I've been through a lot since Karachi. Just as you have . . .'

Ayesha put her hand on mine.

'Yes. It binds us together. The loss. It means we understand each other; we understand what's important.'

I nodded, my throat too tight to speak. Ayesha saw the emotion.

'It's all right, Martin; there's no need to explain. I know what you're feeling. And now you know what I've had to deal with.'

We sat. I said I would put the kettle on. When I returned the table was covered in documents.

'Martin, I want you to see these. This is what I found after you flew home. It changes everything.'

When I sat beside her I sensed she was trembling.

'It was Guddu who told me. We should have gone to him straight away, instead of wasting our time with those awful policemen and bureaucrats. He asked me to explain to him what it was that I was pursuing and I said it was the men who committed the murder. But Guddu told me to think again.

He said that what I was really pursuing was my father; that I was haunted by his absence, by the sorrow and the pain of it, and by the need to reconnect with him. Guddu said we uncover the spirit of the dead in the places that have been dear to them. It's superstition, Martin, but it's got a truth to it. We don't give these things enough credence. So he took me to the house my dad had been building, the mansion with the gold taps that everyone's been getting so worked up about. It's in the country outside Kahin Nahi. You can look back over Orangi to the skyscrapers away in Karachi. Guddu had a key because my dad trusted him. He said the house may hold answers to my questions and he left me there. The place is only half-finished; the walls need plastering and the floors haven't been tiled. But it was quiet and I just sat there on my own. I thought about my dad coming to Pakistan to build it. It was his new dream home, the one he'd been driven to build because his dreams in England had been crushed. And I could feel him there with me. It sounds corny but it's true. I knew he was there with me, Martin. And I knew he was telling me to carry on searching.'

Ayesha looked so serious and so convinced by what she was saying. I felt for her in a way I hadn't done since our first meetings over a year ago.

'So where did the documents come from? You said they change everything . . .'

'Yes. It was obvious no one had been in the house since Dad died. I started looking around and I found his passport – here it is. It was lying on the table, covered in dust. The police hadn't even bothered to come and search the place. And then I found his air tickets. Look, you can see the date he flew to Pakistan; and here on the next coupon you can see he had a return flight to London booked for 20 August, a week after he was murdered. I can't believe no one even thought to look for these things. The police couldn't care less.'

'It's pretty slapdash. But knowing about Ibrahim's travel plans doesn't change much. What else did you find?'

'I found letters that he'd been writing. To my mum in Burnley. They're so sad. When I read them for the first time in Kahin Nahi I was in tears . . .'

Ayesha picked up a sheet of paper covered in Urdu script.

'I'll translate for you. "*Dearest Asma, my sweetest spice*" – he was always calling her by pet names – "*I write to you in the cool of the evening. The sun that warmed the land has set, the fire-flies are flitting in the dusk.*" He's quite lyrical, isn't he? I never realised he was such a poet.' Ayesha laughed. 'Then he tells Mum how things have been going with his own mother. She's quite old and we think she's suffering from dementia, so Dad was looking after her. He writes about the weather and some bits of local news. He asks how things are back in Burnley and . . .' Ayesha swallowed, 'he says how much he misses his children . . . He asks about me and how I'm doing with the government contract I was bidding for. And then he tells her about the house and you can see he's so proud of what he's doing, so excited by the way the place is taking shape. It's exactly how I remember him when he was doing up his first dream home in Burnley; he gets so wrapped up in it, Martin, so carried away by it all. Listen to this bit: "*I am doing all this for you, my little tamarind seed; for you and our beautiful children. This place will be my gift to you – the gift of more than a house, the gift of a country and everything it means to me . . ."* When you read that, how can you even think he was involved in anything crooked? He's an honest, simple man, full of enthusiasm and good intentions. There's nothing hidden or evil!'

I wanted to reply; I wanted to tell her how I had read my brother's messages, how I too had learned things that Tom had never told me in life. But Ayesha held up her hand.

'Wait. There's more. There was a filing cabinet in one of the bedrooms. It had a lock on it, but I found the key under a mat – Dad was never much good at hiding things. Inside it there were papers and documents, all the stuff you can see here now. Lots of it was to do with the house construction; there were receipts for building materials and lists of payments to labourers and so on. But what I couldn't find were any ownership documents for the land, like the ones the patwari showed us. I thought that was odd. There was stuff Dad had obviously been collecting for his records. And there was a sort of diary he'd been keeping. He didn't write it in any systematic way; he just seemed to note things down as they came into his head. So there's a lot about us, his children, and about Mum; and some less nice stuff about my dad's brother, uncle Ahmed, how they fell out as young men and how angry and bitter Ahmed was with him. I'd heard most of that already. But there were also references to an argument he seemed to be having with someone in Karachi. I tried to figure out what that was about, but it wasn't easy. His handwriting is terrible for a start, and it's as if he's trying to disguise some of the details. He uses abbreviations and he doesn't write people's names but just puts initials. At first I couldn't make sense of it. Then at the end of his diary, tucked in the back cover, I found this . . .'

Ayesha opened a folder and took out a newspaper cutting. It was crumpled and torn. The Urdu text meant nothing to me, but half way down the page was a photograph of a smiling, middle-aged man in a suit. I asked who it was.

'That's just it, Martin! Listen to what the article says.

'MAJOR WATER SUPPLY PROJECT PROPOSED FOR ORANGI TOWNSHIP.

Karachi City government is examining a proposed $400 million project to improve water supply to Orangi and its environs. Municipal water supply in Karachi has become grossly inadequate with regard to users' needs. Suburban locations, especially low-income settlements, have no access to piped water. Serious shortages have become a feature of life and nowhere more so than in Orangi township, Karachi's largest informal settlement. In the districts of Ghaziabad, Gulshan-e-Zia, Mansoor Nagar, Gulshan-e-Bihar and Raees Amrohvi Colony, the population must rely on standpipes, awami tanks or private tankers. The proposal now being examined will involve the construction of a new downstream dam on the Hub River to ensure adequate water volume is provided via new feeder canals and underground pipes. The project, which has been put forward by Karachi entrepreneur Mr Javed Shafik, pictured (left), has been granted initial funding with the promise of further large-scale investment by the Karachi Regional Authority.'

Ayesha jabbed her finger at the smiling man. 'That's him, Martin! That's the man who killed my father!'

Her face was lit with passion and anger. I heard the conviction in her voice.

'He does keep cropping up,' I said. 'Javed Shafik, the bad penny. But how does finding a newspaper cutting in your father's papers prove Shafik killed him? The patwari said the two of them were best of friends . . .'

'You're not listening, Martin. I said the newspaper article was the key to Dad's diary. As soon as I found it, everything else made sense. I told you Dad referred to people by their initials; well, I went back and I found references to "JSh". There was "visit by JSh" and "phone call from JSh". Just a few days after he arrived in Pakistan, Dad writes "JSh – my land!" Then there's a list of other local landowners, all with dates next to them. It's obvious, isn't it? Shafik was threatening my dad because he needed Dad's land for his big dam contract – a scam, if ever I saw one! – and Dad was refusing to play ball. He was contacting the other landowners to get them to stand up to Shafik. The diary and the newspaper cutting prove what I've said all along: Dad wouldn't cave in to the mafia, so the mafia killed him. It's as clear as day.'

'Well, that's one way of interpreting it. But couldn't there be a different explanation? Who's to say the phone calls and visits from JSh weren't friendly ones? Who's to say the two of them weren't getting together to discuss mutual business? And who's to say your dad's approaches to the other landowners weren't on behalf of Shafik himself, threatening them into selling up?'

Ayesha shook her head. 'I think I will never understand you, Martin. And you certainly don't understand me. I don't think you understand people at all. I thought your brother dying might make you a bit more compassionate, but you're as cold as ever.'

'I'm not cold, Ayesha. I'm trying to be rational.'

'It can be the same thing. You think you're so clever at analysing stuff and reasoning things out, but you always miss what's most important. You need some emotional intelligence, Martin. You need to put yourself in someone else's shoes, and you can't do that.'

'I'm sorry. I'm just trying to do what's best for you . . .'

'How would you know what's best for me? You don't know anything about me.'

'Ayesha, please——'

'I want to make a success of this. I listen to you when you come up with things. But I don't think you ever listen to me!'

Ayesha dropped her gaze. When she looked up, her face had softened.

'Why have we always argued, Martin? Why are we arguing now, when we both want the same thing? We both want to find the truth about a person we loved . . .'

'Maybe. Or maybe one of us wants to create a sanitised version of the truth, something we can live with, that romanticises the dead and defuses the past . . .'

'Perhaps you're right. Perhaps I do need that. But don't you need it, too? Aren't you doing the same thing with Tom?'

'I know what I am doing with Tom!' I felt the anger; tried to contain it. 'I'm not saying I've got everything figured out . . . But what you are asking me to do is to lie. You want me to accept a version of your father that suits you. You want me to write the story without following it to the end, without tracking down the people involved in it and asking for their version. And it's because you're scared what it might throw up.'

'Yes . . .' Her voice was a whisper. 'Maybe . . . It's just so loaded with meaning. It's about who he was . . . and who I am.'

'What? Finding out that Ibrahim was doing something wrong would make you bad too?'

'No . . . But his death has made me question my own identity. I told you how I used to think I was British and I used to think I was Pakistani too, but now I think I'm neither . . .'

'Come on, Ayesha. I understand all that. And I sympathise with you – even though you think I'm incapable of sympathy. But there's something more, isn't there? You're scared of something. And since we're being frank now, why don't you tell me why you were so angry when I mentioned your mother? Why is that such a painful topic?'

She sighed. 'Yes . . . Okay . . . When I was young, my mother and I were close. I told you how we both had to wait in Pakistan before we could get permission to come to England, and that brought us together. But as I grew up, things changed. Something came between us. At the time I didn't know what it was. But looking back I think I had the sense that my mother was hiding things from me; things she knew but didn't want to share, that she felt she had to cover up.'

'Really? What sort of things?'

'I don't know . . .'

'Things about your father?'

'Perhaps . . .'

'In Burnley you asked her why she didn't tell you what Ibrahim was doing on his trips to Pakistan.'

'That was part of it. But it goes back further. To the time of the Kelly Stafford saga. That was the start of it. And there was another thing . . .'

I could see she was hesitating.

'You need to tell me, Ayesha, if we're ever going to get anywhere with this.'

'It was to do with Tariq, my brother. You met him briefly; he burst in on us when we were talking to my mother . . .'

The image of the wild man with the mobile phone came to me, with his boiling anger and frenzied declarations about slashing the throat of his father's killers.

'Tariq had never been like that before. He'd been a quiet boy, shy even. He made a good career as a surveyor. Then a few years ago he just went crazy. He stormed out of the house and said he was never coming back. I have no idea what happened. My father wouldn't talk about it. And when I asked my mother I could tell she wanted to speak about what had gone wrong, but for some reason she couldn't do it. I thought it was because she didn't trust me any more. I got angry. Things got chilly between us. And they've never recovered.'

CHAPTER 29

When I told Denise about my meeting with Ayesha she laughed. I asked what she found amusing and she said, 'You.'

I must have looked hurt.

'I'm not having a go at you, Martin. And I'm speaking as a friend, not as an analyst. But I think Ayesha has got you to a T. You're bright in many ways, but in others you're a complete illiterate. You're great at reading books, but hopeless at reading people. What do you think Ayesha has been trying to tell you all this time about her father and her feelings and hopes?'

'It's obvious, isn't it? She's terrified of discovering her father was a monster.'

'Partly. But there's more to it. Like many daughters, I'd say she has mixed feelings about her father. She grew up with him; she's seen his loving side and she's seen his moments of ugliness and shame. What she really wants to know is which one is the real Ibrahim. I think she does want you to find the truth, but she wants you to find it *in spite of her* not because of her. She forbids you to probe her father's secrets, but in reality she wants you to. She doesn't want to assume the burden of uncovering the truth herself; that would make her feel disloyal. She wants *you* to bear the responsibility for whatever emerges . . .'

'So when she says No, she actually means Yes? I thought that was something we weren't meant to suggest about women any more.'

'Don't make a joke of it, Martin. If you discover Ibrahim was a saint, that would allay her fears and confirm her memories of the good parent. If you find he was a monster it would destroy her illusions. But at the same time it would confirm the bitterness she has nursed against him. Most daughters harbour a covert anger against the father who chided them and criticised them and maybe even hit or abused them. It would pain her, but it would legitimise the grudges that have made her feel guilty. It would ease the cognitive dissonance of her resentments.'

'I can see that. On an intellectual level. And it's interesting you mentioned abuse: do you think Ayesha might have been abused by her father?'

'That's not what I was saying. Do you have something that makes you think she might have been?'

'It's probably just a reaction to all the talk about Pakistani taxi drivers and underage girls. I did wonder, though, if some of Ayesha's behaviours might suggest an underlying pathology. The excessive defensiveness alternating with extreme neediness; the demands for attention and for absolute compliance with her wishes, coupled with bouts of fear and anxiety. Does some of that sound congruent with symptoms of abuse?'

'Possibly. It could have other causes.'

'Of course. But then when she complained about her mother keeping secrets and how that had spoiled their relationship . . . I wondered if she was hinting that the mother knew about the abuse but failed to stop it. And there's Ayesha's behaviour with men – the flamboyant seeking for attention followed by immediate backing away; her on-off relationship with her fiancé, Peter . . .'

'I haven't met Ayesha, but from what you've told me I'd say there's no overt indication of abuse. The behaviour you've described – the unpredictable reactions and extravagant demands – sounds more like the result of the trauma she's been through. Bereavement is not easily assimilated. Our culture does the impact of death a disservice – in detective books and films and on television it seems so inconsequential. A death may be marked by a few perfunctory tears then we settle back into the familiar, aseptic narrative of clues and detectives sleuthing. The reality is very different . . .'

'That's not something you need to convince me of . . .'

'Freud says the human psyche is stretched between two forces – Eros and Thanatos, the drive for life and the pull of death. In Ayesha you might say the death force – her obsession with her murdered father – is overwhelming the yearning for life, which Freud identifies with sexuality and its outcome, human renewal. Her relationship with Peter is put on hold until the morbid spell of Thanatos can be broken.'

'To a non-Freudian that sounds a bit fanciful.'

'Eros and Thanatos are the two basic instincts, the

primal drives of creation versus destruction, battling in the psyche.'

'Okay. I'm not arguing with Freud—'

'Sorry, Martin, I just want to add one thing that might be relevant to Ayesha. Melanie Klein says that when the mind is overwhelmed by that battle, the deflection of the death instinct can find expression in exaggeratedly aggressive behaviour. I mention that for what it's worth.'

'Well, thank you. As you said last time, we almost always forgive what we understand. I can't pretend I understand all of that, but . . .'

'. . . but you're willing to forgive? Honestly, I think that would be a step forward. Forgiving Ayesha, I mean.'

'Forgiving her for what? She hasn't caused me any harm. I could have walked away from the aggravation of working with her at any time.'

'And yet you didn't. Has your experience with Tom helped you understand what she has been going through?'

It was a question I had thought about.

'Yes,' I said. 'She and I have been grappling with the same conundrum. We lost a person we thought we knew; but when they died we discovered we hadn't known them. Or at least, we discovered there were things about them that we didn't know.'

'You said earlier that you were investigating Tom's death.'

'I would say that Ayesha and I have both been struggling to know the unknown. For her that meant who murdered her father and why they murdered him. But also the things her father did and why he did them.'

'She wanted to know who her father was,' Denise said. 'Because feeling that we have been mistaken about someone we have been close to, someone we have relied on, can be immensely disturbing for our own identity. Is that what you have been feeling about Tom?'

'Yes. In a way. I didn't know Tom had such a dark hinterland. I have been trying to understand where that came from. And also to understand how I could have been so stupid that I didn't recognise it. I spent all those years studying psychology and I couldn't understand my own brother.'

'All I would say is that suicide among middle-aged men is horrifically common. And the constant factor is that they don't talk about it. You said you spoke to Tom in his coffin . . .'

'What I really need is for *him* to talk to *me*. I need an explanation. I need a memoir from beyond the grave . . .'

'I fear you are not going to get that, Martin.'

'Tom and I had the same genes and the same upbringing; we were two halves of a whole. So part of me has been destroyed. It isn't just that I can't ask him – or anyone – about the life we shared for all those years; it's as if part of my identity has been obliterated. I feel his absence terribly.'

'What about Tom's children?'

'It must be terrible for them. I'm sure they loved Tom. And I know he loved them more than anything in the world. I can't take the place of their father, Denise, but I would like to be there for them . . .'

'You should do your best to keep the link with them

alive. I think you know that. In the shorter term, what have you decided about Pakistan?'

'I haven't. The more I think about Ayesha's new information – the stuff she gleaned from her father's documents – the less it proves anything. I told her I would let her know if I'm going to pursue the investigation.'

CHAPTER 30

I rang Imran Hayat in Karachi and asked him to find out as much as he could about the Orangi water-supply project and the new Hub River dam. Then I went to see Ayesha.

She was guarded; she had been expecting my visit, anxious to hear if I had written about the material she'd discovered in her father's house. I said I was pondering how best to incorporate it; I remained dubious about the conclusions she wanted me to draw from it.

'I know you're not convinced, Martin,' she said. 'But at the very least the diary entries about Javed Shafik suggest the murder was connected with my dad's land, right? So surely the next step is to establish if the water-supply contract Shafik's getting from the city government means he needs that land. And if he does, then he has to be our prime suspect!'

I tried to be conciliatory. 'I'm working on that. And your father's diary certainly isn't irrelevant. But neither is it conclusive. You agreed that the entries about Shafik are vague. Most of them were made weeks before Ibrahim was killed.

And there are things that your scenario just doesn't explain: for instance, why did the patwari speak of Ibrahim coming in hand-in-hand with Shafik and signing joint-ownership documents? And where did your father get the money to build his house if it wasn't from Shafik?'

Ayesha acknowledged the inconsistencies. It seemed a good moment to explore a compromise.

'I can't speak for you, Ayesha, but I would very much like to know the answer to those questions. I find not knowing an irritant and a challenge. So what I propose is that we go back to Pakistan—'

'No, not me. I'm not going, Martin.'

'Okay . . . Well, that's a pity. I obviously can't force you to do anything you aren't comfortable with.'

I waited, but Ayesha was silent. I tried again.

'Can I ask about something that's been worrying me? When we were in that awful bar in Karachi – the one where the guy tried to steal your handbag – you said you wouldn't help me write the book unless you got paid for it . . .'

Ayesha shook her head. 'Please don't bring that up. I was angry and we were both drunk. When you reminded me what I'd said about Pakistanis always demanding money, it made me feel ashamed. I don't want people to think I'm like that – the thought that I'd try to make money out of my father's death is repulsive. Please forget I ever said it.'

'Okay. Thank you for that. And the other thing we argued about is control. You've said several times that you want to control what I write in the book, to the extent of wanting me to omit things or bend the facts.'

'Really? Is that how it struck you?'

'Very much so. It seemed like you were trying to manipulate reality, trying to mould real life into your version of how you'd like things to be.'

'Don't exaggerate. I wanted control of the book because I was worried how the investigation might turn out . . .'

'Yes. But I'm not going to cede control to you.'

'So what's the solution?'

'What if I were to tell you that I'm going back to Pakistan on my own; that I'm going to see where the story takes me and I'm not going to stop until I get to the truth. Then I'm going to write the book on my own terms. How would that be?'

'How would it be? I don't suppose I could stop you . . . I mean, if you're that determined. The story is public knowledge, it's been in the newspapers, so I couldn't prevent you writing about it.'

'Sure. That's all true. But what I'm saying to you is that if you tell me now, definitively, that you don't want me to write about your father's murder, then I will respect that. I won't write the book. So let me ask: do you want to say that to me?'

Ayesha lowered her eyes. 'No, Martin. I am not saying that.'

'So we agree. I go?'

'You'll go without my blessing.'

'Yes.'

'On your own initiative.'

'Yes.'

'And without me helping you or being a part of it.'

'Yes, whatever happens and whatever I discover out there, it is my responsibility.'

Ayesha thought for a moment.

'You know that I want to find out what happened to my dad. I've never denied that. But I'm afraid of it. And I'm afraid, too, of what would happen if you use real names and real events in the book.'

'Really? But I've already written 50,000 words . . . I've been writing the book as things happen, putting them in as I discover them . . .'

'I know.'

'And you want me to go back over all that? You want me to change everything to disguise you?'

'Yes. I do. I've been thinking about this for a while. If you use my real name, the people who killed my dad could kill me too. Look what happened to Masood Jilani, the private detective – look at what happened to that young Pakistani girl, Malala, who stood up for herself . . . Anyone who dares to challenge these people puts themselves in danger.'

'But they're not going to come after you in England, surely. That sounds a bit melodramatic.'

'Don't joke about it, Martin. I've heard that Shafik has two brothers who live in Southall and the three of them are constantly going back and forth between Karachi and London transporting drugs or people or whatever they trade in. And now my mum's saying she needs to go to Pakistan to sort out the paperwork for my dad's estate. She's an old woman; she'd be completely defenceless if they go after her. I can't risk you using real names in the book.'

Rewriting the whole of the manuscript was a daunting prospect. I asked her again if it would be better if I didn't write anything. She shook her head.

'No. I do want you to write it, Martin. Because I want the story to be told. I want people to know about the terrible things that go on in Pakistan, about the lawlessness, the warped values and lack of respect for human life. I want them to know about the racism of the British authorities when they're dealing with UK citizens abroad, how they have one set of values for whites and another for the rest of us. I want you to put into words the sense of alienation that creates for hundreds of thousands of Pakistanis in Britain, the sense of being rejected by both our countries.'

I was relieved we had found a way to make things work. It would take a while, but I told Ayesha I would go through the two hundred or so pages I had written and change names and characters to protect the people involved.

'Thank you, Martin. I'm glad we see eye to eye. Do you think your publishers will be okay with what we're doing?'

'I'll have to find that out. But my editor is smart; I'm sure she will understand.'

'Could you maybe explain things in a preface? You know: *This is a novel. But the circumstances it describes, the land disputes, honour killings, corruption and organised crime, as well as the anguish of British Pakistanis affected by such crimes, are all true* – that sort of wording?'

I laughed. 'You need to leave that stuff to me, Ayesha. I told you I'm not going to let you control what I write!'

'Yes. Of course. It's your book and your responsibility. What you do in Pakistan, and whatever you unearth there, is down to you. This is your initiative, not mine.'

She paused for a moment then added, 'But you will keep me informed, won't you?'

CHAPTER 31

Imran rang from Karachi. He had been digging for information about the Orangi water project and the proposed new dam on the Hub River. He was excited.

'Do you remember that Roman Polanski movie, Martin? The one with Jack Nicholson? Well Karachi is Chinatown in spades. Water is everything. In the years after partition the city expanded so rapidly that water supplies were simply exhausted. But the place carried on growing, further and further into the desert, with no one even thinking what all those extra millions were going to drink. Orangi is one of the informal settlements where people have to drink polluted water from filthy streams or awami tanks run by local mosques and community groups. Those who can afford it pay for private tankers; those who can't go thirsty or die from cholera. I have a report from researchers at Karachi University that I can send you, so you can see the scale of the problem.'

I asked Imran what made him think the Orangi dam

project was anything other than a genuine attempt to tackle a pressing problem. He laughed.

'Nothing is genuine here. You need to look behind the headlines. This has a little bit to do with improving people's lives and a lot to do with making other people very rich. Whoever controls the water supply wields power and influence. The politicians and the crooks – the big crime groups – fight for control of it. And this contract is part of their game.'

'Okay, I'm not disagreeing with you, Imran. But we'll need more than just rumour and speculation if we're going to tackle Javed Shafik; if we're going to prove that Ibrahim's death was connected to the building of the dam.'

'As of today I don't have documentary evidence of Javed Shafik's corrupt practices in the Orangi scheme, but I would be surprised if he isn't creaming off millions from public funds. What I do know is that the project is already mired in controversy. When I send you the academic water report I will attach some articles about this.'

'Thank you. And have you been able to establish whether or not Shafik actually needs Ibrahim Rahman's land for the construction scheme? That's the other crucial factor.'

Imran said he was waiting for clearance to view the planning documents connected with the water project and would let me know when he had done so.

'The dam scheme is being trumpeted as a shining example of public–private cooperation to benefit the community. And that will be helpful for us, Martin. I have renewed our request for an interview with Mr Shafik. I have told them we wish to highlight the social impact of his work in deprived areas. Although they have not formally agreed, the noises coming back from them are positive.'

In the weeks that followed, Imran's messages became less cheerful. He was continuing to pursue the information I had asked him for, but with a frustrating lack of success. The Karachi planning office had refused him permission to consult the land documents connected with the dam project, citing considerations of commercial sensitivity. Javed Shafik had still not confirmed our interview. Ayesha, too, had fallen silent, in accord with our agreement.

I used the time to recast my manuscript, removing any details that would identify the real people involved. The book became a fictionalised version of the truth.

Imran's documents arrived. The first was a photocopied sixty-page report on the chequered history of water supply in Karachi. I flicked through the opening section on the establishment in the 1950s of the Joint Water Board and its attempts to secure supplies from Lake Kalri and the Indus River eighty miles from the city. Bureaucratic rivalry, infighting and corruption dogged the JWB's efforts. The network of conduits and pumping stations required to bring the water into Karachi took years to complete, by which time the pipes were leaking so badly that half of the water was lost en route. The Indus would never provide more than 260 million gallons a day; by the 1980s, Karachi needed twice that. The Hub River was dammed north of Karachi to form a reservoir that furnished another 100 million gallons, but the water pumped from it depleted the river's flow and stretches closer to the city began to run dry.

Orangi and other districts were left waterless. People began to break open water mains to siphon off supplies. Illegal hydrants were set up, water was drawn from leakage points and private boreholes, pumped into donkey wagons and pushcarts to be sold to families in the poorest neighbourhoods. The authorities pronounced the water unfit for human consumption but did not intervene. People were forced to use it because they had no alternative.

The shortages fostered entrepreneurial invention then commercial rivalry and finally, inevitably, corruption. The practice of breaking open the existing system of pipes to steal water was done with the connivance of Water Board staff. In cases where the stolen water was contaminated by sewage, officials were bribed to certify its purity. Rival gangs of tanker operators fought turf wars to safeguard their monopoly of deliveries. Each crime group had its own territory; each had political protection from factions in the city government. The profits grew in line with the shortages. A 1,200-gallon tanker would bring in four hundred rupees; a 2,400-gallon tanker seven hundred and a 3,600-gallon tanker over a thousand. At times of drought or breakdowns in the municipal system, the rates would double or treble. Tanker operators learned how to bribe Water Board officials to create artificial crises by shutting down pumping stations.

The city authorities responded by rationing mains water. But more people began to make illegal connections to secure greater than their allotted share. Water mains were vandalised, pipes and equipment stolen. When the city tried to introduce its own fleet of tankers with water purified for drinking, it met fierce resistance from the commercial operators. Municipal tankers were attacked and set on fire. The organised crime groups running the illegal deliveries persuaded their political placemen to force the scheme's abandonment.

The situation got out of hand. With growing numbers of households having to rely on contaminated water, diseases spread. Cases of cholera rose and public protests broke out in Orangi and other settlements. When water riots seemed inevitable in the late 1990s the city called on its last line of defence. The Pakistan Rangers, a paramilitary force used in border security and anti-terrorist operations, were deployed to restore order, tasked with breaking the hold of the crime groups and taking over the tanker distribution system. The Rangers' efforts were opposed by politicians connected to the mafias; the force's commander had his work cut out.

The presence of the troops maintained a precarious equilibrium, but the underlying problems were unresolved. A survey of existing water mains found most of the city's underground pipes to be suffering from leaks, with many damaged beyond repair. The shortfall in water flowing into Karachi was growing larger by the month; demand was rising inexorably, supplies from the Indus and Hub rivers dwindling. The Rangers could not be expected to remain indefinitely and the city's leaders feared the explosion of unrest that might follow their departure.

The academics' report ended with a pessimistic vision

of the future: 'Water has become our city's most pressing and most redoubtable problem,' the authors wrote. 'The authorities must bite the bullet. Big investment schemes, including the building of new downstream dams and the construction of extensive conduits and pumping stations are urgently required. Unless decisions are taken now, Karachi faces economic and social meltdown.'

At the bottom of the report, in red ink, Imran had scribbled, 'Shafik has them over a water barrel!' with a smiley face and two exclamation marks.

The rest of the documents in the envelope were cuttings from Urdu language newspapers, with Imran's translations or synopses. Most of the articles hailed the announcement of the Orangi water scheme and the new Hub River dam, giving official figures for the extra water it would bring into the city and reproducing quotes from government spokesmen lauding the foresight and wisdom of the politicians and entrepreneurs involved. One cutting took a different tack; Imran had underlined the relevant sections.

PROTEST OVER NEW DAM SCHEME: A large number of employees held sit-ins outside the office of the Water and Irrigation Department on Monday in protest against 'massive' corruption in the department. The Sindh Trade Union leaders who organised the protest demanded that the Chief Justice of Pakistan, Chief Justice of the Sindh High Court, army chief, heads of NAB and Rangers and other authorities take notice of the large-scale corruption in the Water and Irrigation Department and deal with the corrupt persons with an iron hand. They alleged while addressing the protesters that higher officials of the department had, in connivance with contractors, usurped Rs4 billion reserved for construction of barrages and excavation of canals. No work was carried out physically but their fake bills were prepared and payment claimed, they said, adding that paper contracts had been awarded for a scheme of Rs40 billion, of which nearly a fifth was swallowed up by corruption. Massive corruption of one billion of rupees was made in the Ghaziabad canal excavation and Rs550 million was made in the excavation of Mansoor Nagar, Gulshan-e-Bihar drain, but nothing was spent on the ground.

When I rang Imran to thank him for the documents he sounded excited.

'Martin! Your call is perfect timing. Javed Shafik's people just telephoned. The interview is all systems go!'

CHAPTER 32

I spotted Imran as soon as I stepped out of customs into the airport concourse. He looked agitated.

'Shukran Allah! We need to go. Shafik has changed the interview time. We need to go right away . . .'

After the weeks of waiting, the onrush of events came as a shock.

'Okay, Imran. Tell me what the arrangements are.'

'I have a car. And a driver. We cannot drive there. First we must meet Shafik's people . . .'

'Calm down, Imran. And go back a bit. Tell me what has happened.'

We were pushing through the crowds, heading towards the exit. Imran's words were a tumbling stream.

'Yes. So we go to the car. The driver is waiting. Shafik agreed tomorrow. But now his people say come at once. Okay. He's seeing us so he can boast to the world about his philanthropy. Bringing the miracle of water to the people. What a philanthropist! But now I think he is suspicious. I think he has been Googling you. This is not good. He is changing the time to upset us. You saw from my documents that the stakes are big in this game. Hundreds of millions of dollars. And Shafik is up to his neck – I found out about this; I will tell you – he will not hesitate to be rough with us . . .'

The doubts and squabbles were coming to an end. Things would be resolved now. One way or another.

In the car, Imran told me what he had discovered. He had been to Orangi and to Kahin Nahi. He had sought out the landowners whose names were listed in Ibrahim's diary. Some were gone – neighbours shrugged their shoulders when Imran asked where – and two were dead; no one would say when or how. Imran saw the fear in people's eyes. In a café two men came to his table. They wanted to know who Imran was, where he came from and why he was asking questions. He gambled: he was investigating reports of blackmail and intimidation against local people. The men hesitated then took him to a house on the edge of the town. They levered off a padlock fixed to the door. In the dining room there were family photographs, tea cups stacked on the sideboard. But the blinds were drawn and dust covered the floor. It was the house of Jahangir Miandad, the men said. He had owned fifty acres of farmland until the dacoits, marauding thugs, came calling on him. Jahangir told them this was his home and he didn't want to sell. His body was found in a dried-out irrigation ditch. Imran asked if the men knew who the bandits were working for, but they shook their heads. He asked if they knew another local landowner by the name of Ibrahim Rahman. They did.

Were they aware that Rahman had also tangled with the dacoits? They laughed. 'Tangled? He was the organiser, the one who got us together to fight them . . .'

I motioned Imran to stop.

'The men confirmed that Ibrahim was standing up to Shafik? That he was leading the resistance to the land-grabbers? It's crucial—'

'The men were categorical, Martin. I got access to the land documents for the Orangi water project – I had to bribe the clerk – and it is one hundred per cent clear that Shafik needs Ibrahim's land. The contract for the dam is worth millions; there are massive profits in it. It will occupy hundreds of acres. Before Ibrahim took up the fight, the locals were being intimidated, bullied and murdered. Ibrahim pulled them together. He got lawyers involved. He did everything possible to keep the dacoits at bay.'

'So the bandits must have gone after Ibrahim? If he was the ringleader . . .'

'They did. According to the locals, the goons came to Rahman's house on many occasions. And their boss came with them. They threatened Ibrahim, but he wouldn't give in. He was fearless – he didn't care a fig for his own safety, for his own life. People kept telling him he was in danger, but he wouldn't budge. He'd staked everything on the thing he was fighting for. He was like a man in a barroom brawl, Martin – his friends were all telling him to back off, for his own safety; but he'd invested so much pride in it that he just kept going despite knowing he could never win.'

'God, Imran . . . If Shafik's thugs were prepared to

murder the little guys like Jahangir Miandad, they'd have had no hesitation in bumping off someone like Ibrahim! Ayesha must be right – Ibrahim died a hero.'

Imran nodded, but something was troubling him. I asked what it was.

'I don't know, Martin. There's something strange I haven't been able to figure out. It seems Ibrahim got away with it . . .'

'How do you mean, he "got away with it"? He's dead . . .'

'Yes. But the thing is that he didn't die when the row over the land was going on. Somehow he survived all that. I don't know why, but the bandits backed off and left him alone. He wasn't killed until much, much later, when all the fuss had faded away . . .'

We sat in silence as the car edged through the Karachi traffic. Imran was right.

'So by the time he died' – I was thinking aloud – 'he had already signed his land over to Shafik. Shafik had no reason to kill him.'

Imran shrugged.

'I think we need to tread carefully when we see Shafik. Don't go blundering in, Martin. He is a clever man. And dangerous. I got written statements from the landowners I spoke to, confirming they were threatened to make them give up their land. But remember – these men spoke to me in confidence; we mustn't divulge their identities to Shafik or they'll be dead meat.'

The car pulled up at a roadside café. The place was rundown, off the beaten track. When I asked why we were stopping, Imran said, 'I told you. We can't drive to Shafik.

He says he will know when we are here and his people will come for us. It's about security.'

'Security? I thought this guy was an entrepreneur. If he's got nothing to hide, why does he hide away?'

'It's not so surprising. In Karachi, even the legitimate businessmen operate like that. There are too many people ready to settle business disputes with a gun. The big conglomerates have headquarters downtown, but most use shell companies. Shafik has an address in Karachi, but you won't find him there. In fact, you won't find him at all unless he wants . . .'

A black Mercedes swung into the car park. We got out of our car and waited awkwardly.

'Okay, Martin. We need to stay calm. We're journalists; we've been invited for an interview . . .'

Imran took a step forward; two men jumped from the car and motioned him back. I saw the tell-tale bulges under their jackets. One of them pulled out a mobile phone while the other strode in our direction.

'Hands in the air! Legs apart!'

The man frisked us and waved to his companion. He spoke into the phone, clicked it off then beckoned us over.

'You appreciate the need for precautions. You are required to wear these.'

He held out two balaclavas with no eye-holes. The man pulled the material over my head and pushed me into the back seat. I felt Imran tumble in next to me as the driver hit the accelerator.

CHAPTER 33

Shafik was smartly dressed, dark suit and green tie; black hair slicked down, neat moustache. Swarthy. Short. Vladimir Putin height. A smiling killer who smelled of cologne. I strove to remember the questions I had rehearsed, the aims and outcomes.

'Whisky?'

I said I'd stick to soda. He shrugged.

'You journalists not such good drinkers after all?'

There was a desk and two armchairs. He motioned me to one of them and sat in the other. Imran took the seat at the desk. The bodyguards stood by the door.

'So you want to hear about pipes and dams?' Javed Shafik sipped his whisky, weighing me up. 'It sounds mundane. But in this country it is vital.'

I nodded encouragement.

'We are doing everything we can, making the utmost efforts to relieve the suffering of the nation. This scheme is a vision of hope. It promises a better future for millions of people.'

'I see that. Do you have a map of the area you will be working on? How much land will the construction affect?'

His eyes narrowed.

'Don't worry about that, man. Don't worry about details. I can show you a map any time. It's the big picture that's important.'

Tension crackled; I was struggling to gauge its pitch.

'Okay. Then perhaps you could give me an idea of the scale – the height of the dam; volume of water; miles of pipe . . .'

Shafik rattled off the figures.

'After Tarbela and Mangla, which are among the largest dams in the world, this is one of the most ambitious projects Pakistan has ever seen. The last dam on the Hub River created as many problems as it solved. This one will save our city from thirst and disease. It will secure the future of our children. We are privileged to be part of it.'

He sounded sincere; I had come here convinced he was a liar.

'I understand this is a commercial scheme. That the proposal came from entrepreneurs like yourself. In other words, it is a moneymaking venture.'

Shafik was unruffled.

'It is a public-private partnership. We have many investors. Including the Chinese – Sinohydro are investing two hundred million. For them, it's a question of profit; Beijing gets the revenues from the hydroelectric power the dam will generate. But for us, it is a matter of national pride. You understand? A question of doing the right thing.'

'Yes. You aren't making a profit from the construction yourself?'

'Don't be naïve, man. Of course I will make a profit. Within recognised commercial parameters. Above board. I am sure you have heard about the philanthropic activities of my companies; about the grants we make to deprived communities, the youth clubs and cricket teams we sponsor . . .'

'Yes. But just on this specific contract: could you give me a breakdown of the costs? And how much you stand to make from it?'

'Are you an idiot? No businessman discusses these things. Have you never heard of commercial confidentiality?'

'I have. I have also heard of the corruption that attends these contracts. About the false invoices, the bribes and the public funds disappearing into private pockets . . .'

Shafik burst into laughter.

'You say you are a serious journalist? There is no way you could know anything about these matters. You are talking through your hat!'

'Perhaps . . .'

'You come here and make accusations. But you have no proof of anything.'

'All right. If we are talking of proof, let me ask you one question: How did you acquire the land you need for the Hub River dam? I know the government was not willing to award the contract until you could guarantee you had the land. So how did you get it?'

'I bought it.'

'No. Not all of it. What about those landowners who

refused your offer? Who asked for a proper market price? Who didn't want to sell at all?'

'Okay, my friend. You need to be clear. What are you accusing me of?'

'Of using illegal means to acquire the land you need for a corruption-ridden contract that will net you massive profits from public funds. Clear enough?'

Shafik's expression had frozen into a caliginous mask.

'What illegal means?'

'Intimidation, blackmail, violence . . .'

'To make an omelette, you break eggs. The project is essential for Karachi. If we twisted a few arms, the end justifies the means.'

'Justifies murder?'

'What murder? Give me a name!'

'Jahangir Miandad.'

'Jahangir Miandad? What proof do you have?'

'Signed statements. Written testimony from the land-owners you bullied and threatened. Evidence that your thugs slit Miandad's throat and dumped him in an irrigation ditch!'

Javed Shafik leapt to his feet. His guards pulled me out of the chair and pinned my arms behind my back. Shafik thrust his face into mine.

'Signed statements? Written testimony? What the hell is this!' His spittle flew. 'If you have statements, you need to hand them over!'

I felt the fist in my face before I saw him raise his arm. Blood trickled from my left nostril.

'Give me the damn statements!'

I remembered Imran's warning and shook my head. Shafik hit me again. Imran jumped up.

'Here! Here are the statements. If anything happens to the men who made them, I will know whom to hold responsible!'

Shafik took the documents. The guards drew their guns. There was silence as Shafik thumbed through the papers. When he looked up his face wore an expression of mock concern.

'Gentlemen, you have given me a decision to make. And I am not a man who takes decisions lightly.' He gestured to the guards. 'Escort Martin sahib and Imran-ji to the waiting room. I will call for them when I am ready.'

At the end of a corridor the men pushed us through a door that they locked behind us. The room was in darkness but I sensed we were not alone. Imran pointed to a corner.

'Don't say anything, Martin. I think someone is here.'

What appeared to be a bundle of rags stirred. Imran addressed it in Urdu. A thin voice answered.

'I think this fellow is in trouble,' Imran said. 'I'm going to take a look.'

My eyes had adjusted enough to see the bloodstained blanket that Imran lifted from the human form beneath it. The man looked in his mid-thirties. His once white shalwar kameez was covered in dirt; a bandage wrapped round his right hand was caked in blood. Imran sat the man upright and began to address him, but the fellow pointed towards the door and raised a finger to his lips. For several minutes they conversed in whispers. When Imran returned he was shaken.

'Martin, this man is a prisoner. He was brought here for reasons of extortion and revenge. We must not speak too loud – he says the jailers listen at the door.'

It was less than twenty-four hours since I had been shopping at Sainsbury's in Pimlico. The situation was surreal. Imran said the man barely knew why he had been abducted; it was to do with a land dispute or with a marriage in his family that had gone wrong. He had been held and beaten in a torture cell run by thugs attached to the UF, the party that dominated Karachi politics, after which he was passed on to Javed Shafik.

'It proves Shafik has political connections,' Imran said. 'And that gives him impunity to act as he likes. Did you see the fellow's hand? Every ten days they are cutting off one of his fingers and sending it to his father. If he collects them all and does not pay the ransom money, they are going to send him his son's head. It's brutal!'

'A complete nightmare . . . for him and for us.'

'I have less concern for ourselves. You are a known journalist. Shafik cannot treat you like an insignificant local . . .'

'Maybe. But he could treat me like Daniel Pearl . . .'

'Stop it, Martin. That sort of talk is not helpful!'

The man in the corner was calling for Imran to come and sit with him. They spoke for a time in Urdu and the discussion became agitated. When the man fell silent, Imran covered him with the blanket and came back to me.

'That was a hard conversation. The fellow was pleading with us to help him. He wants us to tell the police where he is. He told me how to find his family and asked me to implore them to pay the ransom. I said we would do our best, but if the father hasn't paid up I fear he doesn't have the means to do so. I feel sorry for all of them.'

The door opened and a man with a grey beard motioned for us to get up. In the corridor he handed us over to the guards, who took us back to their boss. Javed Shafik flashed a smile.

'These statements are trash. I will not dirty my fingers with such people.'

He gave the papers to one of the guards, who looked questioningly at him then nodded and put them in his pocket.

'But you didn't come here to ask me about scum like Jahangir Miandad. Do you think I don't understand what your real interest is? That I don't know about you and Ibrahim Rahman!'

There was a knock at the door. The grey-bearded jailer came in, bowed and asked permission to speak. Shafik listened to what he had to say then got up and went with him out of the door. Imran turned to me with a look of horror.

'Ya Rasullallah! The jailer was telling Shafik about our conversation with the fellow in the cell. He told him the man was pleading for us to tell the world what they were doing to him. Shafik was really angry . . .'

'Angry with him and angry with us, too . . . How on earth does Shafik know about us and Ibrahim? I thought we were keeping that under wraps.'

'But Shafik isn't stupid, Martin. I told you he's been researching you. He has connections in Pakistan and connections in Britain. He knows much more than he lets on.'

When Shafik returned I took the initiative.

'I should tell you, Mr Shafik, that I have left letters with both the Pakistani and the British police informing them that Imran and I were travelling to see you today. The letters specify that if I do not notify them of our safe return, they should take the necessary measures . . .'

Two shots rang out in the corridor.

'You were saying?' Shafik leaned back in his chair. 'Something about the police? I can assure you there is no need for that . . .'

Unnerved by the gunshots, I was struggling to take in what he was saying.

'You will come to no harm at my hands. For two reasons. First, I had nothing to do with the death of Ibrahim Rahman . . .'

He paused momentarily with a faint smile on his lips.

'And second, if you write anything that suggests I did, I can guarantee there will be consequences. I know, for instance, where Rahman's family live. I would not be able to vouch for their safety.'

Shafik fixed me with unblinking eyes. I blinked.

'Well, okay . . . Thank you for that assurance. I understand what you are saying.'

I was finding it hard to meet his gaze.

'But may I be frank? You are correct that my interest is in Ibrahim Rahman. I am inquiring into his death on behalf of his daughter, and because I have a personal stake in the matter. And, if I am honest, I have to say that the evidence I have discovered points very strongly to your involvement—'

I broke off. I was levelling accusations at someone who had seemingly just ordered a man's execution.

'So do please tell me,' he said. 'What is this evidence you speak of?'

'Well, there are the landowners' statements you have just seen. They indicate pretty clearly that your men were using strong-arm tactics to make them give up their land . . .'

Shafik made a gesture of impatience.

'We have dealt with that. I have said perhaps we used a little force to make the omelette. I don't deny it.'

'Okay. But the men's statements also confirm that Ibrahim was active in resisting your attempts to get the land. In fact, he was the man who did most to rally people against you.'

'Again, I don't deny it. Rahman was a nuisance.'

'Right. Thank you for confirming that. I have seen Ibrahim's diaries and he lists all the threats you made against him. So would you also confirm that you and your men visited him on more than one occasion, that you demanded he hand over his land and that you threatened him with violence if he refused?'

'Yes.'

'What do you mean? You confirm you threatened him?'

'Yes.'

'So why the hell should I believe you when you say you didn't kill him! You killed Jahangir Miandad and probably others, too. Ibrahim was the biggest obstacle to your plans and now he's dead . . .'

'Why should you believe me? Because I am telling the truth. Rahman and I made a deal.'

'He made a deal with you? With a man who makes his money trafficking alcohol and drugs and people . . .'

Shafik grinned.

'Your saintly Ibrahim doing a deal with Javed Shafik? You seem shocked. Rahman handed over his land and came to work in my businesses – the businesses you have just listed with such outrage in your voice.'

'So you're saying that Ibrahim was involved in—'

'Precisely. You've understood. I am sorry to disappoint you, but even saints can be greedy. Rahman worked for me.'

'Ibrahim . . . trafficking? I don't believe you! You keep asking me for proof – so what proof do *you* have?'

The phone rang. Shafik spoke into it hurriedly and hung up.

'I have to go. You are welcome to leave if you wish. My men will drive you back to Karachi.'

'But I have more questions. I need answers.'

'Then you are welcome to enjoy my hospitality until I return.'

Shafik was putting on his coat. From the drawer of the desk he took out a folder and flicked through its contents. For a moment he hesitated then handed it to me.

'You may look at this. When you have finished give it to Abdul.'

He nodded towards one of the guards sitting behind us with his gun in his lap, told the other to follow him and left.

The folder contained photographs. There were pictures of Shafik in restaurants with groups of men in suits, Shafik signing documents, shaking hands, inspecting cargoes in a warehouse. Others showed him at a rural airstrip, talking to officers of the Pakistani army, enjoying a drink with senior policemen. They formed a pictorial record of Shafik's activities, legal and illegal; Imran guessed they had been taken as a prospective blackmail tool, an insurance policy against betrayal by disloyal associates. And in them, to our dismay, we found Ibrahim. There was Ibrahim with Shafik in the room we were now sitting in, poring over papers on Shafik's desk, the two of them sharing a joke. There were photos of Ibrahim counting bundles of money, using a knife to open a bag of white powder. In one shot, Shafik's bodyguard was holding a gun to the temple of a man cowering in terror; in the background was the unmistakable figure of Ibrahim Rahman.

CHAPTER 34

Shafik was away for three hours. Three hours in which to contemplate his photographs with their damning implications. The evidence seemed incontrovertible; Ibrahim had participated in Shafik's criminal activities and had done so willingly. When Imran showed the photos to the gunman guarding us, he nodded a grim confirmation. I dreaded having to tell Ayesha that her father was so far removed from the hero she believed him to be.

We decided to leave then thought again. We debated the dangers of staying. It would mean chancing Shafik's volatile behaviour, risking his fragile benevolence turning to wrath. But there were more questions and I needed to know the answers.

When he returned he was in a spiteful mood. The business he had rushed off to had not gone well. He asked why we were still there and if we believed him now. I said we did.

'I can't argue with the evidence. You and Ibrahim worked together. But will you tell me exactly what he did for you?'

'Import-export. There are commodities which exist in

abundance here but are in short supply and great demand in England. Rahman helped us to meet that demand.'

'What commodities? Drugs? Human traffic?'

'Let's say that the commodities we were transporting could be awkward to distribute. We needed a reliable network at the other end and Rahman was going to provide it. His taxi drivers had experience with the sort of things from which we make our living.'

'What do you mean, "was going to"? He hadn't done that work before? He was starting because of you?'

'Yes. He was a novice, but he showed willing. He could have had a future.'

'I don't understand why you didn't kill him when he refused to sell his land.'

'I told you that my men put pressure on Rahman, just as they did with the other troublemakers. Rahman was stubborn. He said he didn't care if he was killed. And we could not kill him.'

'Why not?'

'Because the bastard had protection. He was smart. He had a deal with one of the top guys in the Karachi police, a guy called Zaid Alam. And this Zaid had political protection. He was on the payroll of powerful people in the deep state, people even we can't afford to tangle with.'

'You mean Commander Zaid? He's the man who helped us get this whole investigation going. Imran, you told me Zaid was an honest cop!'

Imran was about to reply, but Shafik cut in.

'Honest? What does that mean? Honesty's a hazy concept here. Sure, Zaid is honest. And maybe he helped you from good intentions. But no one – not even the most powerful cop or judge or councillor – can survive on honesty. Even guys like Zaid have to play the game. He needs protection and to get it he has to compromise. That's the way this country works.'

'So when Zaid sent us to see the people in Kahin Nahi, the party knew about it? The UF knew what we were looking for and what we suspected?'

'In Karachi you don't go anywhere without people knowing.'

'We were being followed?'

'Followed and reported on.'

'And what about now? Have we been followed here to you?'

Shafik laughed.

'I *do* the following. It is my business to see everything, to know everything.'

I thought back to Aled Parry-Jones's horror when I told him I had approached Mohammed Asif for protection on my visit to the city. The sense of being spied on from all sides was discomfiting.

'So if Ibrahim had protection . . . and if you couldn't kill him or bully him into doing what you wanted, how did you do it? How did you get him to sign over his land? To do all the terrible things we've seen in the photos?'

Shafik looked like a magician about to unveil his best trick.

'When one method fails you must try another. "Thinking without boxes" I think is the expression. We thought without a box. We found a softer way of persuading him.'

'Softer? That's the last thing I associate with you!'

'One of my men came to me. He said he knew how to speak with Rahman, to speak to him nicely. They had a good discussion. And he came back with your Ibrahim in his pocket.'

'Your man just talked to Ibrahim and magically he agreed to come and work for you?'

'You've got it.'

'This fellow spoke so nicely that Ibrahim was convinced, where all your bullying had failed?'

'Exactly. My guy wouldn't say how he did it. But I guessed there was something personal between them, something between my man and your Ibrahim that I didn't understand.'

'Personal? What sort of personal? Who is this man with the power to turn your fearless opponent into your ally, to make him do your bidding without a whimper?'

'His name is Snake Eyes.'

'Snake Eyes? What sort of name is that? I need to speak to him!'

Shafik laughed. 'I thought you might say that. But it isn't that simple. Snake Eyes is in jail.'

'In jail?'

'In the Central Prison in Machh in Balochistan. For murdering a heroin dealer he fell out with.'

I had glimpsed the prospect of a solution; talking to the man who knew Ibrahim and recruited him to the world of crime held out the hope of answers. But a brick wall had sprung up that threatened to bring my investigation to a frustrating end.

'You can't get me in to see him, can you?'

It was worth a try.

'Perhaps. We support our men. Even on death row we don't abandon them.'

'Then you're willing to help me? Will you help me get into the jail?'

Shafik nodded. 'I will do what I can. I cannot guarantee miracles.'

I felt a surge of relief. I had not realised how important the quest to discover the truth had become to me. The prospect of failure had made me reckless, putting myself in the hands of a crime boss I knew I should not trust. I asked Shafik why he was willing to help me, but he told me not to look a gift horse in the mouth.

'To be clear,' I said, 'for my peace of mind – you categorically assure me that you did not murder Ibrahim Rahman?'

'Rahman was going to put his taxi network at our disposal. He was an asset, so why would I kill him? I didn't kill him and I don't know who did.'

Shafik's reply sounded genuine. He escorted us to the car. The guard placed the black hoods over our heads. Shafik helped us climb in and the door slammed. Almost at once I heard a metallic rap on the window. The barrel of a gun? 'Wind down the window!' Could he shoot me through the glass? The driver pressed a switch; the window slid down. Would Shafik shoot me in the car? What about the blood? I flinched.

'Martin sahib?' Shafik's voice was ingratiating. 'You asked me why I am agreeing to help you . . .'

'Yes . . .'

'It is because I admire your work.'

The conversation was taking an odd turn.

'Really?'

'Your books and your films.'

'Oh?'

'And because I hope you might include me as a character.'

I nodded uncomprehendingly.

'My favourite is the movie of your book *Gorky Park*. Lee Marvin is my sort of character – you can make me into Lee Marvin!'

Imran nudged my thigh. I could barely restrain myself. As the car sped away the two of us burst into laughter.

CHAPTER 35

Before I left London I had made a booking at the hotel where Ayesha and I had stayed on our previous visit. But Imran counselled against it. After our meeting with Javed Shafik, he said, it was inevitable that people would be watching us. The big international hotels were constantly monitored; we would be too much on view. Instead, we took a bus to Nazimabad in north-western Karachi then threaded our way through the villa-lined streets of Model Park to Chowrangi. At the crossroads beside the Pakistan air force monument Imran paused and looked around; satisfied we were alone, he beckoned me into the warren of streets beyond the Al Badar Hadi Market.

Night had come, moonless and richly dark. Imran's mother's house was a modest bungalow. She greeted us with smiles and plates of sai bhaji chawal with koki flat bread and pallo machi. Her son had been to London, but London rarely came to Nazimabad and I was feted. The best crockery was dusted off, the table laid with bright-patterned linen, neighbours called to view the exotic visitor. The warmth of the welcome and the animated, incomprehensible chatter calmed me. The horrors of the day receded. When the last guest left, Imran said I should take his room; he would camp on the sofa in the living room. Against my expectations I slept. When I opened the blinds, morning had come and the street was alive with bustle.

Over a breakfast of baked bakarkhani Imran and I reviewed the events of the past two days. The adrenalin had subsided now and the extent of the peril we had been in shook us. To bolster our spirits we joked about Shafik's self-regarding naivety, but we both acknowledged the reality of the danger he posed. Imran was wary of accepting his help. I was sceptical that he could deliver. Gaining access to a prisoner on death row seemed a proposition so outlandish that I had all but dismissed it. Imran was less sure.

'In Pakistan these things happen. The authorities are susceptible to threats and bribes. Prison governors have unchecked power in their kingdom. If they see an advantage in bending the rules, they do so.'

Imran called to his mother and they spoke briefly in Urdu. She turned to me and embarked on an animated explanation before he reminded her of the insurmountable linguistic divide. She laughed and pointed to her son, who took up the narrative.

'I was asking my mother about a young fellow from near here who is also in that jail awaiting the hangman. His name is Saulat Mirza. He has confessed to a dozen killings, but by some means he keeps appearing on our TV screens. I asked about Saulat because his case illustrates the anomalies in our justice system. It is a prime example of the deep state at work.'

'The deep state? It sounds malignant.'

'It is unfamiliar in true democracies. To us the deep state means the shady forces that hold power behind the scenes – corrupt politicians, elements of the intelligence services, the military, security forces, judiciary, organised criminals. They are never in the spotlight, but they influence everything, from dealing with or promoting terrorism, to deciding public appointments and distributing state funds, to covert plots and assassinations. Saulat Mirza's story is tangled up in the machinations of these people.'

'And he's in the same jail as our Snake Eyes fellow?'

'Yes, in Balochistan. But Saulat grew up here in Nazimabad. My mother knew his parents; they were Mohajirs, Muslims who fled from India after partition. Saulat went to Shipowners' College at Shahrah e Noojahan, the same school I went to. I remember he was active in the Mohajir Students Organisation, the youth wing of the MQM, and he evidently got recruited by the party's less savoury elements. In the mid-1990s he was involved in a series of political killings, including two US diplomats who were gunned down at a traffic light, and four American finance officers from the Union Texas Petroleum company.'

'Is that what he was arrested for?'

Imran laughed. 'No chance. He was working for people who guaranteed his immunity. That's what I meant about the deep state: the party in power uses killers like Saulat Mirza to do its dirty business and they just get away with it. In Karachi alone there are hundreds of assassinations every year.'

'But Saulat Mirza's in jail . . .'

'Right. He got unlucky. In 1997 he gunned down the Managing Director of the Karachi Electricity Company, a man called Malik Hamid. Hamid had been investigating allegations of corruption against some of his officials, but it turned out they were on the payroll of the MQM. The party told Hamid to drop it, but he wouldn't; so Saulat Mirza shot him, along with his bodyguard and his driver, as they were leaving to go to work.'

'But if Mirza was acting on behalf of the deep state, how come the deep state didn't protect him?'

'It tried to. But the murdered man had a son who was determined they weren't going to get away with it. Omar Hamid was so obsessed with getting justice for his dead father that he gave up his academic studies and joined the Karachi Police Department. He teamed up with the one cop who had a reputation for integrity amid all the dirt and corruption – Chaudhry Aslam. The two of them caught Saulat Mirza in a sting operation at Karachi airport and before the MQM could intervene they staged a press conference where they exposed all the political assassinations the guy had carried out. It was a pre-emptive strike. Saulat's protectors were taken by surprise; they couldn't stop the case going to court and Saulat got the death penalty. But the politicians had obviously promised to get him out because when the judge announced his verdict, Saulat just sniggered and said, "That's only a formality. Don't worry about it."'

'Yet he's been inside for a decade and a half.'

'Yes. Every time the party was about to get him released, Omar Hamid and Chaudhry Aslam would kick up such a fuss that they had to back down. In the end, someone in high places got sick of being disrespected, because Chaudhry Aslam switched on the ignition of his car and got blown to pieces. Omar was so upset and so angry that he wrote a novel telling the whole story of his father's murder using pseudonyms and invented locations, but revealing the dreadful things the deep state and its killers get up to.'

'So isn't Omar putting himself in danger?'

Imran nodded. 'Since his book came out, Omar Hamid has been living in London. He is safer there. And when your book comes out, I think you should do the same.'

Imran and I sat looking at each other. Then he burst out laughing.

'But a bit of drama's good for book sales, isn't it? And Saulat Mirza has been helping Omar's sales with those TV appearances I mentioned. It seems he has fallen out with his friends at the MQM – they have said publicly that they are washing their hands of him and they won't give him any more help with his defence. The judiciary took the hint and announced that Saulat would be hanged within a week. But the prospect of the noose seems to have jogged his memory, because he somehow got a camera and a cameraman into his cell on death row and recorded a whole series of explosive revelations. Having spent more than a decade denying it was the MQM who gave him his assassination orders, he has changed his tune. In the video he says the instruction to kill Omar's father came directly from the head of the MQM, Nasser Aziz. And he says he and other killers got protection from the Governor of Sindh, a fellow called Mohammed Asif.'

'Mohammed Asif!'

'Have you come across him?'

'Yes . . . Well, tangentially shall we say.'

'The Governor issued a statement denying he had ever protected any criminals, least of all political assassins like Saulat Mirza. Mirza's family responded by leaking photographs of Mohammed Asif and other politicians at their family weddings and visiting Saulat in jail looking very friendly indeed. For a lot of Pakistanis it confirmed what they always suspected about the way the deep state runs the country. Mirza's video was shown on national television the day before he was due to be executed. And he was very clever. In the video he claims he has all sorts of further revelations he can make about the plots and conspiracies of powerful people who operate in the shadows, about the crimes and corruption that go on behind the scenes. So the President was forced to step in and halt the hanging. They needed at the very least to be seen to be listening to what Saulat had to say. My mother has been following the drama in the media and she gave me this cutting.'

Imran handed me an editorial from one of Pakistan's English-language newspapers, headlined 'A killer's confession'.

Many individuals on the verge of being sent to the gallows would conceivably have the desire to unburden themselves. Not many, however, have been provided the opportunity to indulge in such a cathartic exercise on national television as did the MQM worker, convicted in 1999 for multiple murders, on late Wednesday night. Mirza's sensational revelations, which have sent convulsions through Pakistan's fourth largest political party, were followed by the announcement that his execution had been stayed ...

Saulat Mirza's 'confession' has brought some of MQM's most prominent names into the dragnet. It is the latest salvo in the concerted push to tighten the noose around the party that controls much of the country's largest city and its financial hub.

However, the latest development raises several questions: how did a camera find its way into the death cell? ... Why now? What is the long-term objective? The situation – a condemned prisoner looking for any way to delay the inevitable – was conducive to manipulation. But in the eyes of the establishment, no stranger to Machiavellian tactics, there is perhaps considerable political mileage to be gained ... While it is an open secret that the MQM employs heavy-handed tactics to maintain its grip on a city where politics and criminal networks often overlap, such an approach augurs ill for peace in the metropolis. As the deep state orchestrates the MQM's 'remaking' to its current requirements, both the central and the Sindh governments appear to be taking a back seat. By doing so, they do themselves and the democratic project no favours.

I handed the cutting back to Imran.

'Not the sort of thing you would come across in the UK, I suppose?' he said. 'But this is Pakistan. It's impossible to untangle truth from lies. And it's hard to know who you can trust. Shafik's fellow, Snake Eyes, is on death row with Saulat Mirza and the two of them have a lot in common.

Before he died, Chaudhry Aslam revealed that Mirza was continuing to run his network of crooks and assassins from his jail cell. No one dared to stop him. A prison official who tried to interfere was shot dead on his way home. And I suspect it is the same with Shafik and Snake Eyes. These people intimidate and murder their way to the top. They are tools of the deep state, but they use the power that confers on them for their own ends.'

CHAPTER 36

Concerned that his mother would be alarmed by the dangers we were running, Imran said little to her about the business we were engaged in. With an unexpected sense of humour he told her I was in Karachi for a conference on Freudian archetypes and the murdered father figure in Shakespeare's *Hamlet*. In her presence we were cheerful. But mothers are tuned to understand their children and she did. Without saying anything, she fussed over us with food and more food, tea and sweetmeats; she brought us slippers, washed our linen, plumped our eiderdowns.

Imran was in touch with Shafik by text and email, but did not tell him where we were staying. Shafik was working on the jail visit. Snake Eyes had been convicted under the name of Mushtaq Waraich, but Shafik said that too was probably an alias.

On the third day Imran's mother came to us with a parcel. It had been delivered by a very polite man in a shiny black car; he would not come in for tea or say who he was, but he told her that Imran-ji would understand.

Imran beckoned me into the garden. The parcel contained a wooden box and a sealed letter addressed to Sajid Gul, Superintendent, Machh Central Prison. Inside the box we found a curved, ceremonial dagger extravagantly engraved with verses that Imran said were from the Qur'an. Imran's mobile phone pinged. The text was from Javed Shafik with instructions for our trip north.

The following day we woke early. It would take eight hours to drive to Quetta, where we would spend the night. Machh was another forty miles, but there were few hotels and none that was safe for foreigners. Quetta itself was home to senior Taliban commanders and an important staging post for Al Qaeda. I would need to wear Pakistani clothing and cover my face.

The drive was spectacular. Leaving the suburbs of Karachi we crossed the Hub River at Rais Goth and joined the N25, the RDC Highway, skirting the coast then turning north. The British engineers who traced the route had followed the valleys of the Lyari and Winder rivers, before eventually rejoining the northern section of the Hub in the Siahan and Makran mountains of Balochistan. The peaks to the left and right closed on us as we climbed from the valley towards Khuzdar, the halfway point of our journey, 4,000 feet above sea level. Alexander the Great had passed through on his march back to Babylon after conquering India in 300BC. In Kalat we took tea where in 1947 the last Khan of the Princely Kingdom had resisted incorporation into Pakistan, appealing first to India to take his people in, then maintaining a stubborn year-long independence before bowing to the inevitable. The last leg of the drive took us through Mastung and into Balochistan's mountain capital, Quetta; night was falling as we pulled into the city.

Over breakfast we discussed the day ahead. Shafik had texted to say that we should report directly to the Prison Superintendent, without divulging to anyone the reason for our visit. The arrangements sounded fragile, most likely the product of a bribe, a threat or a favour Shafik was owed. The drive to Machh took an hour, through Pakistan's bandit country. But the dacoits and jihadis were otherwise engaged and we saw the town's minarets emerge from the hills that surround it. Machh was a former outpost of the Raj gone to seed. Its mountain setting was dramatic, but tourists didn't come. The jail, located halfway up the rocky northern slope, seemed to be the main enterprise. Its walls, blanched and topped by wire, were visible for miles. Within its thirteen acres, red-roofed cell blocks radiated like spokes from a central parade ground of scrubby grass. The walls were high, but above them rose the wooden crossbeam of the gallows.

A pink gatehouse, flanked by stone watchtowers, bore the date 1929, a time when Machh was a distant holding place for opponents of British rule. Now the green and white crescent flew from the flagpole and the guards carried Heckler and Koch machine guns. They waved us out of the car into the guardroom. A Frontier Corps NCO examined our papers and asked what we wanted. Imran spoke politely, deferentially; the man pointed to a wooden bench. We sat for thirty minutes, forty minutes, an hour. A prison official in a khaki uniform came and took our letter. He returned at once to usher us in to the Superintendent.

Eyes filled with curiosity, Sajid Gul poured us tea and inquired about our journey. Imran explained that I had no Urdu; the Superintendent spoke English.

'I see you are here to call on one of my guests.'

He was weighing us up, trying to decipher what interest a Pakistani academic and a foreigner might have in a man called Snake Eyes. Shafik's letter and the dagger made him deferential.

'Allow me to offer my help. The man you wish to see is in D block.'

Gul had evidently concluded that we were friends of his guest.

'We have been taking care of him. As a man facing, I may say, the ultimate sanction, he should be in solitary confinement. But we have not applied this with undue rigour.'

'Thank you,' Imran said. 'And may I ask for some further information? The person is known to us under his alias of Snake Eyes, but I wonder if you have other details.'

Sajid Gul unlocked a filing cabinet and took out a dossier.

'Yes,' he said. 'There are several known aliases. He is charged under the name Mushtaq Waraich. Also known as Kamran Rafique. And Ahmed Rahman. Birth date stated as 23 March 1951. Birth place Karachi. Charged on multiple counts, including—'

Gul was reading out a list of offences, but I was not listening.

'Wait, Superintendent! Could you repeat the list of aliases?'

He did.

'And I missed some of the charges. The murder of the

heroin dealer we were aware of. Then you mentioned theft and contraband. Did this involve smuggling abroad?'

Gul ran his finger down the page.

'Yes, several counts of drug-running. Human-trafficking. Most of them unproven. In fact, had he not killed the dealer in the bazaar he would be a free man.'

I looked at Imran. We must not let Gul know about Ahmed Rahman.

'Superintendent, did the cross-border offences involve the UK? Was Snake Eyes – Waraich – accused of smuggling offences to Britain?'

Gul nodded. 'He was accused of them. But not convicted.'

'Do you have details of Waraich's connections in the UK? The places he was alleged to be smuggling to?'

Gul turned the page.

'It is stated that the accused had a home ir Burnley, Lancashire. Which is also the alleged destination of the goods.'

My heart was racing. Imran took over.

'Thank you, Superintendent sahib. If you agree, I think Martin would like to see the fellow.'

Gul bowed, summoned the official in the khaki uniform and beckoned us to follow them. At the hub of the wheel from which the cell blocks radiated, a yellow stuccoed building was surrounded by a low wooden palisade. A sleepy-looking guard gave a leisurely salute. The unbarred windows were open and Bollywood film music was audible from inside. I was ready for what lay ahead.

CHAPTER 37

'May I point out the quality of the accommodation?' Gul was pursuing his own agenda. 'This block is for A-class prisoners. Despite Waraich not being entitled to such status, I took it upon myself to grant it to him.'

The door opened into a communal area. The walls were white; white tiles on the floor. A faint smell of bleach gave it the air of a hospital waiting hall. A Nordic Track exercise machine, a rack of barbells and a ping-pong table were at the far end of the room; under the window a colour television was playing music videos from a DVD. Imran could not hide his astonishment.

'Superintendent-ji, this is a hotel! Is your whole jail so luxurious?'

Gul laughed.

'I told you: this is A-class. We have 845 inmates but only two such guests. Saulat Mirza is away in Islamabad spinning his tales to the President, so that leaves your colleague Mushtaq Snake Eyes. Condemned men should normally be in the black cells, but in certain cases I am able to temper justice with mercy. When you speak to Mr Shafik, please confirm to him that Snake Eyes enjoys all the A-class privileges – his own room, bathroom, TV, fridge, superior food and personal cook.'

A hacking cough came from behind a door. Gul lowered his voice.

'That is him. I need to mention something. We cannot shield death row prisoners from the stress of their situation. They wake each morning filled with fear, not knowing if the day will bring bad news. Some collapse under the strain. Saulat Mirza has been smoking a hundred cigarettes a day trying to stave off the noose. Your Snake Eyes spends sleepless nights. It can make them unpredictable, their behaviour unstable. And there are no psychologists in our jails; just the mullahs who lead the inmates in prayer and teach them the religious texts. You need to be prepared for what you are about to see.'

There was a growl from the door.

'Who the hell are you talking to, Gul?' The voice was harsh. 'You are disturbing me, you bastard!'

Gul gave a nervous smile.

'Snake Eyes-ji, you have visitors. Friends of Shafik sahib. Do you wish to receive them?'

There was silence, then a grunt.

'Have you searched them?'

'They are here at the wish of Shafik himself.'

'So send them in. Make yourself scarce. Tell the boy to fetch us coffee.'

Gul and his assistant left us at the door of Snake Eyes' cell.

'Show your faces! I am a busy man!'

It sounded incongruous. With what did a condemned man fill his days? Imran went first.

'Snake Eyes-ji, we have come with Shafik's blessing. To talk to you . . .'

A bearded figure in a white cotton robe that looked freshly laundered was stretched on a daybed. He removed the earphones of a silver iPod from his ears.

'Talk about what?' The figure propped itself on an elbow, pulled out a mobile phone from beneath a pillow. 'Give me your names then wait outside.'

In the white hall we exchanged whispers.

'How does he have a mobile? Why are there no guards? Why are the officials so afraid of him?'

Snake Eyes finished his call and summoned us back.

'Okay. Shafik wishes me to talk to you.'

I let Imran take the lead.

'Snake Eyes-ji,' he began respectfully. 'Are they treating you well? Do you have what you need?'

'I have what I need because we keep the bastards scared. They give me all this' – he swept the room with his hand – 'because we know where their families live.'

Imran smiled. 'And the mobile phone? They don't make problems?'

'They don't make problems because I need the phone for business. And the guards get a cut.' His English was fluent, his tone extravagantly boastful. 'They know the jobs we're doing and they turn a blind eye. We send the C-class jailbirds on awaydays and they readmit them in the evening. The whole prison knows what heists and hits we have planned, but we are in jail so they can't pin it on us.

Last week we did a job in Quetta and the guys were back inside before anyone missed them. This week a bunch of new arrivals come in and they've been charged with our robbery!'

'And how about the other prisoners? They maintain respect?'

'There were some gangsters from Kala Pul who brought a four-wheel drive and gave it to the prison boss. They used to get allowed out to go and party. We had to bring them down a peg. And there are fights over who controls the amenities. Drugs, alcohol, women; you can get them all in here. They're profitable things; the syndicates all want a stake.'

'So who decides?'

'Same as on the outside: the political parties. They provide protection and discipline. The MQM, the UF and the others all have their structures; the jail bosses negotiate with them. Each party has its own territory, its own kitchens and washrooms. And they're ruthless about checking out new recruits because they're scared of infiltrators and spies. We need to know who everyone is and who they work for. I'm talking to you because Shafik told me to, but you haven't told me who you are or what your business is.'

I had expected the question.

'Well, you know our names,' I said. 'And I'm sure Shafik has told you that I am writing about Pakistan. I need the sort of information only you and he can provide. I have promised that anything I write will be anonymised. I will disguise your identities and background, but Shafik wants to be a character in my book and you can be, too.'

I caught the look on Snake Eyes' face that told me he was interested. I pressed ahead.

'So tell me, should I use your alias or a fictionalised version of your real name? Snake Eyes, or Mushtaq Waraich?'

The man on the bed stroked his chin. The beard was the product of jail, but the fastidiously waxed moustache was part of the man.

'Snake Eyes is fine.'

He wanted to be in the book; I had him.

'So tell me how you came to work for Javed Shafik.'

Snake Eyes swung his feet down to the floor. Stiff from lying, he walked uneasily to the window and looked out.

'I knew him in England. A long time ago. We both worked in the cotton mills, but Shafik was smart; he understood things that other people didn't. Even then, back in the 1970s, he knew the English would never accept us. They hated us Pakistanis. Some of us tried being nice to them, tried to integrate and become British. But Shafik said there was no point. We got sworn at and spat on; some of us got smashed up by the bovver boys.'

He ran his finger over his ribs as if resurrecting the memory of a still hurtful injury.

'It was a hard lesson, but it was liberating. Their brutality meant we could hate them. We didn't owe them anything. We didn't need to defer to the whites; we could exploit their weaknesses and take them for whatever we could get. And they had plenty of weaknesses. They had no moral code, no respect and no honour. They didn't live by the values of religion. They were consumed by greed and sensual appetites. So Shafik gave them what they wanted.

In the seventies it was booze and smuggled cigarettes. Then the English started wanting drugs, so he brought them opium from Afghanistan, hashish and heroin from Khyber Pakhtunkhwa trafficked through Karachi and Islamabad. There were plenty of mules ready to swallow a few condoms for a thousand rupees, but most of the time he just parcelled it up and sent it by airmail.

'The trade grew so big that Shafik had to find new transport methods to meet the demand. And that's when I got involved. He and I were travelling back and forth to Pakistan, negotiating with shipping companies to hide the drugs in their containers, stuffing the tyres of cars that were being transported to London or replacing baby powder with heroin. I'm not bigging myself up, but one of my ideas was the best – we got friendly with the funeral homes in Karachi and they used to tip us off whenever a British Pakistani had died and was being flown back to the UK. The amount of heroin you can get into a coffin – under the lining, in the corpse's clothes or rammed into his body – is huge!'

Snake Eyes paused for effect. There was a recklessness in the man's boasting that I found intimidating. When I asked if he was worried about the consequences, he laughed.

'You mean you're wondering why I'm telling you this? It's because I'm proud of it. The English hate us, we make money out of them; it's simple. Being in jail is just a holiday for me. I can take care of business from the comfort of my bed. No one can touch me because they're shit scared of Shafik and the UF. And once things have calmed down I'll be out of here. Shafik has got the party to guarantee it. He's paid the right people the right money. That's how it works.'

I remembered Superintendent Gul's words about the pressures of being on death row. Snake Eyes didn't seem unbalanced, just utterly assured of his own invulnerability. And that gave him licence to brag.

'Can I ask about human-trafficking?' I was testing the limits of his candour. 'There've been a lot of news stories in England about Pakistani men abusing young girls.'

Snake Eyes glanced at me.

'You're confusing things. The abuse happens to English girls in English cities. The trafficking involves Pakistani girls who get smuggled into the UK. And that's usually for marriages, visas . . .'

'And prostitution?'

'Maybe. Sometimes.'

'And which of these do you and Shafik know about?'

'We have acted as intermediaries in the immigration trade. We don't have anything to do with the abuse rings . . .'

'Really? It's just that I heard of a case in Burnley – a young white girl; her name was Kelly Stafford – and I wondered if you knew about it.'

Snake Eyes fixed me with a glare that explained his nickname; intense, disturbing, dark with menace.

'Why are you bringing that up? Why the fuck are you talking about Burnley?'

I had touched a nerve.

'No reason. Just that Superintendent Gul mentioned you lived in Burnley. And that some of the charges against you were connected with the place.'

'Gul showed you my charge sheet? I'll fix that bastard!'

'I'm surprised. You've been quite open about all the other allegations. So why this sudden outrage? Is it because of Kelly Stafford? Or because of Burnley, perhaps?'

'It's because there are things you should not know about! Things that include my connections in England! You'd better not write a single word of this in your book – not if you want to live to see it published, you bastard!'

The ferocity of his rage jolted me. The journalist's impunity had lulled me into thinking of this as a story. But it was perilous reality and I was being sucked into it.

'Okay, look – I am not going to use real names and places. Maybe I'll talk about Bradford instead of Burnley . . .'

I attacked from a different angle.

'But I need to know the truth. And I need to hear it from you. Your name isn't Snake Eyes or Mushtaq Waraich or Kamran Rafique, is it? It's Ahmed Rahman!'

He stared at me, unblinking, calculating. Then he shrugged.

'Maybe. So what if it is?'

'So it explains something that has been puzzling me. You are Ahmed Rahman and your brother was Ibrahim Rahman. Am I right?'

'You tell me. You seem to know a lot of things.'

'You both worked for Javed Shafik—'

'Things that might not be good for you, journalist . . .'

'But Ibrahim died, didn't he?'

'What?'

'He died. He was murdered . . .'

'Just because I'm in this cell . . . just because I'm in this cell doesn't mean I can't squeeze you 'til the blood runs from your veins, you bastard . . .'

'I'm not out to get you, Ahmed . . . I'm not out to get your boss. I'm trying to understand. I'm trying to explain something that's been troubling me . . . Ahmed . . .?'

Hearing his name used seemed to check him. He looked around.

'I too have a brother, Ahmed. I had a brother. Like you, my brother died and I have been looking for explanations. Like you I've had the loss, the absence and the guilt. And Tom's death has become tangled up with Ibrahim's – don't ask me how or why. I need answers to both. Even if I never write anything; even if I throw away all these notes and wipe all the tapes, I need to know. And I think perhaps you do, too . . .'

CHAPTER 38

Ahmed Rahman was silent. What thoughts were stirring behind his expressionless eyes? When he spoke his words were belligerent, but his tone was not.

'Listen to me, journalist. I don't care if you get answers. I don't care about your brother. But I do want to know why you've come here asking questions about mine. An Englishman, with no understanding of me or my people or my country. Why do you come here and ask me these things?'

'I've come because Ibrahim's daughter, your niece, asked me to. Ayesha asked me to find out what happened to her father and I promised her I would. I know about Shafik and Ibrahim and the quarrel over his land. I know Shafik threatened him and I know Ibrahim was ready to die to protect his property. But then something happened and I need to know what it was. You went to Ibrahim. You spoke to him. And you persuaded him to change his mind. I need to know *how* you convinced your brother to give up a law-abiding, family life and enter your world of depravity.'

For the first time in our conversation, Ahmed laughed. It was a laugh of derision and, just possibly, relief.

'How do you think I did it? I persuaded him through brotherly love!'

Ayesha's account of Ahmed's behaviour after Ibrahim's death had conditioned my ideas about her uncle, the men he mixed with at the funeral meal and the long, troubled relationship between the two brothers.

'Can I just go back a bit? Ayesha told me about you and Ibrahim when you were growing up, when the two of you came to England and lived together in Burnley. She told me about the quarrels you had and the problems between your two families. To be honest, it doesn't sound like there was much brotherly love at all.'

Ahmed's laugh was harsh.

'It's not me you should be asking about those things. Those quarrels were my brother's fault. He was the one who refused to show respect. I was his elder; I brought him from Pakistan to England; he lived in a house that I provided, worked at a job that I found for him. I was due deference, but he wouldn't give it. Ibrahim always thought he knew best: he disrespected my advice about how we should live among the whites; he laughed at my warnings not to try to be part of their godless society . . . and he let his children laugh at me.'

The bitterness in his voice was unmistakable; Ahmed was spilling out things that had festered within him, that he had long yearned to share.

'All I wanted was for Ibrahim to acknowledge me.' He was sitting now on the edge of the bed, his swagger gone.

'I collected him at the airport in 1969. I came in a car and I drove him from Gatwick to Burnley. Is that not brotherly love? I looked after him when we were living in our uncle Kabir's house; I took him to the factory and persuaded the foreman to take him on. Is that not brotherly love? I went with him when he wanted to go to a stupid football game and when he wanted to introduce me to his white English friends. Is that not brotherly love? And when it all went wrong, when we were attacked and beaten up, I stood by him. All I wanted was for my brother to respect me. But he didn't. He persisted in trying to be British. He moved to a white area, bought a house in a smart street, sent his children – even his daughter! – to university. When she went to Cambridge I told him to make sure she didn't get big ideas, but he ignored me. He was in my debt, but he thought he was better than me. His family looked down on us. I tried to tell them they were making me a laughing stock in the eyes of the community, but they just sneered.'

Ahmed's eyes were pleading for understanding.

'Ayesha mentioned some of those things, Ahmed. But she told me her father's side of the story. She said that later on, when you'd fallen out, you demanded money for the car from Gatwick to Burnley, that you'd kept a logbook of everything you'd ever done for him and a balance sheet of what he owed you for it. She said it was your way of humiliating him. And she said you tried to blame him publicly for the death of Kelly Stafford at his taxi business . . .'

'Dammit, man! You're talking about Kelly Stafford again!'

'Yes. Because you never answered the question I asked

you about her. Did you have anything to do with her death? Did Ibrahim?'

Ahmed hesitated.

'Ibrahim had nothing to do with it. It was an unfortunate event; that's all I will say on the subject, so don't ask me any more about it.'

He sounded sincere about his brother's innocence.

'Well, let me ask you about something else Ayesha told me. She said that when you were boys in Pakistan you made Ibrahim witness the murder of two young lovers who'd committed some sort of offence against family honour . . .'

'Yes! I did. I did it because he needed to learn a lesson; he needed to see the rewards of treachery and dishonour. But he didn't learn a thing. He didn't understand that broken promises and disrespect bring retribution . . .'

I had the impression that there was something more Ahmed wanted to say.

'Do you mean his disrespect for you, Ahmed? Is that what you are trying to tell me?'

'I will tell you this, journalist. You are right that my brother and I quarrelled. You know enough about the reasons and it doesn't matter now who was to blame. Maybe it was him, maybe it was me. But I want you to know that we found a way to resolve our differences. Several years ago in Burnley, he and I spoke. We both wanted an end to the things that divided us; he was willing and I was willing.'

Ahmed looked at me. I nodded encouragement.

'Ibrahim thought we could just shake hands and everything would be okay. But I said it would take more than that. I had been disrespected by him, and the Pakistani community notices everything. In Burnley people talk. For my self-respect and my family's self-respect Ibrahim needed to acknowledge that he had dishonoured me and that he was atoning for it. I know you English don't understand, but these things are important. I offered him a deal. His son Tariq had done well in the world; he was a surveyor, earning a good salary. His daughter Ayesha had gone to Cambridge. And his youngest, Bilal, was making good money driving a taxi. My daughter and my son hadn't done so well. They were good kids, but not successful. So I told Ibrahim that my price for pardoning him was that he must promise Tariq and Ayesha in marriage to my children. And he agreed. He promised solemnly, before witnesses and before the council of elders. But then he reneged . . .'

'How come?'

'When he told Tariq, the boy refused; he argued with his father and stormed out of the house. I don't know if he even told Ayesha. He should have forced his children to agree, but he was pathetic. He came to me and backed out of our agreement.'

Ahmed's face twisted with anger and regret.

'I couldn't let him get away with it. I told the council of elders that Tariq and Ayesha had broken a solemn arrangement. And what's more, both of them were consorting with whites. I had followed Tariq and saw he was sleeping with a girl from an English family. And I learned that Ayesha was seeing an English boy called Peter. I demanded retribution and the elders agreed. They said my brother and his children had dishonoured me. They asked if I was willing to pardon them and I said I was not; I had an obligation to defend my family's honour. The elders ruled that I had the right to exact the ultimate penalty on both Tariq and Ayesha. They said it would be merciful if I would negotiate financial compensation in lieu of their deaths, but I was not obliged to do so. They issued their judgment and said it was up to me.'

Ahmed smiled.

'I pocketed the judgment and did nothing. I was waiting for the moment to use it. And that moment came when Ibrahim started his stupid histrionics about the land we needed for the Orangi water project. Shafik didn't know Ibrahim was my brother. He tried and failed to persuade him to see sense. In the end I said I would do it. I went to see him and told him that unless he did what Shafik wanted I would invoke the judgment against his son and his daughter. Ibrahim had to come to work for us, or he was condemning his children to death.'

CHAPTER 39

Ahmed Rahman stared at me. He had confessed to a journalist whom he knew was taking notes, compiling evidence against him. The prophet Mohammed said a believer sees his sins as if he were sitting under a mountain which he fears will fall upon him, while the wicked person considers his sins as flies passing over his nose.

'Can we be clear?' I said. 'You are saying Ibrahim refused to compromise himself, until you threatened to kill his children. He sacrificed himself to protect Ayesha and Tariq?'

'If you put it like that.'

'Your brother was a good man.'

'If you say so.'

Ahmed laughed; but he knew his brother had behaved better than he ever could. There was one more question.

'Am I right, then, to assume you killed him?'

The door opened and the boy came in with a tray of coffee.

'Goddamit!' Ahmed rounded on him. 'Why the fuck are you coming in here now! Get out of here, you bastard!'

The boy dropped the tray; cups smashed and a stain of black liquid spread over the tiles. The child burst into tears, turned and ran.

'Okay, journalist; time for you to go.'

The moment of candour had passed. Ahmed had spoken so openly that perhaps now he regretted it. The more I pressed him, the more he rowed back.

'Leave it! I've told you enough. Why would I kill my brother? We'd already got what we needed from him . . .'

The old Ahmed was back, arrogant and angry. He called the guard to take us away. I made a final plea.

'I need to know, Ahmed. I need to know who killed Ibrahim. If it wasn't you, then tell me who it was!'

Ahmed turned his back, snarled at me.

'You figure it out. You think you're so fucking clever, coming here and passing judgment. You tell me who it was. Tell me who deserves to pay for it, who deserves to suffer for it. You tell me who that man is!'

We reached Quetta after midnight and checked back in to the hotel. I asked the night porter to book an international call to London, but he said there was little chance of getting it until the morning. I was eager to tell Ayesha that her father had not been a willing participant in the crimes he had committed; I dreaded having to tell her that the identity of his murderer remained opaque.

My dreams took me to the death cell, to Saulat Mirza's hempen noose and hundred cigarettes. *Did you ever see a hangman tie a hangknot? . . . He winds, he winds; after thirteen times . . .* I found myself on the floodlit stage of Imran's make-believe *Hamlet* conference, with Ahmed as smiling, villainous Uncle Claudius. *O, my offence is rank; it smells to heaven. It hath the primal eldest curse upon't, A brother's murder!* Ahmed as fratricide, king-slayer, outcast from God. *And the Lord had respect unto Abel and to his offering. But unto Cain and to his offering he had not respect.* What did Freud say about the Brudermörder, with his anguish of jealousy and self-disgust, his urge to destroy the being closest to him? *And the Lord said unto Cain, Why art thou wroth? . . . And it came to pass, when they were in the field, that Cain rose up against Abel.* And what would Freud say about me dreaming now – I knew it was a dream, but I knew it *in* my dream – of the Brudermord? *What if this cursed hand were thicker than itself with brother's blood?* Ahmed struggling to confess his guilt, but unable to purge the conscience that pricks and burns. *'Forgive me my foul murder'? That cannot be . . . What then? What rests . . . when one can not repent? O bosom black as death!* Elektra avenges her father, but who shall avenge the brother? *And the Lord said, Now you are cursèd from the ground which has opened its mouth to receive your brother's blood* . . . The ground that Ahmed stole; the land that was his brother's. And what about the widow, Gertrude, who marries her murdered husband's brother? I was back on the floodlit stage, wearing Claudius's robes and crown. I was kneeling, trying to purge my guilt. Loud knocking from somewhere behind me; the revenger come for him who murdered the brother he loved. I tried to rise but my knees were glued to the floor. I tried to run but my guilt weighed me down . . .

The porter had been knocking at the door, concerned that the line might be cut before I roused myself to use it. By the time we reached the lobby the operator had got through to Ayesha. I blurted out the news she had been hoping to hear. Ibrahim was not a villain. There was an explanation for the crimes he had committed. Her image of a loving father was safe.

There was silence on the line. I had expected gratitude and relief. I called her name, asked if she was still there.

'Martin, I already knew . . .'

'What do you mean, you already knew?'

'After you went back to Pakistan I spoke to Tariq. He told me about Dad's promise to marry us off to Ahmed's children. That was why Tariq ran away from home . . .'

'Yes, I know . . .'

'. . . and why he was so angry with Mum, who had gone along with it. But he told me he'd tried to patch things up. He contacted Dad in Kahin Nahi and Dad spoke to him about how Ahmed was using the judgment against us to blackmail him. Tariq was furious. He told Dad not to give in; he said he would come to Pakistan and take care of things – with a knife if necessary. But Dad said that if Tariq showed his face in Kahin Nahi, Shafik's dacoits would slaughter him out of hand.'

'So if you knew, why did you let me come here?'

'Because we don't know who killed our father. Dad told Tariq he was going to work for Shafik and Ahmed and that he would be safe once he had given them what they wanted. Then we heard that Dad had been murdered.'

'And you were hoping I would find out by whom . . .'

'There's more. I showed Tariq the papers from Dad's desk; he went through them all and he found something dangerous. Ahmed kept some of Dad's land for himself – land that he kept secret from Shafik. Can I send you a fax?'

I asked the porter for the fax number. He said it was unreliable, but the machine whirred into life. The pages spewed out, accompanied by a commentary over the phone from Ayesha.

'Look at the first page, Martin. It's the ownership document, the fard, for part of Dad's land – you can see the boundaries outlined on the map. You won't be able to read the Urdu, but Dad's name has been replaced by Ahmed's.'

'So how come Ahmed didn't keep the fard for himself?'

'That's what I'm trying to tell you. Mum's name is also on the document, Asma Rahman. Tariq contacted the patwari and asked him what's been going on. The patwari said Ahmed brought Dad in and asked for the land to be signed over. Dad agreed to have his name removed, but Asma was not present to authorise the removal of hers. So now the land is held jointly by Mum and Ahmed. The patwari drew up two authenticated copies of the fard; we've got one of them and Ahmed has the other.'

'Okay, so why had Ibrahim put Asma's name on that particular piece of land? And how come Ahmed wants to keep that bit for himself, when he let all the rest go to Shafik for his dam scheme?'

'Exactly! Have a look at this . . .'

The fax whirred again; this time the document was in English.

KAHIN NAHI, Pakistan – Huge oil and gas reserves have been discovered at Kahin Nahi, fifteen kilometres from Karachi, according to Oil and Gas Development Co (OGDCL) sources. Other wells in the area include Ahdi, Mastala, Missa and Tobra, all of which are currently in production with Pakistani Petroleum. The sources said OGDCL prospectors estimate the new find could yield up to 4,600 barrels of crude daily, making it one of the largest discoveries of recent years and opening up a new area for exploitation of hydrocarbon potential. (APP)

CHAPTER 40

I showed Imran the faxes over breakfast and he confirmed that the fard registered the land as owned in partnership between Asma Rahman and Ahmed Rahman. There were other documents.

'These are surveyors' reports, Martin. It looks like they were commissioned by Ibrahim to evaluate the potential quantities of oil. There are some differences between them, but all of them say the revenues will be substantial.'

I told Imran about my phone call with Ayesha. She had asked me to go back to Machh to see Ahmed again. She was desperate for answers to the remaining questions about her father, and this might be the last opportunity to get them.

Imran was dubious. It had been dangerous going to the jail once, he said; going twice was patently foolish. We had angered Ahmed, and his power to wreak vengeance extended beyond the prison walls.

I acknowledged Imran's concerns. But for all the antagonism and suspicion our encounter had aroused, I felt Ahmed might welcome another meeting. There were things that still nagged his conscience.

'We should try again, Imran. Would you ring the Superintendent of the jail and see if we can go there today?'

Imran rang. Superintendent Gul said he would ask if Ahmed was willing, but returned to say he had categorically refused. It was a blow. I asked Imran to ring Javed Shafik and see if he would order Ahmed to change his mind. It was mid-afternoon before we heard back: we should go to the prison at once.

Ahmed was surly. He refused to get up from the daybed, kept his eyes fixed on the window, ignored my questions.

'Ahmed. Look, I'm sorry about the way we got in to see you today . . .'

Silence.

'I wouldn't have insisted, but there are important things to talk about . . .'

'Go to hell!'

'. . . important for me and important for you, too, I think.'

He shifted his body, raised his head.

'How do you know what's important for me?'

'I know what I would consider important if I were in your position.'

'What do you mean, my position?'

'On death row . . .'

'Oh, grow up! I'm not going to swing. The party have said they're getting me out of here; next month at the latest.'

'Okay. So maybe you won't die now. But you are going to die . . .'

'It's you who's going to die if you don't stop hassling me!'

'. . . and I don't think you want to die with your conscience heavy.'

'My conscience? Who said anything about my conscience?'

'You did, Ahmed. The last time I was here.'

'Me?'

'Yes. You told me I should figure it out. You asked me who must pay for Ibrahim's death, who is the man who deserves to suffer for it . . .'

I saw the apprehension in his eyes.

'. . . and I did figure it out. You were giving me the answer in the question – it was you who murdered your brother; and you can't live with yourself because of it!'

'Oh, yes? Who says?'

'I think you want to tell me about it. You want to share the burden . . .'

'Fuck off! You know nothing. And anyway, the Qur'an says only Allah can forgive . . .'

Ahmed turned away, mumbling fervent, rapid words, invoking the formulae of forgiveness. 'O son of Adam, so long as you call upon Me, and ask of Me, I shall forgive you. Despair not of the Mercy of Allah: Were your sins to reach the clouds of the sky, I would forgive you. Were you to come to Me with sins as great as the earth and were then to face Me, I would bring you forgiveness . . .'

'Come on, Ahmed . . .'

'For Allah is full of knowledge and wisdom. Turn to Allah for He will remove from you your ills and admit you to the Gardens through which rivers flow . . .'

Unexpectedly, Imran joined in: 'But oh! My servants who have transgressed against their souls! Of no effect is the repentance of those who continue to do evil until death does face them!'

Ahmed hesitated. Imran took over the incantatory verses.

'For lo! Unto those who leave repentance until the time of their death, We have prepared a punishment most griev-ous. On the Day of Judgment they will dwell for ever in ignominy, for the Lord is swift in retribution!'

Ahmed snarled, 'Repenting to anyone other than Allah is forbidden!'

But Imran had an answer: 'The Qur'an says, "Verily, your fellow men on whom ye call for counsel and relief are like unto you; therefore call on them now, so they might soothe your mind and answer your prayer!"'

Ahmed slumped onto the bed. He had lifted his arms so the sleeves of his robe covered his face.

'Enough!' His voice through the white linen was distant, strained. 'What is it you want from me?'

'Who paid the Pathans to strangle Ibrahim? . . . Ahmed . . .'

'Yes . . .'

'It was you?'

'Yes . . .'

There was silence in the white prison; a prisoner in a white robe, grappling with his sin.

'But why? You said yourself you didn't need to kill him. Ibrahim had done what you asked of him. He'd turned over his land; he'd come to work for Javed Shafik; he was ready to hand over his taxi network . . .'

'But it wasn't enough!' he groaned. 'It wasn't enough, because it could never be enough! For all the hurt and all the humiliation, for all the slights and insults, all the sneering, superior . . . He had to die. There was no other way.'

'But did you not feel—?'

'Enough! My brother is dead. And I am alive . . .'

There was anguish in Ahmed's voice; but could I feel pity for a man who had bribed and threatened and lied to cover up his crime? Who had misled his brother's loved ones and condemned them to the hell of unknowing?

'You went to the police and got them to concoct a fictitious version of what you had done . . .'

'The police had no interest in the case. It was an honour killing – they happen; it was justified.'

'There's no honour in murdering a man because you resent his happiness or his success. Because you feel inferior to him. There's no honour in sending thugs to pin down your own brother on a concrete floor and crush his skull with a sledgehammer.'

Ahmed turned away, torn between shame and self-justification, between the need for absolution and the impervious swagger of the hardened killer.

'It was no honour killing,' I said. 'You killed him because you were stealing your brother's land!'

'What are you talking about, journalist? You know nothing about that!'

'Oh, no? So what do you think this is?'

I thrust Ayesha's copy of the fard into Ahmed's hand. As he scanned it the openness in his eyes faded; a veil of unfeeling descended.

'You kept this land for yourself. When you gave the rest to Shafik, you kept this. The water scheme and the dam were a red herring – it was the oil that was the real prize. Right from the beginning.'

'Go to hell, journalist!'

'No. *You* go to hell, Ahmed. I thought there was goodness in you alongside the evil. But I've understood you now.'

'Why should I care what you think you have understood? Or what you think about me?'

'But the land has Asma's name on it, Ahmed. How are you going to deal with that?'

A smile spread across his face.

'Don't worry. I know how to do it.'

'What? By killing Asma?'

'If I have to . . .'

'You're already tormented because you killed your brother; and now you're planning to kill his wife . . .'

Ahmed laughed. 'Kill her . . . or marry her; whichever gets me the oil. I'm getting out of here next month; you won't have long to wait . . .'

There was an angry finality in his farewell.

'Don't forget, journalist – I can have you killed before you even get back to Karachi. You should look out for yourself!'

That evening I told Ayesha the identity of her father's killer.

EPILOGUE

We created man from a drop of semen so that We may test
him . . . And verily, We shall put men to the test with fear
and suffering and loss of wealth and lives and children . . .

— Qur'an 76:2, 2:155

If men divide into those who have suffered and those whose
suffering awaits, this was the year of my graduation. I sit
now by my open window, leaning my cheek on my hand,
watching the breeze blow the cherry blossom, and can
embrace neither the Allah whose suffering winnows the
unbelievers, nor the Christian suffering that strengthens
and ennobles. It is several months since I was in Pakistan;
the things I saw there have settled in the silt of my mind. I
took the manuscript of my book to my editor and explained
that there may be stylistic inconsistencies. I wrote the
first part – the events that happened before my brother's
death – before my brother's death. There was a hiatus while
I staggered; and when I picked it up again my life and my

voice had changed. 'This book has been the journal of your plague year,' she said.

The day after I came back from Karachi I sat with Ayesha; we tried to draw the lessons of what we had discovered. I hoped the common endeavour of our quest, with its lowering disappointments and meagre successes, might outweigh our differences. I hoped we might come together in mutual acknowledgement of the other's grief. But we argued. Over trivial things. I walked out and we didn't communicate. I understood that she was unhappy – my investigation had brought her little cheer and no catharsis – and unhappiness mixed with frustration made her run from comfort. It took me a while to understand that I was the same. Always at the end of a project I feel empty. This time, because the dangers had been survived, the research done and the book written without any of the emotional redemption such stories are held to generate, it was worse. The plague year and Tom's loss had disturbed my balance. The gloom descended. I had to get away. I travelled to avoid thinking, ran to escape from myself. It took time – months – but it helped. The voyage lifted my spirits. I returned to England with new energy, resolved to make good the mistakes I had committed.

I determined to put things right with Ayesha. She had a new address; she invited me to come and see her. I found the house in the long terraced streets of Fulham. She opened the door and pointed to the number on it.

'Look, Martin – 786! That's a lucky number for Muslims!'

'Really?'

'Yes. Because that's what the letters of *Bismillah ir-Rahman ir-Rahim* add up to; *In the name of Allah, the most Merciful . . .*'

'You seem happy . . . Happier than when we last met.'

'I am, Martin. Come in.'

In the kitchen she showed me the cradle and the pram. Wrapped in a pink blanket, her week-old baby was sleeping. We hugged and the hug was long, each of us trying to hide our tears behind the other's back. I thought of the bar in Piccadilly long ago when her heel snapped and she first told me her story.

She went to make tea; it gave us time to compose ourselves. Leaning over the tiny form in the pink blanket I understood that for Ayesha hope had triumphed. Denise's life force, Freud's Eros, had vanquished Thanatos. When she returned, she told me how the resolution of the mystery of her father's death had freed her to marry. His inhibiting shadow had lifted; she had thrown her mind and her body into the union with Peter, and in the months that followed Peter had made her happy. The baby was confirmation that she had done the right thing.

'My father would have disliked me marrying an Englishman. He would have given his blessing because he loved me, but he would have worried about it . . .'

Ayesha bit her lip.

'I can't believe he's dead . . . I still can't believe it . . . And the most terrible thing is that he died to protect me. He died because of the stupid Pakistani code of honour, because Tariq and I should have married our cousins . . .'

'Don't regret, Ayesha. Ibrahim died because he loved you. You should treasure that memory. And you should love your children as he loved you.'

For a moment, neither of us could speak.

'Did you see that Saulat Mirza was executed?' I changed the subject. 'The government held a commission of inquiry to examine the revelations he was promising about the MQM – stuff he hoped would get him reprieved – then they said thank you very much and hanged him anyway!'

Ayesha had news of her own.

'Did you hear about Ahmed, Martin?'

'No. What?'

'He's dead . . .'

'Really?'

'You remember he told you the UF was going to get him released? Well, he was right. He got out while you were away on your odyssey. And a week later he was found murdered by the Karachi-Orangi highway. They'd cut off his right hand and stuffed it into his mouth . . .'

'God!'

'Apparently it's the dacoits' sign that he was caught stealing . . .'

'So it was Javed Shafik who did it? Because Ahmed had kept the land with the oil on it?'

'Yes, probably . . .'

'What do you mean, probably?'

'It's just that . . . you remember you told me on the phone from Quetta how Ahmed was boasting he was going to get the land for himself? How he was going to sort out Asma's claim to it by murdering her or marrying her?'

'Yes. He was bragging. He had a big mouth . . .'

'Maybe. Anyway, I told Tariq about it and he went ape-shit. He went to Pakistan . . .'

I burst out laughing. The vision of Tariq as Hamlet

avenging his father by killing his uncle was so glib that pulp fiction would spurn it. Ayesha looked puzzled.

'Why are you laughing? He hasn't come back and he isn't responding to my messages. I'm worried . . .'

There were other mistakes I needed to put right, other people I had hurt or neglected. I wrote to my brother's children: 'Your dad's death is the most painful thing that has ever happened to me. The deaths of Nana and Papa were sad, but they were in the order of things. Tom dying was wrong in every way. I have found it hard to speak about this, and I think you have, too. I hope you will tell me when you want to talk.'

I could not replace their father, but I wanted to be there for them. I wanted it for me, too. They were the last flesh and blood that linked me to him.

I had spent a year among the dead, looking for answers about the past, driven by the compulsion to understand in order to forgive and be forgiven. But I had discovered that the dead keep their secrets; no one will tell us if and how we could have saved them. My thoughts were turning to the living. Ayesha told me that Ibrahim's dream house in Kahin Nahi was to become a school, offering education to poor as well as rich, girls as well as boys. It would be Ibrahim's gift and Ayesha's. Her joy over her baby daughter had brought her new hope. I could see her life was restarting and I was happy for it. Now I must restart mine.

AFTERWORD

*I thought my book was ended. But a week after I delivered the man-
uscript to my publisher I had a phone call from the coroner's office
in the town where my brother had died. The long-delayed inquest
had been completed, a verdict of suicide returned and Tom's effects
were now available for collection. An apologetic official handed me
a bin sack containing the clothes he had been wearing, his watch,
cigarette lighter and a laptop that I didn't recognise. I recharged
it and hit the Start key. In the index of saved documents I found
one addressed to me. 'Martin, Have a look at this. Can you edit
it for me? If you think it's any good, would you see if you can get
it published?'*

I will always remember my forty-eighth birthday, because I
spent it in the locked ward of a psychiatric hospital and I found
out how old God is. My name is Tom and if you saw me I don't
think you would consider me dangerous. I look ordinary. My
fellow patients, with a few exceptions, are also ordinary. The
men in the lockup are personable or stand-offish, polite or
rude, helpful or selfish, friendly or unfriendly just like the
rest of us. The lockup resembles a mid-priced hotel. You share

toilet facilities, but that's no hardship. Food is served three times a day. The only thing is that the doors are kept locked and some of the guests are criminals.

There is very little to do. There is a secure area, poetically described as 'the garden', which is camouflaged by a fog of cigarette smoke. The TV in the patients' lounge is kept in a Perspex cage to prevent damage. One evening we watched a DVD of *Die Hard 2*. When it finished we found that *Die Hard 1* was about to start on TV. Voices were raised in protest: 'We can't watch *Die Hard 1* after we've watched *Die Hard 2*!' But Sean said, 'We're in a mental hospital; we can do what we like.'

Not many of the patients in Taylor Ward wanted to be there. Sean was an exception. With a broken nose and a face that had taken a few knocks, he was hard as nails. But he was in hospital because he'd tried to hang himself, and he liked it (hospital). He had a young son, a crushing heroin addiction and had known for some time that life wasn't worth living. He also knew how he was going to end it. The rope he bought was the right length and the right strength. He didn't want his family to find him, so he waited until they went out. He had a couple of hours before an unshockable friend was due and he would leave the front door open.

But Sean's wife forgot her purse, came back ten minutes later and found him tying the rope to the roof rafters and down through the loft hatch.

'What are you doing?'

'Just putting up an indoor washing line, love!'

She took him to the psychiatric unit and he found life was good there. He got Methadone and Diazepam, and he was allowed out for an hour each day when he injected his heroin. He told me the ward was the best place he'd ever lived. I don't know what happened to him, but all good things come to an end and I suppose he reverted to Plan A.

There was another heroin addict, whose name to my shame I can't remember. It hurts me a little to say that I didn't like him very much. I tried to avoid his company and spoke to him only when it would have been impolite not to. When I did talk to him, I tried to do so in a civil manner because not many other people, staff or patients, did. I also seemed to be his greatest benefactor of cigarettes.

On one of the regular inspections by the sniffer dogs, they found an empty syringe under his bed. He didn't get the Methadone or Diazepam that Sean had been prescribed and was forced to go cold turkey. I had to stop him when he described his withdrawal symptoms because it was too horrific.

When I was about to be transferred to another ward I went to say goodbye. 'All my friends are leaving,' he said, 'because you're my friend.' I felt guilty and belittled that I had shunned his company.

As an animal lover I enjoyed the visits from the sniffer dogs. The Springer spaniels were so happy to be doing what they had been trained to do. Their tails wagged and they had huge smiles on their faces (don't tell me that dogs can't smile, because I know they can).

Other patients didn't look forward to their visits quite as much as I did. You could tell from their faces which of them had something to hide, and they usually found it – heroin, cannabis, vodka . . .

When I first saw James I thought he was a woman. But I don't think he knew what he was. Thirty years old, of mixed race, very forthright and with mental health issues that defied both definition and treatment, James was a dedicated alcoholic. It was usually his vodka that the sniffer dogs found, much to his annoyance. The reason I thought James was a woman was his long black hair, brushed across his head from a parting on his extreme right to somewhere around his waist on the left, and the fact that he was wearing a skirt. He was from a broken family, had fended for himself all his life and didn't give a shit about anything. He would tell you so at great length.

It wasn't easy to meet the James behind the hair and the skirt, but when you met him you didn't forget him. And your life was richer for it. He had come to the ward directly from a drug-induced coma in his sheltered accommodation. He hadn't intended to kill himself; he just liked drugs and alcohol. I'm not sure why they kept James in the hospital, because every time they asked him if he wanted help to kick his habits his answer was 'Do I fuck'. And when they asked him what he was going to do when he was released, he said, 'I'm going straight to the fucking off licence so I can get pissed.' I guess they knew you can't help someone who doesn't want to be helped.

During my stay here I met two men called Stewart, two men called Dave, and two men called Sean. I haven't changed their names, to protect the innocent. I was going to call the next Sean by another name to make things easier for the reader, but that wouldn't be fair.

Sean Cramer is one of the most talented young men I

have ever met. You should remember his name because Sean Cramer is going to be famous. At least he should be, if his mental condition doesn't get him first. He's twenty-one, tall, slim and handsome. His personality is straightforward and generous. Sean is a singer-songwriter and he's world class. I am his number one fan. He is also bipolar.

Sean's disorder is controlled by a medication called Lithium. But Lithium is known to stifle creativity and that's why Sean was in the hospital; he had stopped taking his medication because it stopped him being creative. I'm not sure why it was so important that he should be forced to take his medication, but that's what they were doing to him.

Sean wandered round the place looking glum. Not even his legions of fans could cheer him up. Our men's ward is on the ground floor and the women's ward up above. The women's windows overlook our garden. Every window in a psychiatric facility has to have a metal grille (to stop people getting in, obviously) and whenever Sean was in the garden the women would gather at the grilles to shout and wave to him. It might have been his music or it might have been his looks (they called him Elvis), I don't know; they never reacted that way with me.

The fact that Sean continued to refuse to take his pills was of great concern to the mental health professionals. Sean had requested a Mental Health Tribunal, at which he intended to argue that the medication was stifling his talent. A Mental Health Tribunal is a sort of trial in a sort of court and its verdict carries the force of law. It takes the medical profession four weeks to prepare for it, during which the patient remains incarcerated. He gets to be interviewed by an independent psychiatrist and has the right to appoint a Mental Health Advocate or a solicitor specialising in mental health issues. Sean and his advocate were certain that they had a good case, and that they were going to win.

I don't know who was the judge at Sean's tribunal, but he or she didn't set much store by artistic talent and the verdict went against him. He accepted it philosophically. On his Facebook page he wrote something like 'I fought the law, and the law won'. I have no idea if he restarted his Lithium but I heard he enrolled at a drama and music college in Liverpool. I got his autograph as an investment in the future.

Stephen was another artist on the ward. His medium was paint on paper. He wasn't as accomplished as Sean, but he was certainly more prolific; Stephen could produce a work of art in a matter of seconds. I've produced a few works of art myself, so I know a bit about these things. My son sometimes tells me a four-year-old could do better, and I know what he means. It is undoubtedly the case with Stephen's paintings, but that's because Stephen has the mind of a four-year-old.

In his thirties with a slouch and bad teeth, he was in most other ways an adult. He was good at smoking for example and he rolled his own cigarettes, although sometimes he would freeze and forget what he was doing until someone reminded him. By then most of his tobacco was on the floor. He had either seven or three children: John, Jennifer, Jonathan and 'I forget the rest'. He was an expert dribbler, although not with a football.

When coffee was served he always took two cups, each with three sugars; at mealtimes he always took a second helping, even though he had barely started the first. The incredible thing (literally) about Stephen is that not only is he highly trained in specialised restraint techniques and high speed pursuit, but he is also a high-ranking police officer working undercover in a mental hospital.

I think it was because he felt vulnerable (without reason; we all liked him, no one would have hurt him) that he needed to keep reminding us he had a radio in his shirt pocket that put him in direct contact with Police Headquarters. At the slightest hint of trouble he would request emergency back-up. We all waited for the blue lights and sirens, but they never came.

I hope Stephen will keep producing his paintings, because in the same way that putting an infinite number of monkeys in front of a typewriter will eventually produce *War and Peace*, I know he will produce a masterpiece. Keep checking The Tate.

After my suicide attempt I was taken to the General Hospital until a bed was available in a mental health ward. I had been sectioned under the Mental Health Act so I wasn't allowed out in the grounds in case I ran away in my pyjamas. That meant I wasn't able to smoke and I saved about fifty quid. When I was transferred to Ramsey Ward I was desperate for a cigarette, but I didn't have any. The first person I met who looked safe to approach was Dave and I asked him if he would lend me one. He did and I was very grateful.

The problem with patients in a psychiatric hospital is that you don't know why they are there unless they tell you.

Dave was in his fifties, smartly dressed with a neat haircut and a well-trimmed moustache. And he was a criminal. I know because he told me.

I had guessed from the way he stood and the way he walked that he was ex-military. He had been a soldier since he left school and had seen some pretty terrible things in war zones around the world. He was traumatised by what he saw in Bosnia and had been receiving treatment since then. Discharged from the army on medical grounds, he had settled in a nice little flat in Liverpool. Then one evening, for no reason he could understand, he set it on fire. 'I called the fire brigade,' he said. 'I told the police what I had done and they arrested me for arson.' So Dave was a criminal awaiting trial. Conviction was a certainty but he was hoping he would be sentenced to treatment rather than punishment. That's why he was on Ramsey Ward; his sentence had already begun.

So the point I was making is that there is no way of knowing why people are in the mental health care system. Sometimes you can guess, but most of the time most of them seem unremarkable.

A new patient arrived. He came into the lounge, walked up to each of us and shook our hands. 'Hello, I'm Steve and I'm so happy to be here.' When I asked him why, he said, 'Because I've just come from the police cells', and that was it; he didn't say another word the whole time he was with us. Not a single word; no telling, no guessing, no label on his forehead. I had no idea why he was there.

Chris, on the other hand, had a ginger beard which, even after he had trimmed it, was never shorter than a foot long.

Together with his moustache it obscured the whole of his lower face. But you could tell that he was always smiling. It wasn't just his face that was smiling, it was all of him. His whole happy, bouncy, bumbling personality was constantly, unfailingly smiling. Even the most depressed depressives, and there were a few of them in there, found it hard to be miserable when Chris was around.

Chris wanted to help everybody. So when Donald arrived it seemed to be a perfect match; he was just what Chris was looking for. Donald was old and confused and he genuinely did need help. Chris was straight there, right at Donald's side. Chris was in his element and Donald was getting the care he clearly craved.

When Donald had been there a few days, and Chris had all but adopted him, two police officers came. They asked to speak to Donald in a private room. Unfortunately they chose a room next to the garden and they didn't close the window. One of the patients heard the whole interview. He came running into the ward shouting, 'He's a paedo! Donald's a fucking paedo!'

Luckily the nurses spotted what had happened and Donald didn't come back. We heard he'd been removed for his own safety. Chris was left feeling upset; the ink on the adoption papers wasn't even dry.

Spike Milligan once wrote, 'What a mental health patient needs is a cuddle, but that unfortunately doesn't seem to be available on the NHS.' I'd like to say that Spike, who knew quite a lot about being mental, was right. Compassion and humanity from the health professionals would go a long way. It would have helped me.

I was brought to the psychiatric ward in a police car (which seemed to impress the inmates) and the first words I heard there were, 'We've been really worried about you.' I liked that. But when I had heard the same words from ten different people at ten different times in ten different places, I started to wonder. When the words became, 'We've all been really worried about you, George' (they'd read my file and didn't realise I never used my first name), it dawned on me that they'd been told to say it and that they were actually thinking, 'Got to pick the kids up at four and we'll have fish for tea, then take Johnny to Scouts', or 'A quick game of squash with Damien after work, then a couple of G&Ts at the club.' If that makes me sound a bitter person then maybe I am. But not about this.

I am in favour of euthanasia if a person's pain is too much to bear. I have taken three of our dearly loved pets, Stella my beautiful Weimaraner, Izzy our stupid chocolate Labrador, and Nat our big fat cat, to the vets when it became kinder not to let them suffer. I was diagnosed with severe depression and I don't understand how we can be so compassionate to animals, but not to humans. When I went to my GP he asked me a series of questions that he downloaded from his computer and said, 'Yes, you're severely depressed' . . . I should have been a doctor! I was prescribed Prozac, but got all the side-effects without any benefit. I was shaking so uncontrollably that I could barely stand up. I got confused and lost. I came off the Prozac and my mood plummeted. That's when I started ruminating about euthanasia.

My wife Tara had been very supportive. But I don't think

she could really understand how I was feeling. There had been a news report about a family on a camping holiday who had taken a disposable barbecue into their tent to keep them warm at night. They had all died in their sleep from carbon monoxide poisoning. Easy!

But it's not easy, and I can testify that it doesn't always work. I bought a disposable barbecue, blocked up any obvious holes in our garden shed and settled down for a long sleep. Perhaps it was the wrong sort of barbecue, or I hadn't found all of the air holes. My wife came home from work and found me alive. She called the emergency services and it all went terribly, irretrievably downhill.

Until 1962 attempted suicide was a prosecutable offence; that's why we talk about committing suicide. It sounds wrong to me. You can commit murder, you can commit armed robbery, you can commit adultery; but the words 'commit' and 'suicide' don't belong together. I haven't yet committed any of the above, but I've tried one of them. So far without success.

I broadly believe that my life is my own to do with what I want. It is about the only thing that the state can't legally take from me. But it makes little practical difference. Even if a suicide attempt is no longer a criminal act, the results are the same. Whether it's a prison sentence or a section under the Mental Health Act, the poor bugger gets locked up.

It isn't easy to take your own life and I am not a brave person. I have gone on to the top of a bridge with a rucksack of bricks on my back. I genuinely intended to jump but got to thinking, 'It's too cold and it's dark. It's raining and miserable; and what if the rucksack comes off, because I'm a good swimmer?' Razor blades would hurt and leave a mess; and pity the poor lorry driver who had me coming through his windscreen, or the train driver whose wheels went over me. They'd never recover. I know you can't just put a bag over your head and breathe in stale air until you collapse, because the survival instinct makes you rip the bag away; I know, I've tried.

I asked Sean, my heroin addict friend I mentioned earlier, why he'd chosen to hang himself when he could just have taken an overdose of heroin. He said, 'With a rope it's quick and final. With an overdose they might find you and revive you.'

It's a good point, except that as I said before, I'm a coward. The idea of putting a rope around my neck and jumping into oblivion doesn't appeal to me. I'd rather take an overdose but again, that isn't as easy as it sounds. I took a whole cocktail of medication over not one but two days, together with a large amount of alcohol. It wasn't a haphazard, spur of the moment attempt; it was carefully planned. So I didn't eat at all on the first day until the evening, when I took a fistful of pills over a few hours then went to bed. The next morning I started again, pills and whisky for breakfast and so on all through the day. I was becoming increasingly drowsy, increasingly other-worldly. I had stayed away from home for those two days, but I wanted to die in my own bed. So I went there to finish the job.

By the time my wife found me, I thought I was too far gone for medical intervention, so I wasn't worried. Mistake number one. I also thought that I could refuse medical treatment. Mistake number two. The paramedic treated me against my will, so I hit him. Mistake number three.

It is certainly true that I would have died without the intervention of the paramedic that evening, but that had been my intention. I would like to apologise for hitting him, but given the state I was in I'm sure it couldn't have been more than a gentle slap. I am angry that he saved my life. But the thing that hurts me most is when people say I was 'attention seeking'.

By the way, in case you were wondering how old God is, the answer depends. Sometimes he is eight thousand years old; that's usually when Stewart is speaking in tongues and blessing us with his big tattooed arms. And at other times he is fifty-three; but that's when Stewart is being Stewart, so I suppose he isn't technically God.